R Deep Learning Essentials
Second Edition

A step-by-step guide to building deep learning models using TensorFlow, Keras, and MXNet

Mark Hodnett
Joshua F. Wiley

BIRMINGHAM - MUMBAI

R Deep Learning Essentials
Second Edition

Commissioning Editor: Sunith Shetty
Acquisition Editor: Aman Singh
Content Development Editor: Snehal Kolte
Technical Editor: Dinesh Chaudhary
Copy Editor: Safis Editing
Project Coordinator: Manthan Patel
Proofreader: Safis Editing
Indexer: Tejal Daruwale Soni
Graphics: Jisha Chirayil
Production Coordinator: Nilesh Mohite

First published: March 2016
Second edition: August 2018

Production reference: 2230818

Published by Packt Publishing Ltd.
Livery Place
35 Livery Street
Birmingham
B3 2PB, UK.

ISBN 978-1-78899-289-3

www.packtpub.com

`mapt.io`

Mapt is an online digital library that gives you full access to over 5,000 books and videos, as well as industry leading tools to help you plan your personal development and advance your career. For more information, please visit our website.

Why subscribe?

- Spend less time learning and more time coding with practical eBooks and Videos from over 4,000 industry professionals

- Improve your learning with Skill Plans built especially for you

- Get a free eBook or video every month

- Mapt is fully searchable

- Copy and paste, print, and bookmark content

PacktPub.com

Did you know that Packt offers eBook versions of every book published, with PDF and ePub files available? You can upgrade to the eBook version at `www.PacktPub.com` and as a print book customer, you are entitled to a discount on the eBook copy. Get in touch with us at `service@packtpub.com` for more details.

At `www.PacktPub.com`, you can also read a collection of free technical articles, sign up for a range of free newsletters, and receive exclusive discounts and offers on Packt books and eBooks.

Contributors

About the authors

Mark Hodnett is a data scientist with over 20 years of industry experience in software development, business intelligence systems, and data science. He has worked in a variety of industries, including CRM systems, retail loyalty, IoT systems, and accountancy. He holds a master's in data science and an MBA.

He works in Cork, Ireland, as a senior data scientist with AltViz.

I would like to thank Sharon for her patience while I worked on this project. I would also like to acknowledge the great work of J. J. Allaire, Hadley Wickham, the entire RStudio team, and all other contributors for their ongoing support of the R language. Finally, I would like to thank the team at Packt and the technical reviewer who helped deliver this project.

Joshua F. Wiley is a lecturer at Monash University, conducting quantitative research on sleep, stress, and health. He earned his Ph.D. from the University of California, Los Angeles and completed post doctoral training in primary care and prevention. In statistics and data science, Joshua focuses on biostatistics and is interested in reproducible research and graphical displays of data and statistical models. He develops or co-develops a number of R packages including varian, a package to conduct Bayesian scale-location structural equation models, and MplusAutomation, a popular package that links R to the commercial Mplus software.

About the reviewer

Vitor Bianchi Lanzetta is an economist with a master's in applied economics from the University of São Paulo, one of the most reputable universities in Latin America. He is very passionate about data science and has done academic research using neural networks, and he has co-authored *Hands-On Data Science with R*. He also authored *R Data Visualization Recipes* and reviewed Mike Bernico's *Deep Learning Quick Reference*.

Packt is searching for authors like you

If you're interested in becoming an author for Packt, please visit `authors.packtpub.com` and apply today. We have worked with thousands of developers and tech professionals, just like you, to help them share their insight with the global tech community. You can make a general application, apply for a specific hot topic that we are recruiting an author for, or submit your own idea.

Table of Contents

Preface

Deep learning is probably the hottest technology in data science right now, and R is one of the most popular data science languages. However, R is not considered as an option for deep learning by many people, which is a shame, as R is a wonderful language for data science. This book shows that R is a viable option for deep learning, because it supports libraries such as MXNet and Keras.

When I decided to write this book, I had numerous goals. First, I wanted to show how to apply deep learning to various tasks, and not just to computer vision and natural language processing. This book covers those topics, but it also shows how to use deep learning for prediction, regression, anomaly detection, and recommendation systems. The second goal was to look at topics in deep learning that are not covered well elsewhere; for example, interpretability with LIME, deploying models, and using the cloud for deep learning. The last goal was to give an overall view of deep learning and not just provide machine learning code. I think I achieved this by discussing topics such as how to create datasets from raw data, how to benchmark models against each other, how to manage data when model building, and how to deploy your models. My hope is that by the end of this book, you will also be convinced that R is a valid choice for use in deep learning.

Who this book is for

If you have some experience with R and are looking for a book that shows some practical examples of how to use R for deep learning, this is the book for you! This book assumes that you are familiar with some of the concepts in machine learning, such as splitting data into train and test sets. Anyone who has built machine learning algorithms in R should have no problem with this book.

What this book covers

Chapter 1, *Getting Started with Deep Learning*, gives an introduction to deep learning and neural networks. It also gives a brief introduction on how to set up your R environment.

Chapter 2, *Training a Prediction Model*, begins with building neural network models using the existing packages in R. This chapter also discusses overfitting, which is an issue in most deep learning models.

Chapter 3, *Deep Learning Fundamentals*, teaches how to build a neural network in R from scratch. We then show how our code relates to MXNet, a deep learning library.

Chapter 4, *Training Deep Prediction Models*, looks at activations and introduces the MXNet library. We then build a deep learning prediction model for a real-life example. We will take a raw dataset of transactional data and develop a data pipeline to create a model that predicts which customers will return in the next 14 days.

Chapter 5, *Image Classification Using Convolutional Neural Networks*, looks at image classification tasks. First, we will introduce some of the core concepts, such as convolutional and pooling layers, and then we will show how to use these layers to classify images.

Chapter 6, *Tuning and Optimizing Models*, discusses how to tune and optimize deep learning models. We look at tuning hyperparameters and using data augmentation.

Chapter 7, *Natural Language Processing Using Deep Learning*, shows how to use deep learning for **Natural Language Processing** (**NLP**) tasks. We show how deep learning algorithms outperform traditional NLP techniques, while also being much easier to develop.

Chapter 8, *Deep Learning Models Using TensorFlow in R*, looks at using the TensorFlow API in R. We also look at some additional packages available within TensorFlow that make developing TensorFlow models simpler and help in hyperparameter selection.

Chapter 9, *Anomaly Detection and Recommendation Systems*, shows how we can use deep learning models to create embeddings that are lower order representations of data. We then show how to use embeddings for anomaly detection and to create a recommendation system.

Chapter 10, *Running Deep Learning Models in the Cloud*, covers how to use AWS, Azure, and Google Cloud services to train deep learning models. This chapter shows how to train your models at low-cost in the cloud.

Chapter 11, *The Next Level in Deep Learning*, concludes the book with an end-to-end solution for image classification. We take a set of image files, train a model, reuse that model for transfer learning and then show how to deploy that model to production. We also briefly discuss **Generative Adversarial Networks** (**GANs**) and reinforcement learning.

To get the most out of this book

This book does not assume that you have access to a high-end machine or even a machine with a GPU. To get the most out of this book, I recommend that you execute all the code examples. Experiment with them, change the parameters, and try to beat the metrics in the book.

Download the example code files

You can download the example code files for this book from your account at www.packtpub.com. If you purchased this book elsewhere, you can visit www.packtpub.com/support and register to have the files emailed directly to you.

You can download the code files by following these steps:

1. Log in or register at www.packtpub.com.
2. Select the **SUPPORT** tab.
3. Click on **Code Downloads & Errata**.
4. Enter the name of the book in the **Search** box and follow the onscreen instructions.

Once the file is downloaded, please make sure that you unzip or extract the folder using the latest version of:

- WinRAR/7-Zip for Windows
- Zipeg/iZip/UnRarX for Mac
- 7-Zip/PeaZip for Linux

The code bundle for the book is also hosted on GitHub at https://github.com/PacktPublishing/R-Deep-Learning-Essentials-Second-Edition. In case there's an update to the code, it will be updated on the existing GitHub repository.

We also have other code bundles from our rich catalog of books and videos available at https://github.com/PacktPublishing/. Check them out!

Download the color images

We also provide a PDF file that has color images of the screenshots/diagrams used in this book. You can download it here: `http://www.packtpub.com/sites/default/files/ downloads/RDeepLearningEssentialsSecondEdition_ColorImages.pdf`.

Conventions used

There are a number of text conventions used throughout this book.

`CodeInText`: Indicates code words in text, database table names, folder names, filenames, file extensions, pathnames, dummy URLs, user input, and Twitter handles. Here is an example: "Mount the downloaded `WebStorm-10*.dmg` disk image file as another disk in your system."

A block of code is set as follows:

```
dfData <- read.csv(fileName)
nobs <- nrow(dfData)
train <- sample(nobs, 0.9*nobs)
test <- setdiff(seq_len(nobs), train)
```

When we wish to draw your attention to a particular part of a code block, the relevant lines or items are set in bold:

```
> dfResults
         w stem stop  nb_acc svm_acc  nn_acc  rf_acc best_acc
12 binary    1    1   86.06   95.24   90.52   94.26    95.24
9  binary    0    1   87.71   95.15   90.52   93.72    95.15
10 tfidf     1    1   91.99   95.15   91.05   94.17    95.15
3  binary    0    0   85.98   95.01   90.29   93.99    95.01
```

Any command-line input or output is written as follows:

```
$ tensorboard --logdir /tensorflow_logs
```

Bold: Indicates a new term, an important word, or words that you see onscreen. For example, words in menus or dialog boxes appear in the text like this. Here is an example: "Select **System info** from the **Administration** panel."

 Warnings or important notes appear like this.

 Tips and tricks appear like this.

Get in touch

Feedback from our readers is always welcome.

General feedback: Email `feedback@packtpub.com` and mention the book title in the subject of your message. If you have questions about any aspect of this book, please email us at `questions@packtpub.com`.

Errata: Although we have taken every care to ensure the accuracy of our content, mistakes do happen. If you have found a mistake in this book, we would be grateful if you would report this to us. Please visit `www.packtpub.com/submit-errata`, selecting your book, clicking on the Errata Submission Form link, and entering the details.

Piracy: If you come across any illegal copies of our works in any form on the Internet, we would be grateful if you would provide us with the location address or website name. Please contact us at `copyright@packtpub.com` with a link to the material.

If you are interested in becoming an author: If there is a topic that you have expertise in and you are interested in either writing or contributing to a book, please visit `authors.packtpub.com`.

Reviews

Please leave a review. Once you have read and used this book, why not leave a review on the site that you purchased it from? Potential readers can then see and use your unbiased opinion to make purchase decisions, we at Packt can understand what you think about our products, and our authors can see your feedback on their book. Thank you!

For more information about Packt, please visit `packtpub.com`.

Getting Started with Deep Learning 1

This chapter discusses deep learning, a powerful multilayered architecture for pattern-recognition, signal-detection, and classification or prediction. Although deep learning is not new, it is only in the past decade that it has gained great popularity, due in part to advances in computational capacity and new ways of more efficiently training models, as well as the availability of ever-increasing amounts of data. In this chapter, you will learn what deep learning is, the R packages available for training such models, and how to get your system set up for analysis. We will briefly discuss **MXNet** and **Keras**, which are the two main frameworks that we will use for many of the examples in later chapters to actually train and use deep learning models.

In this chapter, we will explore the following topics:

- What is deep learning?
- A conceptual overview of deep learning
- Setting up your R environment and the deep learning frameworks available in R
- GPUs and reproducibility

What is deep learning?

Deep learning is a subfield within machine learning, which in turn is a subfield within artificial intelligence. **Artificial intelligence** is the art of creating machines that perform functions that require intelligence when performed by people. **Machine learning** uses algorithms that learn without being explicitly programmed. Deep learning is the subset of machine learning that uses artificial neural networks that mimic how the brain works.

The following diagram shows the relationships between them. For example, self-driving cars are an application of artificial intelligence. A critical part of self-driving cars is to recognize other road users, cars, pedestrians, cyclists, and so on. This requires machine learning because it is not possible to explicitly program this. Finally, deep learning may be chosen as the method to implement this machine learning task:

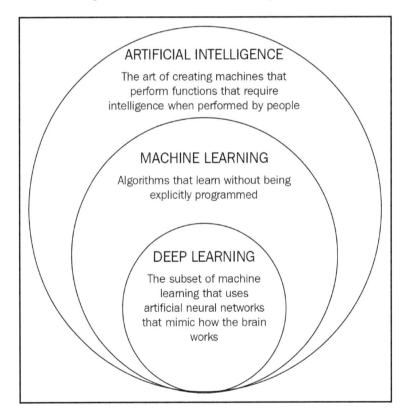

Figure 1.1: The relationship between artificial intelligence, machine learning, and deep learning

Artificial intelligence as a field has existed since the 1940s; the definition used in the previous diagram is from Kurzweil, 1990. It is a broad field that encompasses ideas from many different fields, including philosophy, mathematics, neuroscience, and computer engineering. Machine learning is a subfield within artificial intelligence that is devoted to developing and using algorithms that learn from raw data. When the machine learning task has to predict an outcome, it is known as **supervised learning**. When the task is to predict from a set of possible outcomes, it is a **classification** task, and when the task is to predict a numeric value, it is a **regression** task. Some examples of classification tasks are whether a particular credit card purchase is fraudulent, or whether a given image is of a cat or a dog. An example of a regression task is predicting how much money a customer will spend in the next month. There are other types of machine learning where the learning does not predict values. This is called **unsupervised learning** and includes clustering (segmenting) the data, or creating a compressed format of the data.

Deep learning is a subfield within machine learning. It is called **deep** because it uses multiple layers to map the relationship between input and output. A **layer** is a collection of neurons that perform a mathematical operation on its input. This will be explained in more detail in the next section, *Conceptual overview of neural networks*. This deep architecture means the model is large enough to handle many variables and that it is sufficiently flexible to approximate the patterns in the data. Deep learning can also generate features as part of the overall learning algorithm, rather than feature-creation being a prerequisite step. Deep learning has proven particularly effective in the fields of image-recognition (including handwriting as well as photo- or object-classification) , speech recognition and natural-language. It has completely transformed how to use image, text, and speech data for prediction in the past few years, replacing previous methods of working with these types of data. It has also opened up these fields to a lot more people because it automates a lot of the feature-generation, which required specialist skills.

Deep learning is not the only technique available in machine learning. There are other types of machine learning algorithms; the most popular include regression, decision trees, random forest, and naive bayes. For many use cases, one of these algorithms could be a better choice. Some examples of use cases where deep learning may not be the best choice include when interpretability is an essential requirement, the dataset size is small, or you have limited resources (time and/or hardware) to develop a model. It is important to realize that despite, the industry hype, most machine learning in industry does not use deep learning. Having said that, this book covers deep learning algorithms, so we will move on. The next sections will discuss neural networks and deep neural networks in more depth.

A conceptual overview of neural networks

It can be difficult to understand why neural networks work so well. This introduction will look at them from two viewpoints. If you have an understanding of how linear regression works, the first viewpoint should be useful. The second viewpoint is more intuitive and less technical, but equally valid. I encourage you to read both and spend some time contemplating both overviews.

Neural networks as an extension of linear regression

One of the simplest and oldest prediction models is **regression**. It predicts a continuous value (that is, a number) based on another value. The linear regression function is:

$y=mx+b$

Where y is the value you want to predict and x is your input variable. The linear regression coefficients (or parameters) are m (the slope of the line) and b (the intercept). The following R code creates a line with the $y= 1.4x -2$ function and plots it:

```
set.seed(42)
m <- 1.4
b <- -1.2
x <- 0:9
jitter<-0.6
xline <- x
y <- m*x+b
x <- x+rnorm(10)*jitter
title <- paste("y = ",m,"x ",b,sep="")
plot(xline,y,type="l",lty=2,col="red",main=title,xlim=c(0,max(y)),ylim=c(0,
max(y)))
points(x[seq(1,10,2)],y[seq(1,10,2)],pch=1)
points(x[seq(2,11,2)],y[seq(2,11,2)],pch=4)
```

The *o* or *x* points are the values to be predicted given a value on the *x* axis and the line is the ground truth. Some random noise is added, so that the points are not exactly on the line. This code produces the following output:

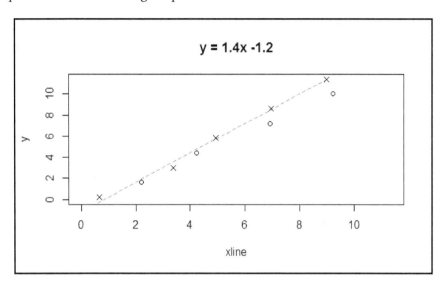

Figure 1.2: Example of a regression line fitted to data (that is, predict *y* from *x*)

In a regression task, you are given some *x* and corresponding *y* values, but are not given the underlying function to map *x* to *y*. The purpose of a supervised machine learning task is that given some previous examples of *x* and *y*, can we predict the *y* values for new data where we only have *x* and not *y*. An example might be to predict house prices based on the number of bedrooms in the house. So far, we have only considered a single input variable, *x*, but we can easily extend the example to handle multiple input variables. For the house example, we would use the number of bedrooms and square footage to predict the price of the house. Our code can accommodate this by changing the input, *x*, from a vector (one-dimensional array) into a matrix (two-dimensional array).

If we consider our model for predicting house prices, linear regression has a serious limitation: it can only estimate linear functions. If the mapping from *x* to *y* is not linear, it will not predict *y* very well. The function always results in a straight line for one variable and a hyperplane if multiple *x* predictor values are used. This means that linear regression models may not be accurate at the low and high extent of the data.

A simple trick to make the model fit nonlinear relationships is to add polynomial terms to the function. This is known as **polynomial regression**. For example, by adding a polynomial of degree 4, our function changes to:

$$y = m_1x^4 + m_2x^3 + m_3x^2 + m_4x + b$$

By adding these extra terms, the line (or decision boundary) is no longer linear. The following code demonstrates this – we create some sample data and we create three regression models to fit this data. The first model has no polynomial terms, the model is a straight line and fits the data very poorly. The second model (blue circles) has polynomials up to degree 3, that is, X, X^2, and X^3. The last model has polynomials up to degree 12, that is, X, X^2,....., X^{12}. The first model (straight line) underfits the data and the last line overfits the data. Overfitting refers to situations where the model is too complex and ends up memorizing the data. This means that the model does not generalize well and will perform poorly on unseen data. The following code generates the data and creates three models with increasing levels of polynomial:

```
par(mfrow=c(1,2))
set.seed(1)
x1 <- seq(-2,2,0.5)

# y=x^2-6
jitter<-0.3
y1 <- (x1^2)-6
x1 <- x1+rnorm(length(x1))*jitter
plot(x1,y1,xlim=c(-8,12),ylim=c(-8,10),pch=1)
x <- x1
y <- y1

# y=-x
jitter<-0.8
x2 <- seq(-7,-5,0.4)
y2 <- -x2
x2 <- x2+rnorm(length(x2))*jitter
points(x2,y2,pch=2)
x <- c(x,x2)
y <- c(y,y2)

# y=0.4 *rnorm(length(x3))*jitter
jitter<-1.2
x3 <- seq(5,9,0.5)
y3 <- 0.4 *rnorm(length(x3))*jitter
points(x3,y3,pch=3)
x <- c(x,x3)
y <- c(y,y3)
```

```
df <- data.frame(cbind(x,y))
plot(x,y,xlim=c(-8,12),ylim=c(-8,10),pch=4)

model1 <- lm(y~.,data=df)
abline(coef(model1),lty=2,col="red")

max_degree<-3
for (i in 2:max_degree)
{
 col<-paste("x",i,sep="")
 df[,col] <- df$x^i
}
model2 <- lm(y~.,data=df)
xplot <- seq(-8,12,0.1)
yplot <- (xplot^0)*model2$coefficients[1]
for (i in 1:max_degree)
 yplot <- yplot +(xplot^i)*model2$coefficients[i+1]
points(xplot,yplot,col="blue", cex=0.5)

max_degree<-12
for (i in 2:max_degree)
{
 col<-paste("x",i,sep="")
 df[,col] <- df$x^i
}
model3 <- lm(y~.,data=df)
xplot <- seq(-8,12,0.1)
yplot <- (xplot^0)*model3$coefficients[1]
for (i in 1:max_degree)
 yplot <- yplot +(xplot^i)*model3$coefficients[i+1]
points(xplot,yplot,col="green", cex=0.5,pch=2)

MSE1 <- c(crossprod(model1$residuals)) / length(model1$residuals)
MSE2 <- c(crossprod(model2$residuals)) / length(model2$residuals)
MSE3 <- c(crossprod(model3$residuals)) / length(model3$residuals)
print(sprintf(" Model 1 MSE = %1.2f",MSE1))
[1] " Model 1 MSE = 14.17"
print(sprintf(" Model 2 MSE = %1.2f",MSE2))
[1] " Model 2 MSE = 3.63"
print(sprintf(" Model 3 MSE = %1.2f",MSE3))
[1] " Model 3 MSE = 0.07"
```

If we were selecting one of these models to use, we should select the middle model, even though the third model has a lower **MSE** (**mean-squared error**). In the following screenshot; the best model is the curved line from the top left corner:

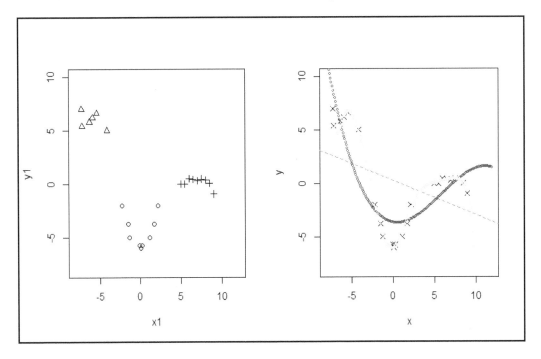

Figure 1.3: Polynomial regression

If we look at the three models and see how they handle the extreme left and right points, we see why overfitting can lead to poor results on unseen data. On the right side of the plot, the last series of points (plus signs) have a local linear relationship. However, the polynomial regression line with degree 12 (green triangles) puts too much emphasis on the last point, which is extra noise and the line moves down sharply. This would cause the model to predict extreme negative values for *y* as *x* increases, which is not justified if we look at the data. Overfitting is an important issue that we will look at in more detail in later chapters.

By adding square, cube, and more polynomial terms, the model can fit more complex data than if we just used linear functions on the input data. Neural networks use a similar concept, except that, instead of taking polynomial terms of the input variable, they chain multiple regression functions together with nonlinear terms between them.

The following is an example of a neural network architecture. The circles are nodes and the lines are the connections between nodes. If a connection exists between two nodes, the output from the node on the left is the input for the next node. The output value from a node is a matrix operation on the input values to the node and the weights of the node:

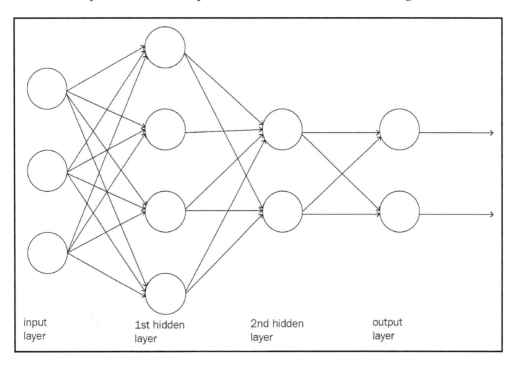

Figure 1.4: An example neural network

Before the output values from a node are passed to the next node as input values, a function is applied to the values to change the overall function to a non-linear function. These are known as **activation functions** and they perform the same role as the polynomial terms.

This idea of creating a machine learning model by combining multiple small functions together is a very common paradigm in machine learning. It is used in random forests, where many small independent decision trees *vote* for the result. It is also used in boosting algorithms, where the misclassified instances from one function are given more prominence in the next function.

By including many layers of nodes, the neural network model can approximate almost any function. It does make training the model more difficult, so we'll give a brief explanation of how to train a neural network. Each node is assigned a set of random weights initially. For the first pass, these weights are used to calculate and pass (or propagate) values from the input layer to the hidden layers and finally to the output layer. This is known as **forward-propagation**. Because the weights were set randomly, the final (prediction) values at the output layer will not be accurate compared to the actual values, so we need a method of calculating how different the predicted values are from the actual values. This is calculated using a **cost function**, which gives a measure of how accurate the model is during training. We then need to adjust the weights in the nodes from the output layer backward to get us nearer to the target values. This is done using **backward-propagation**; we move from right to left, updating the weights of the nodes in each layer very slightly to get us very slightly closer to the actual values. The cycle of forward-propagation and backward-propagation continues until the error value from the loss function stops getting smaller; this may require hundreds, or thousands of iterations, or epochs.

To update the node weights correctly, we need to know that the change will get us nearer to the target, which is to minimize the result from the cost function. We are able to do this because of a clever trick, we use activation functions that have derivative functions.

If your knowledge of calculus is limited, it can be difficult to get an understanding of derivatives initially. But in simple terms, a function may have a derivative formula that tells us how to change the *input* of a function so that the *output* of the function moves in a positive or negative manner. This derivative/formula enables the algorithm to minimize the cost function, which is a measurement of error. In more technical terms, the derivative of the function measures the rate of change in the function as the input changes. If we know the rate of change of a function as the input changes, and more importantly what direction it changes in, then we can use this to get nearer to minimizing that function. An example that you may have seen before is the following diagram:

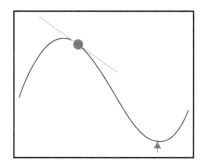

Figure 1.5: A function (curved) line and its derivative at a point

In this diagram, the curved line is a mathematical function we want to minimize over y, that is, we want to get to the lowest point (which is marked by the arrow). We are currently at the point in the red circle, and the derivative at that point is the slope of the tangent. The derivative function indicates the direction we need to move in to get there. The derivative value changes as we get nearer the target (the arrow), so we cannot make the move in one big step. Therefore, the algorithm moves in small steps and re-calculates the derivative after each step, but if we choose too small a step, it will take very long to **converge** (that is, get near the minimum). If we take too big a step, we run the risk of overshooting the minimum value. How big a step you take is known as the **learning rate**, and it effectively decides how long it takes the algorithm to train.

This might seem a bit abstract, so an analogy should make it somewhat clearer. This analogy may be over-simplified, but it explains derivatives, learning rates, and cost functions. Imagine a simple model of driving a car, where the speed must be set to a value that is suitable for the conditions and the speed limit. The difference between your current speed and the target speed is the error rate and this is calculated using a cost function (just simple subtraction, in this case). To change your speed, you apply the gas pedal to speed up or the brake pedal to slow down. The acceleration/deceleration (that is, the rate of change of the speed) is the derivative of the speed. The amount of force that is applied to the pedals changes how fast the acceleration/deceleration occurs, the force is similar to the learning rate in a machine learning algorithm. It controls how long it takes to get to the target value. If only a small change is applied to the pedals, you will eventually get to your target speed, but it will take much longer. However, you usually don't want to apply maximum force to the pedals, to do so may be dangerous (if you slam on the brakes) or a waste of fuel (if you accelerate too hard). There is a happy medium where you apply the change and get to the target speed safely and quickly.

Neural networks as a network of memory cells

Another way to consider neural networks is to compare them to how humans think. As their name suggests, neural networks draw inspiration from neural processes and neurons in the mind. Neural networks contain a series of neurons, or nodes, which are interconnected and process input. The neurons have weights that are learned from previous observations (data). The output of a neuron is a function of its input and its weights. The activation of some final neuron(s) is the prediction.

We will consider a hypothetical case where a small part of the brain is responsible for matching basic shapes, such as squares and circles. In this scenario, some neurons at the basic level fire for horizontal lines, another set of neurons fires for vertical lines, and yet another set of neurons fire for curved segments. These neurons feed into higher-order process that combines the input so that it recognizes more complex objects, for example, a square when the horizontal and vertical neurons both are activated simultaneously.

In the following diagram, the input data is represented as squares. These could be pixels in an image. The next layer of hidden neurons consists of neurons that recognize basic features, such as horizontal lines, vertical lines, or curved lines. Finally, the output may be a neuron that is activated by the simultaneous activation of two of the hidden neurons:

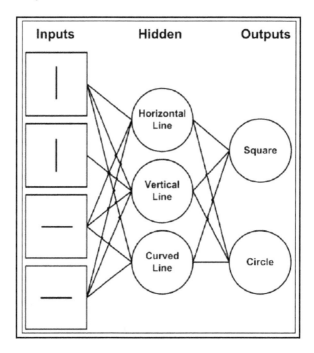

Figure 1.6: Neural networks as a network of memory cells

In this example, the first node in the hidden layer is good at matching horizontal lines, while the second node in the hidden layer is good at matching vertical lines. These nodes *remember* what these objects are. If these nodes combine, more sophisticated objects can be detected. For example, if the hidden layer recognizes horizontal lines and vertical lines, the object is more likely to be a square than a circle. This is similar to how convolutional neural networks work, which we will cover in `Chapter 5`, *Image Classification Using Convolutional Neural Networks*.

We have covered the theory behind neural networks very superficially here as we do not want to overwhelm you in the first chapter! In future chapters, we will cover some of these issues in more depth, but in the meantime, if you wish to get a deeper understanding of the theory behind neural networks, the following resources are recommended:

- Chapter 6 of *Goodfellow-et-al* (2016)
- Chapter 11 of *Hastie, T., Tibshirani, R.,* and *Friedman, J.* (2009), which is freely available at https://web.stanford.edu/~hastie/Papers/ESLII.pdf
- Chapter 16 of *Murphy, K. P.* (2012)

Next, we will turn to a brief introduction to deep neural networks.

Deep neural networks

A **deep neural network** (**DNN**) is a neural network with multiple hidden layers. We cannot achieve good results by just increasing the number of nodes in a neural network with a small number of layers (a shallow neural network). A DNN can fit data more accurately with fewer parameters than a shallow **neural network** (**NN**), because more layers (each with fewer neurons) give a more efficient and accurate representation. Using multiple hidden layers allows a more sophisticated build-up from simple elements to more complex ones. In the previous example, we considered a neural network that could recognize basic shapes, such as a circle or a square. In a deep neural network, many circles and squares could be combined to form other, more advanced shapes. A shallow neural network cannot build more advanced shapes from basic pieces. The disadvantage of a DNN is that these models are harder to train and prone to overfitting.

If we consider trying to recognize handwritten text from image data, then the raw data is pixel values from an image. The first layer captures simple shapes, such as lines and curves. The next layer uses these simple shapes and recognizes higher abstractions, such as corners and circles. The second layer does not have to directly learn from the pixels, which are noisy and complex. In contrast, a shallow architecture may require far more parameters, as each hidden neuron would have to be capable of going directly from pixels in the image to the target value. It would also not be able to combine features, so for example, if the image data were in a different location (for example, not centered), it would fail to recognize the text.

One of the challenges in training deep neural networks is how to efficiently learn the weights. The models are complex with a huge number of parameters to train. One of the major advancements in deep learning occurred in 2006, when it was shown that **deep belief networks** (**DBNs**) could be trained one layer at a time (See *Hinton, G. E., Osindero, S., and Teh, Y. W. (2006)*). A DBN is a type of deep neural network with multiple hidden layers and connections between (but not within) layers (that is, a neuron in layer 1 may be connected to a neuron in layer 2, but may not be connected to another neuron in layer 1). The restriction of no connections within a layer allows for much faster training algorithms to be used, such as the **contrastive divergence algorithm**. Essentially, the DBN can then be trained layer by layer; the first hidden layer is trained and used to transform raw data into hidden neurons, which are then treated as a new set of input in the next hidden layer, and the process is repeated until all the layers have been trained.

The benefits of the realization that DBNs could be trained one layer at a time extend beyond just DBNs. DBNs are sometimes used as a pre-training stage for a deep neural network. This allows comparatively fast, greedy, layer-by-layer training to be used to provide good initial estimates, which are then refined in the deep neural network using other, less efficient, training algorithms, such as back-propagation.

So far we have primarily focused on feed-forward neural networks, where the results from one layer and neuron feed forward to the next. Before closing this section, two specific kinds of deep neural network that have grown in popularity are worth mentioning. The first is a **recurrent neural network** (**RNN**), where neurons send feedback signals to each other. These feedback loops allow RNNs to work well with sequences. An example of an application of RNNs is to automatically generate click-bait, such as *Top 10 reasons to visit Los Angeles: #6 will shock you!* or *One trick great hair salons don't want you to know*. RNNs work well for such jobs as they can be seeded from a large initial pool of a few words (even just trending search terms or names) and then predict/generate what the next word should be. This process can be repeated a few times until a short phrase is generated, the click-bait. We will see examples of RNNs in `Chapter 7`, *Natural Language Processing using Deep Learning*.

The second type is a **convolutional neural network** (**CNN**). CNNs are most commonly used in image-recognition. CNNs work by having each neuron respond to overlapping subregions of an image. The benefits of CNNs are that they require comparatively minimal preprocessing but still do not require too many parameters through weight-sharing (for example, across subregions of an image). This is particularly valuable for images as they are often not consistent. For example, imagine ten different people taking a picture of the same desk. Some may be closer or farther away or at positions resulting in essentially the same image having different heights, widths, and the amount of image captured around the focal object. We will cover CNNs in depth in `Chapter 5`, *Image Classification Using Convolutional Neural Networks*.

This description only provides the briefest of overviews as to what deep neural networks are and some of the use cases to which they can be applied. The seminal reference for deep learning is *Goodfellow-et-al* (2016).

Some common myths about deep learning

There are many misconceptions, half-truths, and downright misleading opinions on deep learning. Here are some common mis-conceptions regarding deep learning:

- Artificial intelligence means deep learning and replaces all other techniques
- Deep learning requires a PhD-level understanding of mathematics
- Deep learning is hard to train, almost an art form
- Deep learning requires lots of data
- Deep learning has poor interpretability
- Deep learning needs GPUs

The following paragraphs discuss these statements, one by one.

Deep learning is not artificial intelligence and does not replace all other machine learning algorithms. It is only one family of algorithms in machine learning. Despite the hype, deep learning probably accounts for less than 1% of the machine learning projects in production right now. Most of the recommendation engines and online adverts that you encounter when you browse the net are not powered by deep learning. Most models used internally by companies to manage their subscribers, for example *churn analysis*, are not deep learning models. The models used by credit institutions to decide who gets credit do not use deep learning.

Deep learning does not require a deep understanding of mathematics unless your interest is in researching new deep learning algorithms and specialized architectures. Most practitioners use existing deep learning techniques on their data by taking an existing architecture and modifying it for their work. This does not require a deep mathematical foundation, the mathematics used in deep learning are taught at high school level throughout the world. In fact, we demonstrate this in Chapter 3, *Deep Learning Fundamentals*, where we build an entire neural network from basic code in less than 70 lines of code!

Training deep learning models is difficult but it is not an art form. It does require practice, but the same problems occur over and over again. Even better, there is often a prescribed fix for that problem, for example, if your model is overfitting, add regularization, if your model is not training well, build a more complex model and/or use *data augmentation*. We will look at this in more depth in Chapter 6, *Tuning and Optimizing Models*.

There is a lot of truth to the statement that deep learning requires lots of data. However, you may still be able to apply deep learning to the problem by using a pre-trained network, or creating more training data from existing data (data augmentation). We will look at these in later Chapter 6, *Tuning and Optimizing Models* and Chapter 11, *The Next Level in Deep Learning*.

Deep learning models are difficult to interpret. By this, we mean being able to explain how the models came to their decision. This is a problem in many machine learning algorithms, not just deep learning. In machine learning, generally there is an inverse relationship between accuracy and interpretation – the more accurate the model needs to be, the less interpretable it is. For some tasks, for example, online advertising, interpretability is not important and there is little cost from being wrong, so the most powerful algorithm is preferred. In some cases, for example, credit scoring, interpretability may be required by law; people could demand an explanation of why they were denied credit. In other cases, such as medical diagnoses, interpretability may be important for a doctor to see why the model decided someone had a disease.

If interpretability is important, some methods can be applied to machine learning models to get an understanding of why they predicted the output for an instance. Some of them work by perturbing the data (that is, making slight changes to it) and trying to find what variables are most influential in the model coming to its decision. One such algorithm is called **LIME (Local Interpretable Model-Agnostic Explanations)**. (*Ribeiro, Marco Tulio, Sameer Singh, and Carlos Guestrin. Why should I trust you?: Explaining the predictions of any classifier. Proceedings of the 22nd ACM SIGKDD international conference on knowledge discovery and data mining. ACM, 2016.*) This has been implemented in many languages including R; there is a package called lime. We will use this package in Chapter 6, *Tuning and Optimizing Models*.

Finally, while deep learning models can run on CPUs, the truth is that any real work requires a workstation with a GPU. This does not mean that you need to go out and purchase one, as you can use cloud-computing to train your models. In Chapter 10, *Running Deep Learning Models in the Cloud*, will look at using AWS, Azure, and Google Cloud to train deep learning models.

Setting up your R environment

Before you begin your deep learning journey, the first step is to install R, which is available at `https://cran.r-project.org/`. When you download R and use it, only a few core packages are installed by default, but new packages can be added by selecting from a menu option or by a single line of code. We will not go into detail on how to install R or how to add packages, we assume that most readers are proficient in these skills. A good **integrated development environment** (IDE) for working with R is essential. By far the most popular IDE, and my recommendation, is RStudio, which can be downloaded from `https://www.rstudio.com/`. Another option is **Emacs**. An advantage of both Emacs and RStudio is that they are available on all major platforms (Windows, macOS, and Linux), so even if you switch computers, you can have a consistent IDE experience. The following is a screenshot of the RStudio IDE:

Figure 1.7 RStudio IDE

Using RStudio is a major improvement over the R GUI in Windows. There are a number of panes in RStudio that provide different perspectives on your work. The top-left pane shows the code, the bottom-left pane shows the console (results of running the code). The top-right pane shows the list of variables and their current values, the bottom-right pane shows the plots created by the code. All of these panes have further tabs to explore further perspectives.

As well as an IDE, RStudio (the company) have either developed or heavily supported other tools and packages for the R environment. We will use some of these tools, including the R Markdown and R Shiny applications. R Markdown is similar to Jupyter or IPython notebooks; it allows you to combine code, output (for example, plots), and documentation in one script. R Markdown was used to create sections of this book where code and descriptive text are interwoven. R Markdown is a very good tool to ensure that your data science experiments are documented correctly. By embedding the documentation within the analysis, they are more likely to stay synchronized. R Markdown can output to HTML, Word, or PDF. The following is an example of an R Markdown script on the left and the output on the right:

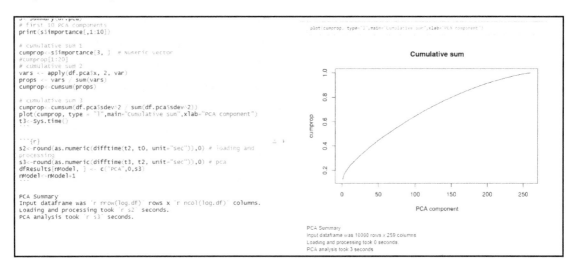

Figure 1.8: R Markdown example; on the left is a mixture of R code and text information. The output on the right is HTML generated from the source script.

We will also use R Shiny to create web applications using R. This is an excellent method to create interactive applications to demonstrate key functionality. The following screenshot is an example of an R Shiny web application, which we will see in Chapter 5, *Image Classification Using Convolutional Neural Networks*:

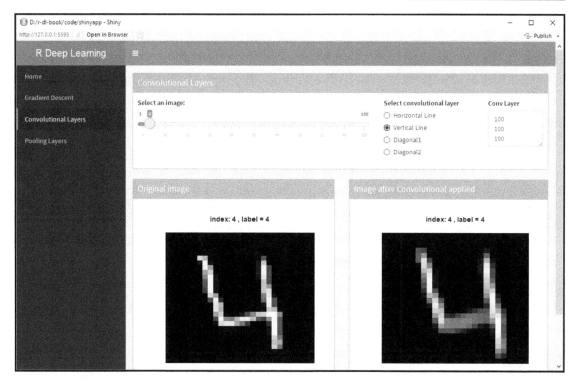

Figure 1.9: An example of an R Shiny web application

Once you have R installed, you can look at adding packages that can fit basic neural networks. The `nnet` package is one package and it can fit feed-forward neural networks with one hidden layer, such as the one shown in *Figure* 1.6. For more details on the `nnet` package, see *Venables, W. N.* and *Ripley, B. D.* (2002). The `neuralnet` package fits neural networks with multiple hidden layers and can train them using back-propagation. It also allows custom error and neuron-activation functions. We will also use the `RSNNS` package, which is an R wrapper of the **Stuttgart Neural Network Simulator** (**SNNS**). The SNNS was originally written in C, but was ported to C++. The `RSNNS` package makes many model components from SNNS available, making it possible to train a wide variety of models. For more details on the `RSNNS` package, see *Bergmeir, C.,* and *Benitez, J. M.* (2012). We will see examples of how to use these models in `Chapter 2`, *Training a Prediction Model*.

The `deepnet` package provides a number of tools for deep learning in R. Specifically, it can train RBMs and use these as part of DBNs to generate initial values to train deep neural networks. The `deepnet` package also allows for different activation functions, and the use of dropout for regularization.

Deep learning frameworks for R

There are a number of R packages available for neural networks, but few options for deep learning. When the first edition of this book came out, it used the deep learning functions in h2o (`https://www.h2o.ai/`). This is an excellent, general machine learning framework written in Java, and has an API that allows you to use it from R. I recommend you look at it, especially for large datasets. However, most deep learning practitioners had a preference preferred other deep learning libraries, such as TensorFlow, CNTK, and MXNet, which were not supported in R when the first edition of this book was written. Today, there is a good choice of deep learning libraries that are supported in R—MXNet and Keras. Keras is actually a frontend abstraction for other deep learning libraries, and can use TensorFlow in the background. We will use MXNet, Keras, and TensorFlow in this book.

MXNet

MXNet is a deep learning library developed by Amazon. It can run on CPUs and GPUs. For this chapter, running on CPUs will suffice.

Apache MXNet is a flexible and scalable deep learning framework that supports **convolutional neural networks** (**CNNs**) and **long short-term memory networks** (**LSTMs**). It can be distributed across multiple processors/machines and achieves almost linear scale on multiple GPUs/CPUs. It is easy to install on R and it supports a good range of deep learning functionality for R. It is an excellent choice for writing our first deep learning model for image-classification.

MXNet originated at *Carnegie Mellon University* and is heavily supported by Amazon; they chose it as their default deep learning library in 2016. In 2017, MXNet was accepted as the *Apache Incubator* project, ensuring that it would remain open source software. It has a higher-level programming model similar to Keras, but the reported performance is better. MXNet is very scalable as additional GPUs are added.

To install the MXNet package for Windows, run the following code from an R session:

```
cran <- getOption("repos")
cran["dmlc"] <-
"https://apache-mxnet.s3-accelerate.dualstack.amazonaws.com/R/CRAN"
options(repos = cran)
install.packages("mxnet")
```

This installs the CPU version; for the GPU version, you need to change the second line to:

```
cran["dmlc"] <-
"https://apache-mxnet.s3-
accelerate.dualstack.amazonaws.com/R/CRAN/GPU/cu92"
```

You have to change `cu92` to `cu80`, `cu90` or `cu91` based on the version of CUDA installed on your machine. For other operating systems (and in case the this does not work, as things change very fast in deep learning), you can get further instructions at `https://mxnet.incubator.apache.org/install/index.html`.

Keras

Keras is a high-level, open source, deep learning framework created by Francois Chollet from Google that emphasizes iterative and fast development; it is generally regarded as one of the best options to use to learn deep learning. Keras has a choice of backend lower-level frameworks: TensorFlow, Theano, or CNTK, but it is most commonly used with TensorFlow. Keras models can be deployed on practically any environment, for example, a web server, iOS, Android, a browser, or the Raspberry Pi.

To learn more about Keras, go to `https://keras.io/`. To learn more about using Keras in R, go to `https://keras.rstudio.com`; this link will also has more examples of R and Keras, as well as a handy Keras cheat sheet that gives a thorough reference to all of the functionality of the R Keras package. To install the `keras` package for R, run the following code:

```
devtools::install_github("rstudio/keras")
library(keras)
install_keras()
```

This will install the CPU-based package of Keras and TensorFlow. If your machine has a suitable GPU, you can refer to the documentation for `install_keras()` to find out how to install it.

Do I need a GPU (and what is it, anyway)?

Probably the two biggest reasons for the exponential growth in deep learning are:

- The ability to accumulate, store, and process large datasets of all types
- The ability to use GPUs to train deep learning models

So what exactly are GPUs and why are they so important to deep learning? Probably the best place to start is by actually looking at the CPU and why this is not optimal for training deep learning models. The CPU in a modern PC is one of the pinnacles of human design and engineering. Even the chip in a mobile phone is more powerful now than the entire computer systems of the first space shuttles. However, because they are designed to be good at all tasks, they may not be the best option for niche tasks. One such task is high-end graphics.

If we take a step back to the mid-1990s, most games were 2D, for example, platform games where the character in the game jumps between platforms and/or avoids obstacles. Today, almost all computer games utilize 3D space. Modern consoles and PCs have co-processors that take the load of modelling 3D space onto a 2D screen. These co-processors are known as **GPUs**.

GPUs are actually far simpler than CPUs. They are built to just do one task: massively parallel matrix operations. CPUs and GPUs both have *cores*, where the actual computation takes place. A PC with an Intel i7 CPU has four physical cores and eight virtual cores by using *Hyper Threading*. The NVIDIA TITAN Xp GPU card has 3,840 CUDA® cores. These cores are not directly comparable; a core in a CPU is much more powerful than a core in a GPU. But if the workload requires a large amount of matrix operations that can be done independently, a chip with lots of simple cores is much quicker.

Before deep learning was even a concept, researchers in neural networks realized that doing high-end graphics and training neural networks both involved workloads: large amounts of matrix multiplication that could be done in parallel. They realized that training the models on the GPU rather than the CPU would allow them to create much more complicated models.

Today, all deep learning frameworks run on GPUs as well as CPUs. In fact, if you want to train models from scratch and/or have a large amount of data, you almost certainly need a GPU. The GPU must be an NVIDIA GPU and you also need to install the CUDA® Toolkit, NVIDIA drivers, and cuDNN. These allow you to interface with the GPU and *hijack* its use from a graphics card to a maths co-processor. Installing these is not always easy, you have to ensure that the versions of CUDA, cuDNN and the deep learning libraries you use are compatible. Some people advise you need to use Unix rather than Windows, but support on Windows has improved greatly. This code on this book was developed on a Windows workstation. Forget about using a macOS, because they don't support NVIDIA cards.

That was the bad news. The good news is that you can learn everything about deep learning if you don't have a suitable GPU. The examples in the early chapters of this book will run perfectly fine on a modern PC. When we need to scale up, the book will explain how to use cloud resources, such as AWS and Google Cloud, to train large deep learning models.

Setting up reproducible results

Software for data science is advancing and changing rapidly. Although this is wonderful for progress, it can make reproducing someone else's results a challenge. Even your own code may not work when you go back to it a few months later. This is one of the biggest issues in scientific research today, across all fields, not just artificial intelligence and machine learning. If you work in research or academia and you want to publish your results in scientific journals, this is something you need to be concerned about. The first edition of this book partially addressed this problem by using the R checkpoint package provided by Revolution Analytics. This makes a record of what versions of software were used and ensures there is a snapshot of them available.

For the second edition, we will not use this package for a number of reasons:

- Most readers are probably not publishing their work and are more interested in other concerns (maximizing accuracy, interpretability, and so on).
- Deep learning requires large datasets. When you have a large amount of data, it should mean that, while we may not get precisely the same result each time, it will be very close (fractions of percentages).

- In production systems, there is more to reproducibility than software. You also have to consider data pipelines and random seed-generation.
- In order to ensure reproducibility, the libraries used must stay frozen. New versions of deep learning APIs are released constantly and may contain enhancements. If we limited ourselves to old versions, we would get poor results.

If you are interested in learning more about the `checkpoint` package, you can read the online vignette for the package at `https://cran.r-project.org/web/packages/checkpoint/vignettes/checkpoint.html`.

This book was written using R version 3.5 on Windows 10 Professional x64, which is the latest version of R at the time of writing. The code was run on a machine with an Intel i5 processor and 32 GB RAM; it should run on an Intel i3 processor with 8 GB RAM.

You can download the example code files for this book from your account at `http://www.packtpub.com/`. If you purchased this book elsewhere, you can visit `http://www.packtpub.com/support` and register to have the files emailed directly to you.

You can download the code files by following these steps:

1. Log in or register to our website using your email address and password.
2. Hover the mouse pointer on the **SUPPORT** tab at the top.
3. Click on **Code Downloads & Errata**.
4. Enter the name of the book in the **Search box**.
5. Select the book for which you're looking to download the code files.
6. Choose from the drop-down menu where you purchased this book from.
7. Click on **Code Download**.

Once the file is downloaded, please make sure that you unzip or extract the folder using the latest version of:

- WinRAR I 7-Zip for Windows
- Zipeg I iZip I UnRarX for Mac
- 7-Zip I PeaZip for Linux

Summary

This chapter presented a brief introduction to neural networks and deep neural networks. Using multiple hidden layers, deep neural networks have been a revolution in machine learning. They consistently outperform other machine learning tasks, especially in areas such as computer vision, natural-language processing, and speech-recognition.

The chapter also looked at some of the theory behind neural networks, the difference between shallow neural networks and deep neural networks, and some of the misconceptions that currently exist concerning deep learning.

We closed this chapter with a discussion on how to set up R and the importance of using a GUI (RStudio). This section discussed the deep learning libraries available in R (MXNet, Keras, and TensorFlow), GPUs, and reproducibility.

In the next chapter, we will begin to train neural networks and generate our own predictions.

Training a Prediction Model 2

This chapter shows you how to build and train basic neural networks in R through hands-on examples and shows how to evaluate different hyper-parameters for models to find the best set. Another important issue in deep learning is dealing with overfitting, which is when a model performs well on the data it was trained on but poorly on unseen data. We will briefly look at this topic in this chapter, and cover it in more depth in Chapter 3, *Deep Learning Fundamentals*. The chapter closes with an example use case classifying activity data from a smartphone as walking, going up or down stairs, sitting, standing, or lying down.

This chapter covers the following topics:

- Neural networks in R
- Binary classification
- Visualizing a neural network
- Multi-classification using the nnet and RSNNS packages
- The problem of overfitting data—the consequences explained
- Use case—building and applying a neural network

Neural networks in R

We will build several neural networks in this section. First, we will use the neuralnet package to create a neural network model that we can visualize. We will also use the `nnet` and RSNNS (Bergmeir, C., and Benítez, J. M. (2012)) packages. These are standard R packages and can be installed by the `install.packages` command or from the packages pane in RStudio. Although it is possible to use the `nnet` package directly, we are going to use it through the `caret` package, which is short for **Classification and Regression Training**. The `caret` package provides a standardized interface to work with many **machine learning** (**ML**) models in R, and also has some useful features for validation and performance assessment that we will use in this chapter and the next.

For our first examples of building neural networks, we will use the MNIST dataset, which is a classic classification problem: recognizing handwritten digits based on pictures. The data can be downloaded from the Apache MXNet site (`https://apache-mxnet.s3-accelerate.dualstack.amazonaws.com/R/data/mnist_csv.zip`). It is in the CSV format, where each column of the dataset, or feature, represents a pixel from the image. Each image has 784 pixels (28 x 28) and the pixels are in grayscale and range from 0 to 255. The first column contains the digit label, and the rest are pixel values, to be used for classification.

Building neural network models

The code is in the `Chapter2` folder of the code for this book. If you have not already downloaded and unzipped the code, go back to `Chapter 1`, *Getting Started with Deep Learning*, for the link to download the code. Unzip the code into a folder in your machine, and you will see folders for different chapters. The code we will be following is `Chapter2\chapter2.R`.

We will use the `MNIST` dataset to build some neural network models. The first few lines in the script look to see whether the data file (`train.csv`) is in the data directory. If the file already exists in the data directory then it proceeds; if it isn't, it downloads a ZIP file from `https://apache-mxnet.s3-accelerate.dualstack.amazonaws.com/R/data/mnist_csv.zip`, and unzips it into the data folder. This check means that you don't have to download the data manually and the program only downloads the file once. Here is the code to download the data:

```
dataDirectory <- "../data"
if (!file.exists(paste(dataDirectory,'/train.csv',sep="")))
{
  link <-
'https://apache-mxnet.s3-accelerate.dualstack.amazonaws.com/R/data/mnist_cs
v.zip'
  if (!file.exists(paste(dataDirectory,'/mnist_csv.zip',sep="")))
    download.file(link, destfile =
paste(dataDirectory,'/mnist_csv.zip',sep=""))
  unzip(paste(dataDirectory,'/mnist_csv.zip',sep=""), exdir =
dataDirectory)
  if (file.exists(paste(dataDirectory,'/test.csv',sep="")))
    file.remove(paste(dataDirectory,'/test.csv',sep=""))
}
```

As an alternative, the `MNIST` data is also available in Keras, so we can download it from that library and save it as a CSV file:

```
if (!file.exists(paste(dataDirectory,'/train.csv',sep="")))
{
 library(keras)
 mnist <- dataset_mnist()
 c(c(x_train,y_train),c(x_test,y_test)) %<-% dataset_mnist()
 x_train <-
array_reshape(x_train,c(dim(x_train)[1],dim(x_train)[2]*dim(x_train)[3]))
 y_train <- array_reshape(y_train,c(length(y_train),1))
 data_mnist <- as.data.frame(cbind(y_train,x_train))
 colnames(data_mnist)[1] <- "label"
 colnames(data_mnist)[2:ncol(data_mnist)] <-
paste("pixel",seq(1,784),sep="")
 write.csv(data_mnist,paste(dataDirectory,'/train.csv',sep=""),row.names =
FALSE)
}
```

When you load any new dataset for the first time, the first thing you should do is a quick check on the data to ensure that the number of rows and columns are as expected, as shown in the following code:

```
digits <- read.csv("../data/train.csv")
dim(digits)
[1] 42000 785

head(colnames(digits), 4)
[1] "label" "pixel0" "pixel1" "pixel2"

tail(colnames(digits), 4)
[1] "pixel780" "pixel781" "pixel782" "pixel783"

head(digits[, 1:4])
  label pixel0 pixel1 pixel2
1     1      0      0      0
2     0      0      0      0
3     1      0      0      0
4     4      0      0      0
5     0      0      0      0
6     0      0      0      0
```

The data looks OK, we have `42000` rows and `785` columns. The header was imported correctly and the values are numeric. Now that we have loaded the data and performed some validation checks on it, we can move on to modeling. Our first model will use the `neuralnet` library as this allows us to visualize the neural net. We will select only the rows where the label is either 5 or 6, and create a binary classification task to differentiate between them. Of course, you can pick any digits you choose, but using 5 and 6 is a good choice because they are similar graphically, and therefore our model will have to work harder than if we picked two digits that were not so similar, for example, 1 and 8. We rename the labels as 0 and 1 for modeling and then separate that data into a train and a test split.

We then perform dimensionality-reduction using **principal components analysis** (**PCA**) on the training data—we use PCA because we want to reduce the number of predictor variables in our data to a reasonable number for plotting. PCA requires that we remove columns that have zero variance; these are the columns that have the same value for each instance. In our image data, there is a border around all images, that is, the values are all zero. Note how we find the columns that have zero variance using only the data used to train the model; it would be incorrect to apply this check first and then split the data for modelling.

Dimensionality-reduction: Our image data is grayscale data with values from 0 (black) to 255 (white). These values are highly correlated, that is, if a pixel is black (that is, 0), it is likely that the pixels around it are either black or dark gray. Similarly if a pixel is white (255), it is likely that the pixels around it are either white or light gray. Dimensionality-reduction is an unsupervised machine learning technique that takes an input dataset and produces an output dataset with the same number of rows but fewer columns. Crucially though, these fewer columns can explain most of the signal in the input dataset. PCA is one dimensionality-reduction algorithm. We use it here because we want to create a dataset with a small number of columns to plot the network, but we still want our algorithm to produce good results.

The following code selects the rows where the label is either 5 or 6 and creates a train/test split. It also removes columns where the variance is zero; these are columns that have the same value for every row:

```
digits_nn <- digits[(digits$label==5) | (digits$label==6),]
digits_nn$y <- digits_nn$label
digits_nn$label <- NULL
table(digits_nn$y)
   5    6
3795 4137

digits_nn$y <- ifelse(digits_nn$y==5, 0, 1)
table(digits_nn$y)
   0    1
3795 4137

set.seed(42)
sample <- sample(nrow(digits_nn), nrow(digits_nn)*0.8)
test <- setdiff(seq_len(nrow(digits_nn)), sample)

digits.X2 <- digits_nn[,apply(digits_nn[sample,1:(ncol(digits_nn)-1)], 2,
var, na.rm=TRUE) != 0]
length(digits.X2)
[1] 624
```

We have reduced the number of column data from 784 to 624, that is, 160 columns had the same value for all rows. Now, we perform PCA on the data and plot the cumulative sum of the variances:

```
df.pca <- prcomp(digits.X2[sample,],center = TRUE,scale. = TRUE)
s<-summary(df.pca)
cumprop<-s$importance[3, ]
plot(cumprop, type = "l",main="Cumulative sum",xlab="PCA component")
```

The cumulative sum of PCA explained variance shows how many principal components are needed to explain the proportion of variance in the input data. In layman's terms, this plot shows that we can use the first 100 variables (the *principal components*) and this will account for over 80% of the variance in the original data:

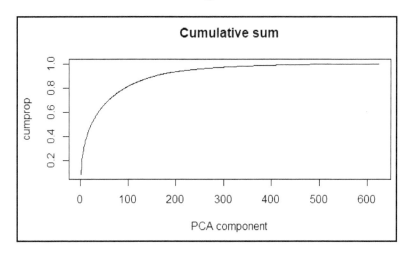

Figure 2.1: Cumulative sum of the Principal Components explained variance.

The next code block selects out the principal components that account for 50% of our variance and use those variables to create a neural network:

```
num_cols <- min(which(cumprop>0.5))
cumprop[num_cols]
  PC23
0.50275

newdat<-data.frame(df.pca$x[,1:num_cols])
newdat$y<-digits_nn[sample,"y"]
col_names <- names(newdat)
f <- as.formula(paste("y ~", paste(col_names[!col_names %in%
"y"],collapse="+")))
nn <- neuralnet(f,data=newdat,hidden=c(4,2),linear.output = FALSE)
```

We can see that 50% of the variance in the original data can be accounted by only 23 principal components. Next, we plot the neural network by calling the `plot` function:

```
plot(nn)
```

This produces a plot similar to the following screenshot. We can see the input variables (**PC1** to **PC23**), the hidden layers and biases, and even the network weights:

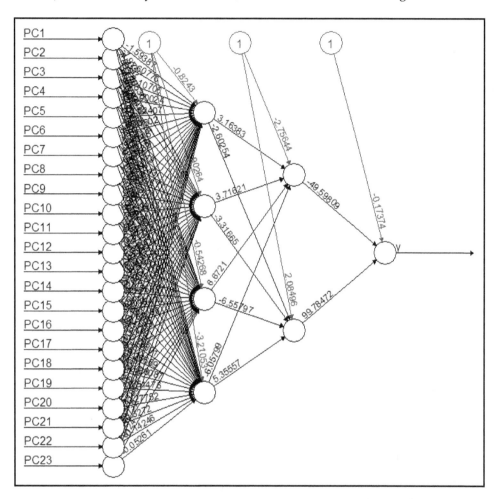

Figure 2.2: An example of a neural network with weights and biases

We selected 23 principal components to use as predictors for our neural network library. We chose to use two hidden layers, the first with four nodes and the second with two nodes. The plot outputs the coefficients, which are not all decipherable from the plot, but there are functions to access them if required.

Next, we will create predictions on a holdout or test dataset that was not used to build either the dimensionality-reduction or the neural network model. We have to first pass the test data into the `predict` function, passing in the `df.pca` object created earlier, to get the principal components for the test data. We can then pass this data into the neural network prediction (filtering the columns to the first 23 principal components) and then show the confusion matrix and overall accuracy:

```
test.data <- predict(df.pca, newdata=digits_nn[test,colnames(digits.X2)])
test.data <- as.data.frame(test.data)
preds <- compute(nn,test.data[,1:num_cols])
preds <- ifelse(preds$net.result > 0.5, "1", "0")
t<-table(digits_nn[test,"y"], preds,dnn=c("Actual", "Predicted"))
acc<-round(100.0*sum(diag(t))/sum(t),2)
print(t)
        Predicted
Actual 0    1
    0  740  17
    1   17 813
print(sprintf(" accuracy = %1.2f%%",acc))
[1] " accuracy = 97.86%"
```

We achieved `97.86%` accuracy, which is not bad considering we only used 23 principal components in our neural network. It is important to note that these 23 variables are not directly comparable to any columns in the input dataset or each other. In fact, the whole point of PCA, or any dimensionality-reduction algorithm, is to produce columns that are not correlated with each other.

Next, we will move on to create models that perform multi-classification, that is, they can classify digits 0-9. We will convert the labels (the digits 0 to 9) to a factor so R knows that this is a classification not a regression problem. For real-world problems, you should use all the data available, but if we used all 42,000 rows, it would take a very long time to train using the neural network packages in R. We will select 5,000 rows for training and 1,000 rows for test purposes. We should select the rows at random and ensure that there is no overlap between the rows in our training and test datasets. We also separate the data into the features or predictors (`digits.x`) and the outcome (`digits.Y`). We are using all the columns except the labels as the predictors here:

```
sample <- sample(nrow(digits), 6000)
train <- sample[1:5000]
test <- sample[5001:6000]
```

```
digits.X <- digits[train, -1]
digits.y_n <- digits[train, 1]
digits$label <- factor(digits$label, levels = 0:9)
digits.y <- digits[train, 1]

digits.test.X <- digits[test, -1]
digits.test.y <- digits[test, 1]
rm(sample,train,test)
```

Finally, before we get started building our neural network, let's quickly check the distribution of the digits. This can be important as, for example, if one digit occurs very rarely, we may need to adjust our modeling approach to ensure that, it's given enough weight in the performance evaluation if we care about accurately predicting that specific digit. The following code snippet creates a bar plot showing the frequency of each digit label:

```
barplot(table(digits.y),main="Distribution of y values (train)")
```

We can see from the plot that the categories are fairly evenly distributed so there is no need to increase the weight or importance given to any particular one:

Figure 2.3: Distribution of *y* values for train dataset

Now let's build and train our first neural network using the `nnet` package through the `caret` package wrapper. First, we use the `set.seed()` function and specify a specific seed so that the results are reproducible. The exact seed is not important, what matters is that the same seed is used each time you run the script. The `train()` function first takes the feature or predictor data (x), and then the outcome variable (y), as arguments. The `train()` function can work with a variety of models, determined via the method argument. Although many aspects of machine learning models are learned automatically, some parameters have to be set. These vary by the method used; for example, in neural networks, one parameter is the number of hidden units. The `train()` function provides an easy way to try a variety of these tuning parameters as a named data frame to the `tuneGrid` argument. It returns the performance measures for each set of tuning parameters and returns the best trained model. We will start with just five hidden neurons in our model, and a modest decay rate. The learning rate controls how much each iteration or step can influence the current weights. The decay rate is the regularization hyper-parameter, which is used to prevent the model from overfitting. Another argument, `trcontrol`, controls additional aspects of `train()`, and is used, when a variety of tuning parameters are being evaluated, to tell the caret package how to validate and pick the best tuning parameter.

For this example, we will set the method for training control to *none* as we only have one set of tuning parameters being used here. Finally, at the end, we can specify additional, named arguments that are passed on to the actual `nnet()` function (or whatever algorithm is specified). Because of the number of predictors (784), we increase the maximum number of weights to 10,000 and specify a maximum of 100 iterations. Due to the relatively small amount of data, and the paucity of hidden neurons, this first model does not take too long to run:

```
set.seed(42)
tic <- proc.time()
digits.m1 <- caret::train(digits.X, digits.y,
          method = "nnet",
          tuneGrid = expand.grid(
            .size = c(5),
            .decay = 0.1),
          trControl = trainControl(method = "none"),
          MaxNWts = 10000,
          maxit = 100)
print(proc.time() - tic)
   user system elapsed
  54.47 0.06 54.85
```

The `predict()` function generates a set of predictions for the data. We will use the test dataset to evaluate the model; this contains records that were not used to train the model. We examine the distribution of the predicted digits in the following diagram.

```
digits.yhat1 <- predict(digits.m1,newdata=digits.test.X)
accuracy <- 100.0*sum(digits.yhat1==digits.test.y)/length(digits.test.y)
print(sprintf(" accuracy = %1.2f%%",accuracy))
[1] " accuracy = 54.80%"
barplot(table(digits.yhat1),main="Distribution of y values (model 1)")
```

It is clear that this is not a good model because the distribution of the predicted values is very different from the distribution of the actual values:

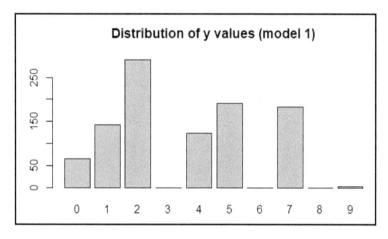

Figure 2.4: Distribution of *y* values from prediction model

The `barplot` is a simple check of the predictions, and shows us that our model is not very accurate. We can also calculate the accuracy by finding the percentage of rows from the predictions that match the actual value. The accuracy for this model is `54.8%`, which is not good. A more formal evaluation of the model's performance is possible using the `confusionMatrix()` function in the `caret` package. Because there is a function by the same name in the `RSNNS` package, they are masked so we call the function using `caret::confusionMatrix` to ensure the function from the `caret` package is used. The following code shows the confusion matrix and performance metrics on the test set:

```
caret::confusionMatrix(xtabs(~digits.yhat1 + digits.test.y))
Confusion Matrix and Statistics

          digits.test.y
digits.yhat1    0   1   2   3   4   5   6   7   8   9
          0    61   1   0   1   0   2   0   0   0   1
```

```
        1    1  104   0    2    0    4    3    9   12    8
        2    6    2  91   56    4   20   68    1   41    1
        3    0    0   0    0    0    0    0    0    0    0
        4    2    0   4    1   67    1   22    4    2   21
        5   39    0   6   45    4   46    0    5   30   16
        6    0    0   0    0    0    0    0    0    0    0
        7    0    0   0    6    9    0    0   91    2   75
        8    0    0   0    0    0    0    0    0    0    0
        9    0    0   0    0    0    0    0    3    0    0
```

```
Overall Statistics
              Accuracy : 0.46
                95% CI : (0.4288, 0.4915)
    No Information Rate : 0.122
    P-Value [Acc > NIR] : < 2.2e-16
                 Kappa : 0.4019
 Mcnemar's Test P-Value : NA
```

Statistics by Class:

	Class: 0	Class: 1	Class: 2	Class: 3	Class: 4	Class: 5 Class: 6
Sensitivity	0.5596	0.9720	0.9010	0.000	0.7976	0.6301 0.000
Specificity	0.9944	0.9563	0.7786	1.000	0.9378	0.8436 1.000
Pos Pred Value	0.9242	0.7273	0.3138	NaN	0.5403	0.2408 NaN
Neg Pred Value	0.9486	0.9965	0.9859	0.889	0.9806	0.9666 0.907
Prevalence	0.1090	0.1070	0.1010	0.111	0.0840	0.0730 0.093
Detection Rate	0.0610	0.1040	0.0910	0.000	0.0670	0.0460 0.000
Detection Prevalence	0.0660	0.1430	0.2900	0.000	0.1240	0.1910 0.000
Balanced Accuracy	0.7770	0.9641	0.8398	0.500	0.8677	0.7369 0.500

	Class: 7	Class: 8	Class: 9
Sensitivity	0.8053	0.000	0.0000
Specificity	0.8963	1.000	0.9966
Pos Pred Value	0.4973	NaN	0.0000
Neg Pred Value	0.9731	0.913	0.8776
Prevalence	0.1130	0.087	0.1220
Detection Rate	0.0910	0.000	0.0000
Detection Prevalence	0.1830	0.000	0.0030
Balanced Accuracy	0.8508	0.500	0.4983

Because we had multiple digits, there are three main sections to the performance output. First, the actual frequency cross tab is shown. Correct predictions are on the diagonal, with various frequencies of misclassification on the off diagonals. Next are the overall statistics, which refer to the model's performance across all classes. Accuracy is simply the proportion of cases correctly classified, along with a 95% confidence interval, which can be useful, especially for smaller datasets where there may be considerable uncertainty in the estimate.

`No Information Rate` refers to what accuracy could be expected without any information by merely guessing the most frequent class, in this case, 1, which occurred 11.16% of the time. The p-value tests whether the observed accuracy (44.3%) is significantly different from `No Information Rate` (11.2%). Although statistically significant, this is not very meaningful for digit-classification, where we would expect to do far better than simply guessing the most frequent digit! Finally, individual performance metrics for each digit are shown. These are based on calculating that digit versus every other digit, so that each is a binary comparison.

Now that we have some basic understanding of how to set up, train, and evaluate model performance, we will try increasing the number of hidden neurons, which is one key way to improve model performance, at the cost of greatly increasing the model complexity. Recall from `Chapter 1`, *Getting Started with Deep Learning*, that every predictor or feature connects to each hidden neuron, and each hidden neuron connects to each outcome or output. With `784` features, each additional hidden neuron adds a substantial number of parameters, which also results in longer run times. Depending on your computer, be prepared to wait a number of minutes for these next model to finish:

```
set.seed(42)
tic <- proc.time()
digits.m2 <- caret::train(digits.X, digits.y,
          method = "nnet",
          tuneGrid = expand.grid(
            .size = c(10),
            .decay = 0.1),
          trControl = trainControl(method = "none"),
          MaxNWts = 50000,
          maxit = 100)
print(proc.time() - tic)
   user system elapsed
 154.49 0.09 155.33

digits.yhat2 <- predict(digits.m2,newdata=digits.test.X)
accuracy <- 100.0*sum(digits.yhat2==digits.test.y)/length(digits.test.y)
print(sprintf(" accuracy = %1.2f%%",accuracy))
[1] " accuracy = 66.30%"
barplot(table(digits.yhat2),main="Distribution of y values (model 2)")
```

This model is better than the previous model but the distribution of the predicted values is still uneven:

Figure 2.5: Distribution of *y* values from prediction model

Increasing the number of hidden neurons from 5 to 10 improved our in-sample performance from an overall accuracy of `54.8%` to `66.3%`, but this is still quite some way from ideal (imagine character-recognition software that mixed up over 30% of all the characters!). We increase again, this time to 40 hidden neurons, and wait even longer for the model to finish training:

```
set.seed(42)
tic <- proc.time()
digits.m3 <- caret::train(digits.X, digits.y,
          method = "nnet",
          tuneGrid = expand.grid(
            .size = c(40),
            .decay = 0.1),
          trControl = trainControl(method = "none"),
          MaxNWts = 50000,
          maxit = 100)
print(proc.time() - tic)
   user system elapsed
2450.16 0.96 2457.55

digits.yhat3 <- predict(digits.m3,newdata=digits.test.X)
accuracy <- 100.0*sum(digits.yhat3==digits.test.y)/length(digits.test.y)
print(sprintf(" accuracy = %1.2f%%",accuracy))
[1] " accuracy = 82.20%"
barplot(table(digits.yhat3),main="Distribution of y values (model 3)")
```

The distribution of the predicted values is even in this model, which is what we are looking for. However the accuracy is still only at 82.2%, which is quite low:

Figure 2.6: Distribution of *y* values from prediction model

Using 40 hidden neurons has improved accuracy to `82.2%` overall and it took over 40 minutes to run on an i5 computer. Model performance for some digits is still not great. If this were a real research or business problem, we might continue trying additional neurons, tuning the decay rate, or modifying features in order to try to boost model performance further, but for now we will move on.

Next, we will take a look at how to train neural networks using the RSNNS package. This package provides an interface to a variety of possible models using the **Stuttgart Neural Network Simulator** (**SNNS**) code; however, for a basic, single hidden-layer, feed-forward neural network, we can use the `mlp()` convenience wrapper function, which stands for multi-layer perceptron. The RSNNS package is a bit trickier to use than the convenience of nnet via the `caret` package, but one benefit is that it can be far more flexible and allows for many other types of neural network architecture to be trained, including recurrent neural networks, and also has a greater variety of training strategies.

One difference between the nnet and RSNNS packages is that, for multi-class outcomes (such as digits), RSNNS requires a dummy encoding (that is, one-hot encoding), where each possible class is represented as a column coded as 0/1. This is facilitated using the `decodeClassLabels()` function, as shown in the following code snippet:

```
head(decodeClassLabels(digits.y))
     0 1 2 3 4 5 6 7 8 9
[1,] 0 0 0 0 0 0 0 0 0 1
[2,] 0 0 0 0 1 0 0 0 0 0
```

```
[3,] 1 0 0 0 0 0 0 0 0 0
[4,] 0 0 0 0 0 1 0 0 0 0
[5,] 0 0 0 0 1 0 0 0 0 0
[6,] 0 0 0 1 0 0 0 0 0 0
```

Since we had reasonably good success with 40 hidden neurons, we will use the same size here. Rather than standard propagation as the learning function, we will use resilient propagation, based on the work of Riedmiller, M., and Braun, H. (1993). Resilient back-propagation is an **optimization** to standard back-propagation that applies faster weight-update mechanisms. One of the problems that occurs as the neural network increases in complexity is that they take a long time to train. We will discuss this in depth in subsequent chapters, but for now, you just need to know that this neural network is faster because it keeps track of past derivatives and takes bigger steps if they were in the same direction during back-propagation. Note also that, because a matrix of outcomes is passed, although the predicted probability will not exceed 1 for any single digit, the sum of predicted probabilities across all digits may exceed 1 and also may be less than 1 (that is, for some cases, the model may not predict they are very likely to represent any of the digits). The `predict` function returns a matrix where each column represents a single digit, so we use the `encodeClassLabels()` function to convert back into a single vector of digit labels to plot and evaluate the model's performance:

```
set.seed(42)
tic <- proc.time()
digits.m4 <- mlp(as.matrix(digits.X),
            decodeClassLabels(digits.y),
            size = 40,
            learnFunc = "Rprop",
            shufflePatterns = FALSE,
            maxit = 80)
print(proc.time() - tic)
   user system elapsed
 179.71 0.08 180.99

digits.yhat4 <- predict(digits.m4,newdata=digits.test.X)
digits.yhat4 <- encodeClassLabels(digits.yhat4)
accuracy <- 100.0*sum(I(digits.yhat4 -
1)==digits.test.y)/length(digits.test.y)
print(sprintf(" accuracy = %1.2f%%",accuracy))
[1] " accuracy = 81.70%"
barplot(table(digits.yhat4),main="Distribution of y values (model 4)")
```

The following bar plot shows that the predicted values are relatively evenly distributed among the categories. This matches the distribution of the actual category values:

Figure 2.7: Distribution of *y* values from prediction model

The accuracy is 81.70% and it ran in 3 minutes on my computer. This is only slightly lower than when we used nnet with 40 hidden nodes, which took 40 minutes on the same machine! This demonstrates the importance of using an optimizer, which we will see in subsequent chapters.

Generating predictions from a neural network

For any given observation, there can be a probability of membership in any of a number of classes (for example, an observation may have a 40% chance of being a 5, a 20% chance of being a 6, and so on). To evaluate the performance of the model, some choices have to be made about how to go from the probability of class membership to a discrete classification. In this section, we will explore a few of these options in more detail.

As long as there are no perfect ties, the simplest method is to classify observations based on the highest predicted probability. Another approach, which the RSNNS package calls the **winner takes all** (**WTA**) method, chooses the class with the highest probability, provided the following conditions are met:

- There are no ties for highest probabilities
- The highest probability is above a user-defined threshold (the threshold could be zero)
- The remaining classes all have a predicted probability under the maximum minus another user-defined threshold

Otherwise, observations are classified as unknown. If both thresholds are zero (the default), this equates to saying that there must be one unique maximum. The advantage of such an approach is that it provides some quality control. In the digit-classification example we have been exploring, there are 10 possible classes.

Suppose 9 of the digits had a predicted probability of 0.099, and the remaining class had a predicted probability of 0.109. Although one class is technically more likely than the others, the difference is fairly trivial and we may conclude that the model cannot with any certainty classify that observation. A final method, called 402040, classifies if only one value is above a user-defined threshold, and all other values are below another user-defined threshold; if multiple values are above the first threshold, or any value is not below the second threshold, it treats the observation as unknown. Again, the goal here is to provide some quality control.

It may seem like this is unnecessary because uncertainty in predictions should come out in the model performance. However, it can be helpful to know if your model was highly certain in its prediction and right or wrong, or uncertain and right or wrong.

Finally, in some cases, not all classes are equally important. For example, in a medical context where a variety of biomarkers and genes are collected on patients and used to classify whether they are, at risk of cancer, or at risk of heart disease, even a 40% chance of having cancer may be enough to warrant further investigation, even if they have a 60% chance of being healthy. This has to do with the performance measures we saw earlier where, beyond overall accuracy, we can assess aspects such as sensitivity, specificity, and positive and negative predictive values. There are cases where overall accuracy is less important than making sure no one is missed.

The following code shows the raw probabilities for the in-sample data, and the impact these different choices have on the predicted values:

```
digits.yhat4_b <- predict(digits.m4,newdata=digits.test.X)
head(round(digits.yhat4_b, 2))
      [,1] [,2] [,3] [,4] [,5] [,6] [,7] [,8] [,9] [,10]
18986 0.00 0.00 0.00 0.98 0.00 0.02 0.00 0.00 0.00 0.00
41494 0.00 0.00 0.03 0.00 0.13 0.01 0.95 0.00 0.00 0.00
21738 0.00 0.00 0.02 0.03 0.00 0.46 0.01 0.00 0.74 0.00
37086 0.00 0.01 0.00 0.63 0.02 0.01 0.00 0.00 0.03 0.00
35532 0.00 0.00 0.00 0.00 0.01 0.00 0.00 0.99 0.00 0.00
17889 0.03 0.00 0.00 0.00 0.00 0.34 0.01 0.00 0.00 0.00

table(encodeClassLabels(digits.yhat4_b,method = "WTA", l = 0, h = 0))

  1   2   3   4  5  6  7   8  9 10
102 116 104 117 93 66 93 127 89 93

table(encodeClassLabels(digits.yhat4_b,method = "WTA", l = 0, h = .5))
```

```
 0  1  2  3  4  5  6  7  8   9  10
141 95 113 86 93 67 53 89 116 73 74

table(encodeClassLabels(digits.yhat4_b,method = "WTA", l = .2, h = .5))
 0  1  2  3  4  5  6  7  8   9  10
177 91 113 77 91 59 50 88 116 70 68

table(encodeClassLabels(digits.yhat4_b,method = "402040", l = .4, h = .6))
  0  1   2  3  4  5  6  7   8  9  10
254 89 110 71 82 46 41 79 109 65 54
```

We now proceed to examine problems related to overfitting the data and the impact on the evaluation of the model's performance.

The problem of overfitting data – the consequences explained

A common issue in machine learning is overfitting data. Generally, overfitting is used to refer to the phenomenon where the model performs better on the data used to train the model than it does on data not used to train the model (holdout data, future real use, and so on). Overfitting occurs when a model memorizes part of the training data and fits what is essentially noise in the training data. The accuracy in the training data is high, but because the noise changes from one dataset to the next, this accuracy does not apply to unseen data, that is, we can say that the model does not generalize very well.

Overfitting can occur at any time, but tends to become more severe as the ratio of parameters to information increases. Usually, this can be thought of as the ratio of parameters to observations, but not always. For example, suppose we have a very imbalanced dataset where the outcome we want to predict is a rare event that occurs in 1 in 5 million cases. In that case, a sample size of 15 million may only have 3 positive cases. Even though the sample size is large, the information is low. To consider a simple-but-extreme case, imagine fitting a straight line to two data points. The fit will be perfect, and in those two training data, your linear-regression model will appear to have fully accounted for all variations in the data. However, if we then applied that line to another 1,000 cases, it might not fit very well at all.

In the previous sections, we generated out-of-sample predictions for the our models, that is, we evaluated accuracy on test (or holdout) data. But we never checked whether our models were overfitting, that is, the accuracy levels on the test data. We can examine how well the model generalizes by checking the accuracy on the in-sample predictions. We can see that the accuracy on the in-sample data is 84.7%, compared to 81.7% on the holdout data. There is a 3.0% loss; or, put differently, using training data to evaluate model performance resulted in an overly optimistic estimate of the accuracy, and that overestimate was 3.0%:

```
digits.yhat4.train <- predict(digits.m4)
digits.yhat4.train <- encodeClassLabels(digits.yhat4.train)
accuracy <- 100.0*sum(I(digits.yhat4.train - 1)==digits.y)/length(digits.y)
print(sprintf(" accuracy = %1.2f%%",accuracy))
[1] " accuracy = 84.70%"
```

Since we fitted several models earlier of varying complexity, we could examine the degree of overfitting or overly optimistic accuracy from in-sample versus out of-sample performance measures across them. The code here should be easy enough to follow. We call the predict function for our models and do not pass in any new data; this returns the predictions for the data the model was trained with. The rest of the code is boilerplate code to create the graphic plot.

```
digits.yhat1.train <- predict(digits.m1)
digits.yhat2.train <- predict(digits.m2)
digits.yhat3.train <- predict(digits.m3)
digits.yhat4.train <- predict(digits.m4)
digits.yhat4.train <- encodeClassLabels(digits.yhat4.train)

measures <- c("AccuracyNull", "Accuracy", "AccuracyLower", "AccuracyUpper")
n5.insample <- caret::confusionMatrix(xtabs(~digits.y +
digits.yhat1.train))
n5.outsample <- caret::confusionMatrix(xtabs(~digits.test.y +
digits.yhat1))
n10.insample <- caret::confusionMatrix(xtabs(~digits.y +
digits.yhat2.train))
n10.outsample <- caret::confusionMatrix(xtabs(~digits.test.y +
digits.yhat2))
n40.insample <- caret::confusionMatrix(xtabs(~digits.y +
digits.yhat3.train))
n40.outsample <- caret::confusionMatrix(xtabs(~digits.test.y +
digits.yhat3))
n40b.insample <- caret::confusionMatrix(xtabs(~digits.y +
I(digits.yhat4.train - 1)))
n40b.outsample <- caret::confusionMatrix(xtabs(~ digits.test.y +
I(digits.yhat4 - 1)))

shrinkage <- rbind(
```

```
    cbind(Size = 5, Sample = "In",
  as.data.frame(t(n5.insample$overall[measures]))),
    cbind(Size = 5, Sample = "Out",
  as.data.frame(t(n5.outsample$overall[measures]))),
    cbind(Size = 10, Sample = "In",
  as.data.frame(t(n10.insample$overall[measures]))),
    cbind(Size = 10, Sample = "Out",
  as.data.frame(t(n10.outsample$overall[measures]))),
    cbind(Size = 40, Sample = "In",
  as.data.frame(t(n40.insample$overall[measures]))),
    cbind(Size = 40, Sample = "Out",
  as.data.frame(t(n40.outsample$overall[measures]))),
    cbind(Size = 40, Sample = "In",
  as.data.frame(t(n40b.insample$overall[measures]))),
    cbind(Size = 40, Sample = "Out",
  as.data.frame(t(n40b.outsample$overall[measures])))
    )
shrinkage$Pkg <- rep(c("nnet", "RSNNS"), c(6, 2))
dodge <- position_dodge(width=0.4)

ggplot(shrinkage, aes(interaction(Size, Pkg, sep = " : "), Accuracy,
                      ymin = AccuracyLower, ymax = AccuracyUpper,
                      shape = Sample, linetype = Sample)) +
  geom_point(size = 2.5, position = dodge) +
  geom_errorbar(width = .25, position = dodge) +
  xlab("") + ylab("Accuracy + 95% CI") +
  theme_classic() +
  theme(legend.key.size = unit(1, "cm"), legend.position = c(.8, .2))
```

The code produces the following plot, which shows the accuracy metrics and the confidence intervals for those metrics. One thing we notice from this plot is that, as the models get more complex, the gap between performance on the in-sample performance measures and the out-sample performance measures increases. This highlights that more complex models tend to overfit, that is, they perform better on the in-sample data than the unseen out-sample data:

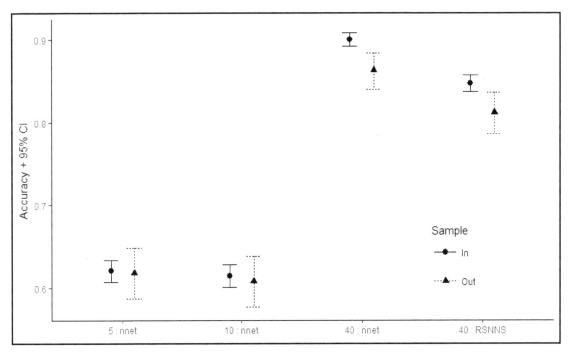

Figure 2.8: In-sample and out-sample performance measures for on neural network models

Use case – building and applying a neural network

To close the chapter, we will discuss a more realistic use case for neural networks. We will use a public dataset by Anguita, D., Ghio, A., Oneto, L., Parra, X., and Reyes-Ortiz, J. L. (2013) that uses smartphones to track physical activity. The data can be downloaded at https://archive.ics.uci.edu/ml/datasets/ human+activity+recognition+using+smartphones. The smartphones had an accelerometer and gyroscope from which 561 features from both time and frequency were used.

The smartphones were worn during walking, walking upstairs, walking downstairs, standing, sitting, and lying down. Although this data came from phones, similar measures could be derived from other devices designed to track activity, such as various fitness-tracking watches or bands. So this data can be useful if we want to sell devices and have them automatically track how many of these different activities the wearer engages in.

This data has already been normalized to range from -1 to + 1; usually we might want to perform some normalization if it has not already been applied. Download the data from the link and unzip it into the data folder that is on the same level as the chapter folder; we will use it in later chapters as well. We can import the training and testing data, as well as the labels. We will then take a quick look at the distribution of the outcome variable in the following code:

```
use.train.x <- read.table("../data/UCI HAR Dataset/train/X_train.txt")
use.train.y <- read.table("../data/UCI HAR Dataset/train/y_train.txt")[[1]]

use.test.x <- read.table("../data/UCI HAR Dataset/test/X_test.txt")
use.test.y <- read.table("../data/UCI HAR Dataset/test/y_test.txt")[[1]]

use.labels <- read.table("../data/UCI HAR Dataset/activity_labels.txt")

barplot(table(use.train.y),main="Distribution of y values (UCI HAR
Dataset)")
```

This produces the following bar plot, which shows that the categories are relatively evenly balanced:

Figure 2.9: Distribution of *y* values for UCI HAR dataset

We are going to evaluate a variety of tuning parameters to show how we might experiment with different approaches to try to get the best possible model. We will use different hyper-parameters and evaluate which model performs the best.

Because the models can take some time to train and R normally only uses a single core, we will use some special packages to enable us to run multiple models in parallel. These packages are `parallel`, `foreach`, and `doSNOW`, which should have been loaded if you ran the script from the first line.

Now we can pick our tuning parameters and set up a local cluster as the backend for the `foreach` R package for parallel for loops. Note that if you do this on a machine with fewer than five cores, you should change `makeCluster(5)` to a lower number:

```
## choose tuning parameters
tuning <- list(
  size = c(40, 20, 20, 50, 50),
  maxit = c(60, 100, 100, 100, 100),
  shuffle = c(FALSE, FALSE, TRUE, FALSE, FALSE),
  params = list(FALSE, FALSE, FALSE, FALSE, c(0.1, 20, 3)))

## setup cluster using 5 cores
## load packages, export required data and variables
## and register as a backend for use with the foreach package
cl <- makeCluster(5)
clusterEvalQ(cl, {source("cluster_inc.R")})
clusterExport(cl,
  c("tuning", "use.train.x", "use.train.y",
    "use.test.x", "use.test.y")
  )
registerDoSNOW(cl)
```

Now we are ready to train all the models. The following code shows a parallel for loop, using code that is similar to what we have already seen, but this time setting some of the arguments based on the tuning parameters we previously stored in the list:

```
## train models in parallel
use.models <- foreach(i = 1:5, .combine = 'c') %dopar% {
  if (tuning$params[[i]][1]) {
    set.seed(42)
    list(Model = mlp(
      as.matrix(use.train.x),
      decodeClassLabels(use.train.y),
      size = tuning$size[[i]],
      learnFunc = "Rprop",
      shufflePatterns = tuning$shuffle[[i]],
```

```
      learnFuncParams = tuning$params[[i]],
      maxit = tuning$maxit[[i]]
      ))
  } else {
    set.seed(42)
    list(Model = mlp(
      as.matrix(use.train.x),
      decodeClassLabels(use.train.y),
      size = tuning$size[[i]],
      learnFunc = "Rprop",
      shufflePatterns = tuning$shuffle[[i]],
      maxit = tuning$maxit[[i]]
    ))
  }
}
```

Because generating out-of-sample predictions can also take some time, we will do that in parallel as well. However, first we need to export the model results to each of the workers on our cluster, and then we can calculate the predictions:

```
## export models and calculate both in sample,
## 'fitted' and out of sample 'predicted' values
clusterExport(cl, "use.models")
use.yhat <- foreach(i = 1:5, .combine = 'c') %dopar% {
  list(list(
    Insample = encodeClassLabels(fitted.values(use.models[[i]])),
    Outsample = encodeClassLabels(predict(use.models[[i]],
                                    newdata = as.matrix(use.test.x)))
  ))
}
```

Finally, we can merge the actual and fitted or predicted values together into a dataset, calculate performance measures on each one, and store the overall results together for examination and comparison. We can use almost identical code to the code that follows to generate out-of-sample performance measures. That code is not shown in the book, but is available in the code bundle provided with the book. Some additional data-management is required here as sometimes a model may not predict each possible response level, but this can make for non-symmetrical frequency cross tabs, unless we convert the variable to a factor and specify the levels. We also drop o values, which indicate the model was uncertain about how to classify an observation:

```
use.insample <- cbind(Y = use.train.y,
  do.call(cbind.data.frame, lapply(use.yhat, `[[`, "Insample")))
colnames(use.insample) <- c("Y", paste0("Yhat", 1:5))

performance.insample <- do.call(rbind, lapply(1:5, function(i) {
  f <- substitute(~ Y + x, list(x = as.name(paste0("Yhat", i))))
```

```
    use.dat <- use.insample[use.insample[,paste0("Yhat", i)] != 0, ]
    use.dat$Y <- factor(use.dat$Y, levels = 1:6)
    use.dat[, paste0("Yhat", i)] <- factor(use.dat[, paste0("Yhat", i)],
levels = 1:6)
    res <- caret::confusionMatrix(xtabs(f, data = use.dat))

    cbind(Size = tuning$size[[i]],
          Maxit = tuning$maxit[[i]],
          Shuffle = tuning$shuffle[[i]],
          as.data.frame(t(res$overall[c("AccuracyNull", "Accuracy",
"AccuracyLower", "AccuracyUpper")])))
}))

use.outsample <- cbind(Y = use.test.y,
    do.call(cbind.data.frame, lapply(use.yhat, `[[`, "Outsample")))
colnames(use.outsample) <- c("Y", paste0("Yhat", 1:5))
performance.outsample <- do.call(rbind, lapply(1:5, function(i) {
    f <- substitute(~ Y + x, list(x = as.name(paste0("Yhat", i))))
    use.dat <- use.outsample[use.outsample[,paste0("Yhat", i)] != 0, ]
    use.dat$Y <- factor(use.dat$Y, levels = 1:6)
    use.dat[, paste0("Yhat", i)] <- factor(use.dat[, paste0("Yhat", i)],
levels = 1:6)
    res <- caret::confusionMatrix(xtabs(f, data = use.dat))

    cbind(Size = tuning$size[[i]],
          Maxit = tuning$maxit[[i]],
          Shuffle = tuning$shuffle[[i]],
          as.data.frame(t(res$overall[c("AccuracyNull", "Accuracy",
"AccuracyLower", "AccuracyUpper")])))
}))
```

If we print the in-sample and out-of-sample performance, we can see how each of our models did and the effect of varying some of the tuning parameters. The output is shown in the following code. The fourth column (null accuracy) is dropped as it is not as important for this comparison:

```
options(width = 80, digits = 3)
performance.insample[,-4]
  Size Maxit Shuffle Accuracy AccuracyLower AccuracyUpper
1   40    60   FALSE    0.984         0.981         0.987
2   20   100   FALSE    0.982         0.978         0.985
3   20   100    TRUE    0.982         0.978         0.985
4   50   100   FALSE    0.981         0.978         0.984
5   50   100   FALSE    1.000         0.999         1.000

performance.outsample[,-4]
  Size Maxit Shuffle Accuracy AccuracyLower AccuracyUpper
1   40    60   FALSE    0.916         0.906         0.926
```

2	20	100	FALSE	0.913	0.902	0.923
3	20	100	TRUE	0.913	0.902	0.923
4	50	100	FALSE	0.910	0.900	0.920
5	50	100	FALSE	0.938	0.928	0.946

As a reminder, the in-sample results evaluate the predictions on the training data and the out-sample results evaluate the predictions on the holdout (or test) data. The best set of hyper-parameters is the last set, where we get an accuracy of 93.8% on unseen data. This shows that we are able to classify the types of activity people are engaged in quite accurately based on the data from their smartphones. We can also see that the more complex models perform better on the in-sample data, which is not always the case with out-of-sample performance measures.

For each model, we have large differences between the accuracy for the in-sample data against the out-of-sample data; the models clearly overfit. We will get into ways to combat this overfitting in Chapter 3, *Deep Learning Fundamentals*, as we train deep neural networks with multiple hidden layers.

Despite the slightly worse out-of-sample performance, the models still do well – far better than chance alone – and, for our example use case, we could pick the best model and be quite confident that using this will provide a good classification of a user's activities.

Summary

This chapter showed how to get started building and training neural networks to classify data, including image recognition and physical activity data. We looked at packages that can visualize a neural network and we created a number of models to perform classification on data with 10 different categories. Although we only used some neural network packages rather than deep learning packages, our models took a long time to train and we had issues with overfitting.

Some of the basic neural network models in this chapter took a long time to train, even though we did not use all the data available. For the MNIST data, we used approx. 8,000 rows for our binary classification task and only 6,000 rows for our multi-classification task. Even so, one model took almost an hour to train. Our deep learning models will be much more complicated and should be able to process millions of records. You can now see why specialist hardware is required for training deep learning models.

Secondly, we see that a potential pitfall in machine learning is that more complex models will be more likely to overfit the training data, so that evaluating performance in the same data used to train the model results in biased, overly optimistic estimates of the model performance. Indeed, this can even make a difference as to which model is chosen as the best. Overfitting is also an issue for deep neural networks. In the next chapter, we will discuss various techniques used to prevent overfitting and obtain more accurate estimates of model performance.

In the next chapter we will look at building a neural network from scratch and see how it applies to deep learning. We will also discuss some methods to deal with overfitting.

3
Deep Learning Fundamentals

In the previous chapter, we created some machine learning models using neural network packages in R. This chapter will look at some of the fundamentals of neural networks and deep learning by creating a neural network using basic mathematical and matrix operations. This application sample will be useful for explaining some key parameters in deep learning algorithms and some of the optimizations that allow them to train on large datasets. We will also demonstrate how to evaluate different hyper-parameters for models to find the best set. In the previous chapter, we briefly looked at the problem of overfitting; this chapter goes into that topic in more depth and looks at how you can overcome this problem. It includes an example use case using dropout, the most common regularization technique in deep learning.

This chapter covers the following topics:

- Building neural networks from scratch in R
- Common parameters in deep learning
- Some key components in deep learning algorithms
- Using regularization to overcome overfitting
- Use case—improving out-of-sample model performance using dropout

Building neural networks from scratch in R

Although we have already used some neural network algorithms, it's time to dig a bit deeper into how they work. This section demonstrates how to code a neural network from scratch. It might surprise you to see that the core code for a neural network can be written in fewer than 80 lines! The code for this chapter does just that using an interactive web application written in R. It should give you more of an intuitive understanding of neural networks. First we will look at the web application, then we will delve more deeply into the code for the neural network.

Neural network web application

First, we will look at an R Shiny web application. I encourage you to run the application and follow the examples as it will really help you to get a better understanding of how neural networks work. In order to run it, you will have to open the `Chapter3` project in RStudio.

What is R Shiny?

R Shiny is an R package from the RStudio company that allows you to create interactive web apps using only R code. You can build dashboards and visualizations, and use the full functionality of R. You can extend R Shiny apps with CSS, widgets, and JavaScript. It is also possible to host your applications online. It is a great tool with which to showcase data science applications and I encourage you to look into it if you are not already familiar with it. For more information, see `https://shiny.rstudio.com/`, and, for examples of what is possible with R Shiny, see `https://shiny.rstudio.com/gallery/`.

1. Open the `server.R` file in RStudio and click on the **Run App** button:

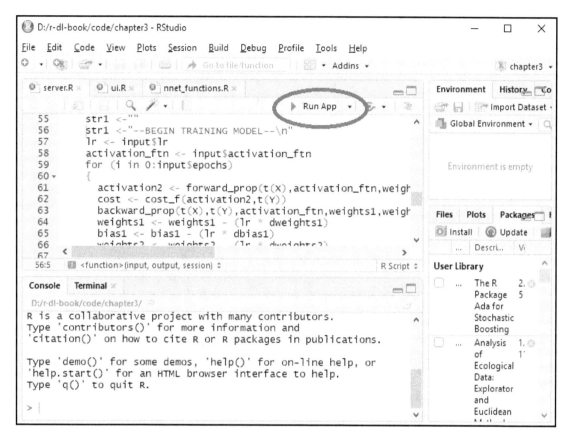

Figure 3.1: How to run an R Shiny application

2. When you click on the **Run App** button, you should get a pop-up screen for your web application. The following is a screenshot of the web application after it starts up:

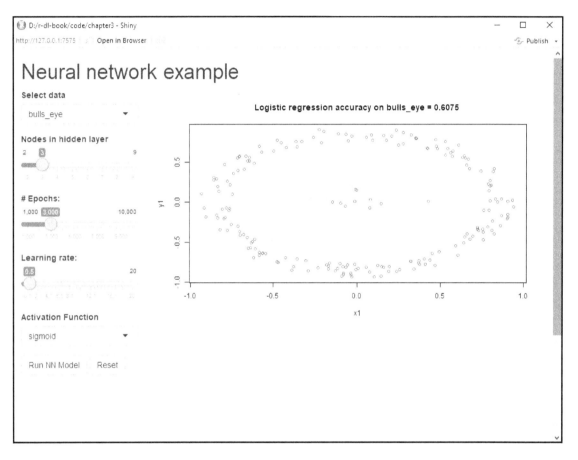

Figure 3.2: R Shiny application on startup

This web application can be used in the pop-up window or opened in a browser. On the left, there is a set of input choices; these are parameters for the neural network. These are known as hyper-parameters, in order to distinguish between the *parameters* that the model is trying to optimize. From top to bottom, these hyper-parameters are:

- **Select data**: There are four different datasets that you can use as training data.

- **Nodes in hidden layer**: The number of nodes in the hidden layer. The neural network has only one hidden layer.
- **# Epochs**: The number of times that the algorithm iterates over the data during model-building.
- **Learning rate**: The learning rate applied during backpropagation. The learning rate affects how much the algorithm changes the weights during every epoch.
- **Activation function**: The activation function applied to the output of each node.
- The **Run NN Model** button trains a model with the selection of input. The **Reset** button restores input choices to the default values.

There are four different datasets to choose from, each with a different data distribution; you can select them from the drop-down box. They have descriptive names; for example, the data that is plotted in *Figure 3.2* is called `bulls_eye`. These datasets are from another R package that is used to test clustering algorithms. The data has two classes of equal size and is composed of various geometric shapes. You can explore these datasets using the web application. The only change we make to the data is to randomly switches labels for 5% of the data. When you run the application, you will notice that there are some red points in the inner circle and some blue points in the outer circle. This is done so that our models should only achieve a maximum accuracy of 0.95 (95%). This gives us confidence that the model is working correctly. If the accuracy is higher than this, the model could be overfitting because the function it has learned is too complex. We will discuss overfitting again in the next section.

One of the first steps in machine learning should be to establish a benchmark score, this is useful for gauging your progress. A benchmark score could be a rule of thumb, or a simple machine learning algorithm; it should not be something that you spend a lot of time working on. In this application, we use a basic logistic regression model as a benchmark. We can see that in the previous screenshot, the accuracy for the logistic regression model is only 0.6075, or 60.75% accuracy. This is not much over 50%, but recall that logistic regression can only fit a straight line and this data cannot be separated using a straight line. A neural network should improve on the logistic regression benchmark, so if we get an accuracy of less than 0.6075 on this dataset, something is wrong with our model and we should review it.

So let's begin! Click on the **Run NN Model** button, which runs a neural network model on the data using the input choices. After a few seconds, the application should change to resemble the following screenshot:

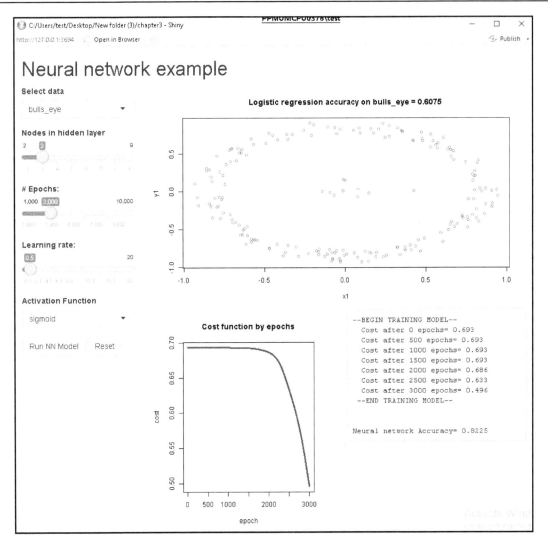

Figure 3.3: Neural network model execution with default settings

The application takes a few seconds and then it creates a graph of the cost function over the # **Epochs** and outputs cost function values as the algorithm iterates over the data. The text output also includes the final accuracy for the model in the text at the bottom right of the screen. In the diagnostic messages in the bottom right, we can see that the cost decreases during training and we achieved a final accuracy rate of 0.825. The cost is what the model is trying to minimize – a lower cost means better accuracy. It took some time for the cost to start decreasing as the model struggled initially to get the right weights.

In deep learning models, weights and biases should be not initialized with random values. If random values are used, this can lead to problems with training, such as vanishing or exploding gradients. This is where the weights get too small or too large and the model fails to train successfully. Also, if the weights are not correctly initialized, the model will take longer to train, as we saw earlier. Two of the most popular techniques to initialize weights to avoid these problems are the Xavier initialization and the He initialization (named after their inventors).

We can see in *Figure 3.3* that the cost has not plateaued, the last few values show it is still decreasing. This indicates that the model can be improved if we train it for longer. Change # **Epochs** to **7000** and click the **Run NN Model** button again; the screen will change to resemble the following plot:

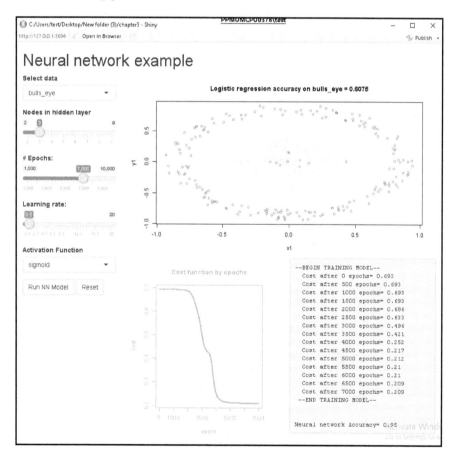

Figure 3.4: Neural network model execution with more epochs

Now we get an accuracy of 0.95, which is the maximum possible accuracy rate. We notice that the cost values have plateaued (that is, are not decreasing further) to around 0.21. This indicates that training the model for longer (that is, more epochs) will probably not improve the results, regardless of the current accuracy number. If the model is under training and the cost values have plateaued, we would need to consider changing the architecture of the model or getting more data to improve our accuracy. Let's look at changing the number of nodes in our model. Click the **Reset** button to change the input values to their defaults, then change the number of nodes to 7, and click the **Run NN Model** button. Now the screen will change to the following:

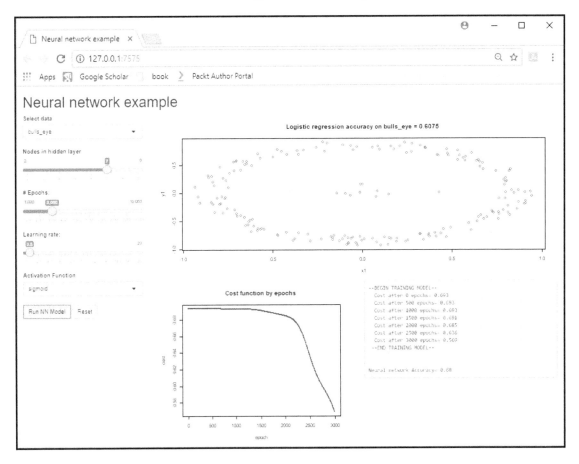

Figure 3.5: Neural network model execution with more nodes

Our accuracy here is 0.68, but compare this to the earlier examples, when we used the same input and only three nodes. We actually get worse performance with more nodes! This is because our data has a relatively simple pattern, and a model with seven nodes might be too complex and will take longer to train. Adding more nodes to a layer will increase training time but does not always improve performance.

Let's look at the **Learning rate**. Click the **Reset** button to change the input values to their defaults, then change the **Learning rate** to around **5**, and click the **Run NN Model** button again to replicate the following screen:

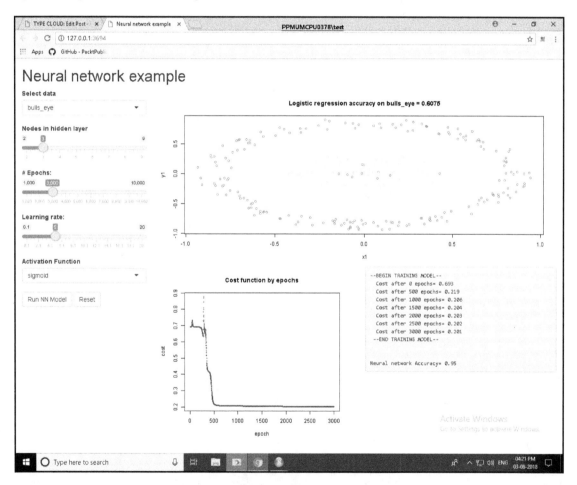

Figure 3.6: Neural network model execution with larger learning rate

We get 0.95 accuracy again, which is the best possible accuracy. If we compare it to the previous examples, we can see that the model *converged* (that is, the length of time it took for the cost function to plateau) much quicker, after just **500** epochs. We needed fewer epochs, so we can see an inverse relationship between learning rates and training epochs. A higher learning rate may mean you need fewer epochs. But are bigger learning rates always better? Well, no.

Click the **Reset** button to change the input values to their defaults, then change the **Learning rate** to the maximum value (**20**), and click the **Run NN Model** button again. When you do, you will get similar output to the following:

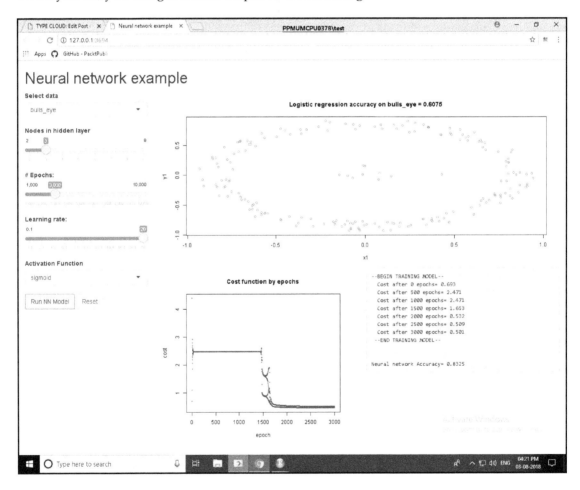

Figure 3.7: Neural network model execution with too great a learning rate

We get an accuracy rate of 0.83. What just happened? By selecting a huge learning rate, our model failed to converge at all. We can see that the cost function actually increases at the start of training, which indicates that the Learning rate is too high. Our cost function graph seems to have repeating values, which indicates that the gradient-descent algorithm is overshooting the minima at times.

Finally, we can look at how the choice of activation function affects model training. By changing the activation function, you may also need to change the **Learning rate**. Click the **Reset** button to change the input values to their defaults and select tanh for the activation function. When we select tanh as the activation function and 1.5 as the **Learning rate**, the cost gets stuck at 0.4 from epochs 500-3,500 before suddenly decreasing to 0.2. This can occur in neural networks when they get stuck in local optima. This phenomena can be seen in the following plot:

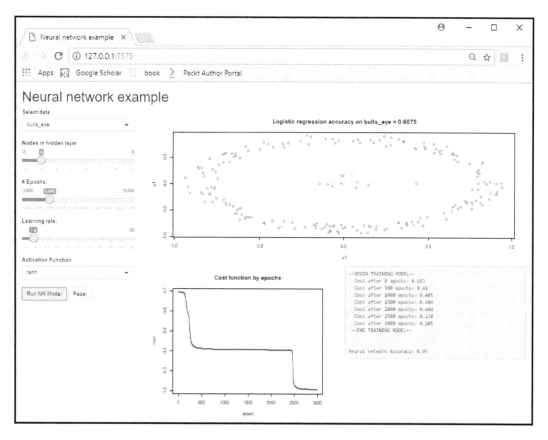

Figure 3.8: Neural network model execution with the tanh activation function

In contrast, using relu activation results in the model training faster. The following is an example where we only run 1,500 epochs with the relu activation to get the maximum possible accuracy of 0.95:

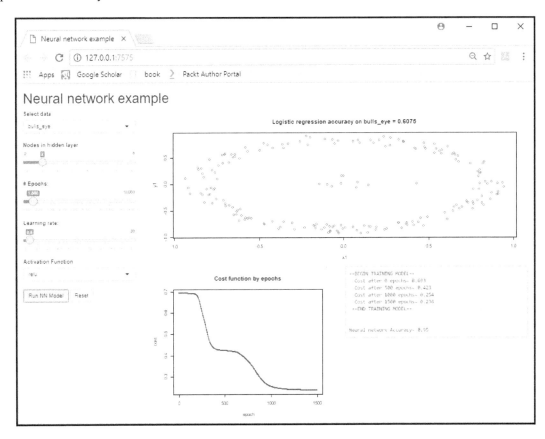

Figure 3.9: Neural network model execution with the relu activation function

I encourage you to experiment with the other datasets. For reference purposes, here is the max accuracy I got for each of those datasets. An interesting experiment is to see how different activation functions and learning rates work with these datasets:

- **worms (accuracy=0.95)**: 3 nodes, 3,000 epochs, Learning rate = 0.5, activation = tanh
- **moon (accuracy=0.95)**: 5 nodes, 5,000 epochs, Learning rate = 5, activation = sigmoid
- **blocks (accuracy=0.9025)**: 5 nodes, 5,000 epochs, Learning rate = 10, activation = sigmoid

In general, you will see the following:

- Using more epochs means a longer training time, which may not always be needed.
- If the model has not achieved the best accuracy and the cost function has plateaued (that is, it is not decreasing by much) toward the end of the training, then running it longer (that is, more epochs) or increasing the learning rate is unlikely to improve performance. Instead, look at changing the model's architecture, such as by changing the # layers (not an option in this demo), adding more nodes, or changing the activation functions.
- The learning rate must be selected carefully. If the value selected is too low, it will take a long time for the model to train. If the value selected is too high, the model will fail to train.

Neural network code

While the web application is useful to see the output of the neural network, we can also run the code for the neural network to really see how it works. The code in `Chapter3/nnet.R` allows us to do just that. This code has the same hyper-parameters as in the web application; this file allows you to run the neural network from the RStudio IDE. The following is the code that loads the data and sets the initial hyper-parameters for the neural network:

```
source("nnet_functions.R")
data_sel <- "bulls_eye"

. . . . . . . .

##################### neural network ####################
hidden <- 3
epochs <- 3000
lr <- 0.5
activation_ftn <- "sigmoid"

df <- getData(data_sel) # from nnet_functions
X <- as.matrix(df[,1:2])
Y <- as.matrix(df$Y)
n_x=ncol(X)
n_h=hidden
n_y=1
m <- nrow(X)
```

This code should not be too difficult to understand, it loads a dataset and sets some variables. The data is created in the `getData` function from the `Chapter3/nnet_functions.R` file. The data is created from functions in the `clustersim` package. The `Chapter3/nnet_functions.R` file contains the core functionality of our neural network that we will look at here. Once we load our data, the next step is to initialize our weights and biases. The `hidden` variable controls the number of nodes in the hidden layer; we set it to 3. We need two sets of weights and biases, one for the hidden layer and one for the output layer:

```
# initialise weights
set.seed(42)
weights1 <- matrix(0.01*runif(n_h*n_x)-0.005, ncol=n_x, nrow=n_h)
weights2 <- matrix(0.01*runif(n_y*n_h)-0.005, ncol=n_h, nrow=n_y)
bias1 <- matrix(rep(0,n_h),nrow=n_h,ncol=1)
bias2 <- matrix(rep(0,n_y),nrow=n_y,ncol=1)
```

This creates matrices for the (`weights1`, `bias1`) hidden layer and the (`weights2`, `bias2`) output layer. We need to ensure our matrices have the correct dimensions. For example, the `weights1` matrix should have the same number of columns as the input layer and the same number of rows as the hidden layer. Now we move on to the actual processing loop of the neural network:

```
for (i in 0:epochs)
{
   activation2 <- forward_prop(t(X),activation_ftn,weights1,bias1,
weights2,bias2)
   cost <- cost_f(activation2,t(Y))
   backward_prop(t(X),t(Y),activation_ftn,weights1,weights2,
activation1,activation2)
   weights1 <- weights1 - (lr * dweights1)
   bias1 <- bias1 - (lr * dbias1)
   weights2 <- weights2 - (lr * dweights2)
   bias2 <- bias2 - (lr * dbias2)

   if ((i %% 500) == 0)
     print (paste(" Cost after",i,"epochs =",cost))
}
[1] " Cost after 0 epochs = 0.693147158995952"
[1] " Cost after 500 epochs = 0.69314587328381"
[1] " Cost after 1000 epochs = 0.693116915341439"
[1] " Cost after 1500 epochs = 0.692486724429629"
[1] " Cost after 2000 epochs = 0.687107068792801"
[1] " Cost after 2500 epochs = 0.660418522655335"
[1] " Cost after 3000 epochs = 0.579832913091798"
```

We first run the forward-propagation function, then calculate a cost. We then call a backward-propagation step that calculates our derivatives, (dweights1, dbias1, dweights2, dbias2). Then we update the weights and biases, (weights1, bias1, weights2, bias2), using our Learning rate, (lr). We run this loop for the number of epochs (3000) and print out a diagnostic message every 500 epochs. This describes how every neural network and deep learning model works: first call forward-propagation, then calculate costs and derivative values, use those to update the weights through back-propagation and repeat.

Now let's look at some of the functions in the nnet_functions.R file. The following is the forward propagation function:

```
forward_prop <- function(X,activation_ftn,weights1,bias1,weights2,bias2)
{
  # broadcast hack
  bias1a<-bias1
  for (i in 2:ncol(X))
    bias1a<-cbind(bias1a,bias1)
  bias2a<-bias2
  for (i in 2:ncol(activation1))
    bias2a<-cbind(bias2a,bias2)
  Z1 <<- weights1 %*% X + bias1a
  activation1 <<- activation_function(activation_ftn,Z1)
  bias2a<-bias2
  for (i in 2:ncol(activation1))
    bias2a<-cbind(bias2a,bias2)
  Z2 <<- weights2 %*% activation1 + bias2a
  activation2 <<- sigmoid(Z2)
  return (activation2)
}
```

If you looked at the code carefully, you may have noticed that the assignment to the activation1, activation2, Z1, and Z2 variables uses <<- rather than <-. This makes those variables global in scope; we also want to use these values during back propagation. Using global variables is generally frowned upon and I could have returned a list, but it is acceptable here to use them because this application is for learning purposes.

The two for loops expand the bias vectors into matrices, then repeat the vector n times. The interesting code starts with the Z1 assignment. Z1 is a matrix multiplication, followed by an addition. We call the `activation_function` function on that value. We then use that output value and perform a similar operation for Z2. Finally, we apply a sigmoid activation to our output layer because our problem is binary classification.

The following is the code for the activation function; the first parameter decides which function to use (`sigmoid`, `tanh`, or `relu`). The second parameter is the value to be used as input:

```
activation_function <- function(activation_ftn,v)
{
  if (activation_ftn == "sigmoid")
    res <- sigmoid(v)
  else if (activation_ftn == "tanh")
    res <- tanh(v)
  else if (activation_ftn == "relu")
  {
    v[v<0] <- 0
    res <- v
  }
  else
    res <- sigmoid(v)
  return (res)
}
```

The following is the `cost` function:

```
cost_f <- function(activation2,Y)
{
  cost = -mean((log(activation2) * Y)+ (log(1-activation2) * (1-Y)))
  return(cost)
}
```

As a reminder, the output of the `cost` function is what we are trying to minimize. There are many types of `cost` functions; in this application we are using binary cross-entropy. The formula for binary cross-entropy is $-1/m \sum log(\bar{y}_i) * y_i + (log(1 - \bar{y}_i) * (1-y_i)$. Our target values ($y_i$) are always either *1* or *0*, so for instances where $y_i = 1$, this reduces to $\sum log(\bar{y}_i)$. If we have two rows where $y_i = 1$ and suppose that our model predicts *1.0* for the first row and the *0.0001* for the second row, then the costs for the rows are *log(1)=0* and *log(0.0001)=-9.1*, respectively. We can see that the closer to *1* the prediction is for these rows, the lower the `cost` value. Similarly, for rows where $y_i = 0$, this reduces to $log(1-\bar{y}_i)$, so the closer to 0 the prediction is for these rows, the lower the `cost` value.

If we are trying to maximize accuracy, why don't we just use what during model training? Binary cross-entropy is a better `cost` function because our model does not just output 0 or 1, but instead outputs continuous values from 0.0 to 1.0. For example, if two input rows had a target value=1 (that is, y=1), and our model gave probabilities of 0.51 and 0.99, then binary cross-entropy would give them a cost of 0.67 and 0.01, respectively. It assigns a higher cost to the first row because the model is unsure about it (the probability is close to 0.5). If instead we just looked at accuracy, we might decide that both rows have the same cost value because they are classified correctly (assuming we assign class=0 where predicted values < 0.5, and class=1 where predicted values >= 0.5).

The following is the code for the backward-propagation function:

```
backward_prop <-
function(X,Y,activation_ftn,weights1,weights2,activation1,activation2)
{
  m <- ncol(Y)
  derivative2 <- activation2-Y
  dweights2 <<- (derivative2 %*% t(activation1)) / m
  dbias2 <<- rowSums(derivative2) / m
  upd <- derivative_function(activation_ftn,activation1)
  derivative1 <- t(weights2) %*% derivative2 * upd
  dweights1 <<- (derivative1 %*% t(X)) / m
  dbias1 <<- rowSums(derivative1) / m
}
```

Backward propagation processes the network in reverse, starting at the last hidden layer and finishing at the first hidden layer, that is, in the direction of the output layer to the input layer. In our case, we only have one hidden layer, so it first calculates the loss from the output layer and calculates `dweight2` and `dbias2`. It then calculates the `derivative` of the `activation1` value, which was calculated during the forward-propagation step. The `derivative` function is similar to the activation function, but instead of calling an activation function, it calculates the `derivative` of that function. For example, the `derivative` of `sigmoid(x)` is *sigmoid(x) * (1 - sigmoid(x))*. The `derivative` values of simple functions can be found in any calculus reference or online:

```
derivative_function <- function(activation_ftn,v)
{
  if (activation_ftn == "sigmoid")
   upd <- (v * (1 - v))
  else if (activation_ftn == "tanh")
   upd <- (1 - (v^2))
  else if (activation_ftn == "relu")
   upd <- ifelse(v > 0.0,1,0)
```

```
    else
      upd <- (v * (1 - v))
    return (upd)
  }
```

That's it! A working neural network using basic R code. It can fit complex functions and performs better than logistic regression. You might not get all the parts at once, that's OK. The following is a quick recap of the steps:

1. Run a forward-propagation step, which involves multiplying the weights by the input for each layer and passing the output to the next layer.

2. Evaluate the output from the final layer using the `cost` function.

3. Based on the error rate, use backpropagation to make small adjustments to the weights in the nodes in each layer. The learning rate controls how much of an adjustment we make each time.

4. Repeat steps 1-3, maybe thousands of times, until the `cost` function begins to plateau, which indicates our model is trained.

Back to deep learning

Many of the concepts in the previous section apply to deep learning because deep learning is simply neural networks with two or more hidden layers. To demonstrate this, let's look at the following code in R that loads the `mxnet` deep learning library and calls the help command on the function in that library that trains a deep learning model. Even though we have not trained any models using this library yet, we have already seen many of the parameters in this function:

```
library(mxnet)
?mx.model.FeedForward.create
```

If you get errors saying the `mxnet` package is unavailable, see Chapter 1, *Getting Started with Deep Learning*, for installation instructions. However, we are not running any `mxnet` code in this chapter, we only want to display the help page for a function. So feel free to just continue reading and you can install the package later when we use it in the next chapter.

This brings up the help page for the `FeedForward` function in the `mxnet` library, which is the forward-propagation/model train function. `mxnet` and most deep learning libraries do not have a specific *backward*-propagation function, they handle this implicitly:

```
mx.model.FeedForward.create(symbol, X, y = NULL, ctx = NULL,
  begin.round = 1, num.round = 10, optimizer = "sgd",
```

```
initializer = mx.init.uniform(0.01), eval.data = NULL,
eval.metric = NULL, epoch.end.callback = NULL,
batch.end.callback = NULL, array.batch.size = 128
...)
```

We will see more of this function in subsequent chapters; for now we will just look at the parameters.

The symbol, X, y, and ctx parameters

The symbol parameter defines the deep learning architecture; X and y are the input and output data structures. The ctx parameter controls which device (for example, CPU/GPU) the model is trained on.

The num.round and begin.round parameters

num.round is equivalent to epochs in our code; that is, however many times we iterate over the data. begin.round is where we resume training the model if we paused training previously. If we pause training, we can save the partially-trained model, reload it later, and resume training.

The optimizer parameter

Our implementation of neural networks used gradient descent. When researchers started creating more complicated multilayer neural network models, they found that they took an extraordinarily long time to train. This is because the basic gradient-descent algorithm with no optimization is not very efficient; it makes small steps towards its goal in each epoch regardless of what occurred in previous epochs. We can compare it with a guessing game: one person has to guess a number in a range and for each guess, they are told to go higher or lower (assuming they do not guess the correct number!). The higher/lower instruction is similar to the derivative value, it indicates the direction we must travel. Now let's say that the range of possible numbers is 1 to 1,000,000 and the first guess is 1,000. The person is told to go higher, which should they do:

- Try 1001.
- Take the difference between the guess and the max value and divide by 2. Add this value to the previous guess.

The second option is much better and should mean the person gets to the right answer in 20 guesses or fewer. If you have a background in computer science, you may recognize this as the binary-search algorithm. The first option, guessing 1,001, 1,002, ..., 1,000,000, is a terrible choice and will probably fail as one party will give up! But this is similar to how gradient descent works. It moves incrementally towards the target. If you try increasing the learning rate to overcome this problem, you can overshoot the target and the model fails to converge.

Researchers came up with some clever optimizations to speed up training. One of the first optimizers was called momentum, and it does exactly what its name states. It looks at the extent of the derivative and takes bigger *steps* for each epoch if the previous steps were all in the same direction. It should mean that the model trains much quicker. There are other algorithms that are enhancements of these, such as RMS-Prop and Adam. You don't usually need to know how they work, just that, when you change the optimizer, you may also have to adjust other hyper-parameters, such as the learning rate. In general, look for previous examples done by others and copy those hyper-parameters.

We actually used one of these optimizers in an example in the previous chapter. In that chapter, we had 2 models with a similar architecture (40 hidden nodes). The first model (`digits.m3`) used the `nnet` library and took 40 minutes to train. The second model (`digits.m3`) used resilient backpropagation and took 3 minutes to train. This shows the benefit of using an optimizer in neural networks and deep learning.

The initializer parameter

When we created the initial values for our weights and biases (that is, model parameters), we used random numbers, but limited them to the values of -0.005 to +0.005. If you go back and review some of the graphs of the `cost` functions, you see that it took 2,000 epochs before the `cost` function began to decline. This is because the initial values were not in the right range and it took 2,000 epochs to get to the correct magnitude. Fortunately, we do not have to worry about how to set these parameters in the `mxnet` library because this parameter controls how the weights and biases are initialized before training.

The eval.metric and eval.data parameters

These two parameters control what data and which metric are used to evaluate the model. `eval.metric` is equivalent to the `cost` function we used in our code. `eval.data` is used if you want to evaluate the model on a holdout dataset that is not used in training.

The epoch.end.callback parameter

This is a `callback` function that allows you to register another function that is called after *n* epochs. Deep learning models take a long time to train, so you need some feedback to know they are working correctly! You can write a custom `callback` function to do whatever you need, but usually it outputs to the screen or log after *n* epochs. This is equivalent to the code in our neural network that printed a diagnostic message every *500* epochs. The `callback` function can also be used to save the model to disk, for example, if you wanted to save the model before it begins to overfit.

The array.batch.size parameter

We only had 400 instances (rows) in our data, which can easily fit into memory. However, if your input data has millions of instances, the data needs to be split into batches during training in order to fit in the memory of the CPU/GPU. The number of instances you train at a time is the batch size. Note, you still iterate over all the data for the number of epochs, you just split the data into batches during each iteration and run the forward-propagation, backpropagation step over each batch for each epoch. For example, if you had 100 instances and selected a batch size of *32* with *6* epochs, you would need *4* batches for each epoch (*100/32 = 3.125*, so we need *4* batches to process all the data), for a total of *24* loops.

There is a trade-off in choosing the batch size. If you choose too low a value, the model will take a longer time to train because it's running more operations and batches will have more variability because of the small size. You cannot choose an enormous batch size either, this might cause your model to crash because it loads too much data into either the CPU or GPU. In most cases, you either take a sensible default that works from another deep learning model, or you set it at some value (for example, 1,024) and if your model crashes, then try again with a value of half the previous value (512).

There is a relationship between **Batch size**, **Learning rates**, and **# Epochs** for training. But there are no hard and fast rules in selecting values. However, in general, consider changing these values together and do not use an extreme value for one of these hyper-parameters. For example, picking a large Learning rate should mean fewer epochs, but if your batch size is too small, the model may fail to train. The best advice is to look at similar architectures and pick a similar set and range of values.

Now that we can see that deep learning still uses many of the concepts from neural networks, we will move on to talk about an important issue that you will probably encounter with every deep learning model: overfitting.

Using regularization to overcome overfitting

In the previous chapter, we saw the diminishing returns from further training iterations on neural networks in terms of their predictive ability on holdout or test data (that is, data not used to train the model). This is because complex models may memorize some of the noise in the data rather than learning the general patterns. These models then perform much worse when predicting new data. There are some methods we can apply to make our model generalize, that is, fit the overall patterns. These are called **regularization** and aim to reduce testing errors so that the model performs well on new data.

The most common regularization technique used in deep learning is dropout. However, we will also discuss two other regularization techniques that have a basis in regression and deep learning. These two regularization techniques are **L1 penalty**, which is also known as **Lasso**, and **L2 penalty**, which is also known as **Ridge**.

L1 penalty

The basic concept of the **L1 penalty**, also known as the **least-absolute shrinkage and selection operator** (**Lasso**–Hastie, T., Tibshirani, R., and Friedman, J. (2009)), is that a penalty is used to shrink weights toward zero. The penalty term uses the sum of the absolute weights, so some weights may get shrunken to zero. This means that Lasso can also be used as a type of variable selection. The strength of the penalty is controlled by a hyper-parameter, alpha (λ), which multiplies the sum of the absolute weights, and it can be a fixed value or, as with other hyper-parameters, optimized using cross-validation or some similar approach.

It is easier to describe Lasso if we use an **ordinary least squares** (**OLS**) regression model. In regression, a set of coefficients or model weights is estimated using the least-squared error criterion, where the weight/coefficient vector, Θ, is estimated such that it minimizes $\sum(y_i - \bar{y}_i)$ where $\bar{y}_i = b + \Theta x$, y_i is the target value we want to predict and $\bar{y}_i$ is the predicted value. Lasso regression adds an additional penalty term that now tries to minimize $\sum(y_i - \bar{y}_i) + \lambda \lfloor \Theta \rfloor$, where $\lfloor \Theta \rfloor$ is the absolute value of Θ. Typically, the intercept or offset term is excluded from this constraint.

There are a number of practical implications for Lasso regression. First, the effect of the penalty depends on the size of the weights, and the size of the weights depends on the scale of the data. Therefore, data is typically standardized to have unit variance first (or at least to make the variance of each variable equal). The L1 penalty has a tendency to shrink small weights to zero (for explanations as to why this happens, see Hastie, T., Tibshirani, R., and Friedman, J. (2009)). If you only consider variables for which the L1 penalty leaves non-zero weights, it can essentially function as feature-selection. The tendency for the L1 penalty to shrink small coefficients to zero can also be convenient for simplifying the interpretation of the model results.

Applying the L1 penalty to neural networks works exactly the same for neural networks as it does for regression. If X represents the input, Y is the outcome or dependent variable, B the parameters, and F the objective function that will be optimized to obtain B, that is, we want to minimize $F(B; X, Y)$. The L1 penalty modifies the objective function to be F(B; X, Y) $+ \lambda \lfloor \Theta \rfloor$, where Θ represents the weights (typically offsets are ignored). The L1 penalty tends to result in a sparse solution (that is, more zero weights) as small and larger weights result in equal penalties, so that at each update of the gradient, the weights are moved toward zero.

We have only considered the case where λ is a constant, controlling the degree of penalty or regularization. However, it is possible to set different values with deep neural networks, where varying degrees of regularization can be applied to different layers. One reason for considering such differential regularization is that it is sometimes desirable to allow a greater number of parameters (say by including more neurons in a particular layer) but then counteract this somewhat through stronger regularization. However, this approach can be quite computationally demanding if we are allowing the L1 penalty to vary for every layer of a deep neural network and using cross-validation to optimize all possible combinations of the L1 penalty. Therefore, usually a single value is used across the entire model.

L1 penalty in action

To see how the L1 penalty works, we can use a simulated linear regression problem. The code for the rest of this chapter is in `Chapter3/overfitting.R`. We simulate the data, using a correlated set of predictors:

```
set.seed(1234)
X <- mvrnorm(n = 200, mu = c(0, 0, 0, 0, 0),
  Sigma = matrix(c(
    1, .9999, .99, .99, .10,
    .9999, 1, .99, .99, .10,
    .99, .99, 1, .99, .10,
```

```
        .99,  .99,  .99,  1,  .10,
        .10,  .10,  .10,  .10,  1
    ), ncol = 5))
  y <- rnorm(200, 3 + X %*% matrix(c(1, 1, 1, 1, 0)), .5)
```

Next, we can fit an OLS regression model to the first 100 cases, and then use `lasso`. To use `lasso`, we use the `glmnet()` function from the `glmnet` package. This function can actually fit the L1 or the L2 (discussed in the next section) penalties, and which one occurs is determined by the argument, alpha. When `alpha = 1`, it is the L1 penalty (that is, `lasso`), and when `alpha = 0`, it is the L2 penalty (that is, ridge regression). Further, because we don't know which value of `lambda` we should pick, we can evaluate a range of options and tune this hyper-parameter automatically using cross-validation, which is the `cv.glmnet()` function. We can then plot the `lasso` object to see the mean squared error for a variety of `lambda` values to allow us to select the correct level of regularization:

```
m.ols <- lm(y[1:100] ~ X[1:100, ])
m.lasso.cv <- cv.glmnet(X[1:100, ], y[1:100], alpha = 1)
plot(m.lasso.cv)
```

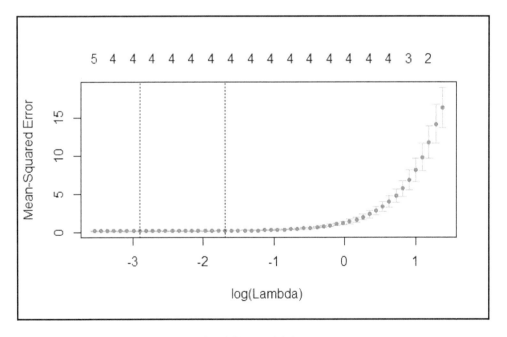

Figure 3.10: Lasso regularization

One thing that we can see from the graph is that, when the penalty gets too high, the cross-validated model increases. Indeed, `lasso` seems to do well with very low lambda values, perhaps indicating `lasso` does not help improve out-of-sample performance/generalizability much for this dataset. For the sake of this example, we will continue but in actual use, this might give us pause to consider whether `lasso` was really helping. Finally, we can compare the coefficients with those from `lasso`:

```
cbind(OLS = coef(m.ols),Lasso = coef(m.lasso.cv)[,1])
                   OLS  Lasso
(Intercept)     2.958  2.99
X[1:100, ]1    -0.082  1.41
X[1:100, ]2     2.239  0.71
X[1:100, ]3     0.602  0.51
X[1:100, ]4     1.235  1.17
X[1:100, ]5    -0.041  0.00
```

Notice that the OLS coefficients are noisier and also that, in `lasso`, predictor 5 is penalized to 0. Recall from the simulated data that the true coefficients are 3, 1, 1, 1, 1, and 0. The OLS estimates have much too low a value for the first predictor and much too high a value for the second, whereas `lasso` has more accurate values for each. This demonstrates that `lasso` regression generalizes better than OLS regression for this dataset.

L2 penalty

The **L2 penalty**, also known as **ridge regression**, is similar in many ways to the L1 penalty, but instead of adding a penalty based on the sum of the absolute weights, the penalty is based on the squared weights. This means that larger absolute weights are penalized more. In the context of neural networks, this is sometimes referred to as weight decay. If you examine the gradient of the regularized objective function, there is a penalty such that, at every update, there is a multiplicative penalty to the weights. As for the L1 penalty, although they could be included, biases or offsets are usually excluded from this.

From the perspective of a linear regression problem, the L2 penalty is a modification to the objective function minimized, from $\sum(y_i - \bar{y}_i)$ to $\sum(y_i - \bar{y}_i) + \lambda\Theta^2$.

L2 penalty in action

To see how the L2 penalty works, we can use the same simulated linear regression problem we used for the Ll penalty. To fit a ridge regression model, we use the `glmnet()` function from the `glmnet` package. As mentioned previously, this function can actually fit the L1 or the L2 penalties, and which one occurs is determined by the argument, alpha. When `alpha = 1`, it fits `lasso`, and when `alpha = 0`, it fits ridge regression. This time, we choose `alpha = 0`. Again, we evaluate a range of lambda options and tune this hyper-parameter automatically using cross-validation. This is accomplished by using the `cv.glmnet()` function. We plot the ridge regression object to see the error for a variety of lambda values:

```
m.ridge.cv <- cv.glmnet(X[1:100, ], y[1:100], alpha = 0)
plot(m.ridge.cv)
```

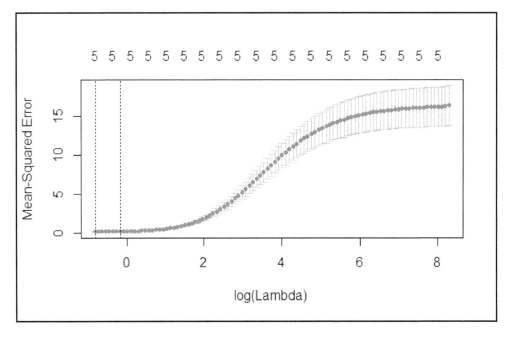

Figure 3.11: Ridge regularization

Although the shape is different from `lasso` in that the error appears to asymptote for higher lambda values, it is still clear that, when the penalty gets too high, the cross-validated model error increases. As with `lasso`, the ridge regression model seems to do well with very low lambda values, perhaps indicating the L2 penalty does not improve out-of-sample performance/generalizability by much.

Finally, we can compare the OLS coefficients with those from `lasso` and the ridge regression model:

```
> cbind(OLS = coef(m.ols),Lasso = coef(m.lasso.cv)[,1],Ridge =
coef(m.ridge.cv)[,1])
               OLS Lasso   Ridge
(Intercept)  2.958  2.99   2.9919
X[1:100, ]1 -0.082  1.41   0.9488
X[1:100, ]2  2.239  0.71   0.9524
X[1:100, ]3  0.602  0.51   0.9323
X[1:100, ]4  1.235  1.17   0.9548
X[1:100, ]5 -0.041  0.00  -0.0023
```

Although ridge regression does not shrink the coefficient for the fifth predictor to exactly 0, it is smaller than in the OLS, and the remaining parameters are all slightly shrunken, but quite close to their true values of 3, 1, 1, 1, and 0.

Weight decay (L2 penalty in neural networks)

We have already unknowingly used regularization in the previous chapter. The neural network we trained using the `caret` and `nnet` package used a weight decay of 0.10. We can investigate the use of weight decay by varying it, and tuning it using cross-validation:

1. Load the data as before. Then we create a local cluster to run the cross-validation in parallel:

```
set.seed(1234)
## same data as from previous chapter
if (!file.exists('../data/train.csv'))
{
  link <-
'https://apache-mxnet.s3-accelerate.dualstack.amazonaws.com/R/data/
mnist_csv.zip'
  if (!file.exists(paste(dataDirectory,'/mnist_csv.zip',sep="")))
    download.file(link, destfile =
paste(dataDirectory,'/mnist_csv.zip',sep=""))
  unzip(paste(dataDirectory,'/mnist_csv.zip',sep=""), exdir =
dataDirectory)
  if (file.exists(paste(dataDirectory,'/test.csv',sep="")))
    file.remove(paste(dataDirectory,'/test.csv',sep=""))
}

digits.train <- read.csv("../data/train.csv")

## convert to factor
digits.train$label <- factor(digits.train$label, levels = 0:9)
```

```
sample <- sample(nrow(digits.train), 6000)
train <- sample[1:5000]
test <- sample[5001:6000]

digits.X <- digits.train[train, -1]
digits.y <- digits.train[train, 1]
test.X <- digits.train[test, -1]
test.y <- digits.train[test, 1]

## try various weight decays and number of iterations
## register backend so that different decays can be
## estimated in parallel
cl <- makeCluster(5)
clusterEvalQ(cl, {source("cluster_inc.R")})
registerDoSNOW(cl)
```

2. Train a neural network on the digit classification, and vary the weight-decay penalty at 0 (no penalty) and 0.10. We also loop through two sets of the number of iterations allowed: 100 or 150. Note that this code is computationally intensive and takes some time to run:

```
set.seed(1234)
digits.decay.m1 <- lapply(c(100, 150), function(its) {
  caret::train(digits.X, digits.y,
            method = "nnet",
            tuneGrid = expand.grid(
              .size = c(10),
              .decay = c(0, .1)),
            trControl = caret::trainControl(method="cv", number=5,
repeats=1),
            MaxNWts = 10000,
            maxit = its)
})
```

3. Examining the results, we see that, when we limit to only 100 iterations, both the non-regularized model and regularized model have the same accuracy at 0.56, based on cross-validated results, which is not very good on this data:

```
digits.decay.m1[[1]]
Neural Network

5000 samples
 784 predictor
  10 classes: '0', '1', '2', '3', '4', '5', '6', '7', '8', '9'

No pre-processing
Resampling: Cross-Validated (5 fold)
```

```
Summary of sample sizes: 4000, 4001, 4000, 3998, 4001
Resampling results across tuning parameters:

  decay  Accuracy   Kappa
   0.0      0.56    0.51
   0.1      0.56    0.51


Tuning parameter 'size' was held constant at a value of 10
Accuracy was used to select the optimal model using the
 largest value.
The final values used for the model were size = 10 and decay = 0.1.
```

4. Examine the model with 150 iterations to see whether the regularized or non-regularized model performs better:

```
digits.decay.m1[[2]]
Neural Network

5000 samples
 784 predictor
  10 classes: '0', '1', '2', '3', '4', '5', '6', '7', '8', '9'

No pre-processing
Resampling: Cross-Validated (5 fold)
Summary of sample sizes: 4000, 4002, 3998, 4000, 4000
Resampling results across tuning parameters:

  decay  Accuracy   Kappa
   0.0      0.64    0.60
   0.1      0.63    0.59


Tuning parameter 'size' was held constant at a value of 10
Accuracy was used to select the optimal model using the
 largest value.
The final values used for the model were size = 10 and decay = 0.
```

Overall, the model with more iterations outperforms the model with fewer iterations, regardless of the regularization. However, comparing both models with 150 iterations, the regularized model is superior (accuracy= 0.66) to the non-regularized model (accuracy= 0.65), although here the difference is relatively small.

These results highlight that regularization is often most useful for more complex models that have greater flexibility to fit (and overfit) the data. In models that are appropriate or overly simplistic for the data, regularization will probably decrease performance. When developing a new model architecture, you should avoid adding regularization until the model is performing well on the training data. If you add regularization beforehand and the model performs poorly on the training data, you will not know whether the problem is with the model's architecture or because of the regularization. In the next section, we'll discuss ensemble and model averaging techniques, the last forms of regularization that are highlighted in this book.

Ensembles and model-averaging

Another approach to regularization involves creating multiple models (ensembles) and combining them, such as by model-averaging or some other algorithm for combining individual model results. There is a rich history of using ensemble techniques in machine learning, such as bagging, boosting, and random forest, that use this technique. The general idea is that, if you build different models using the training data, each model has different errors in the predicted values. Where one model predicts too high a value, another may predict too low a value, and when averaged, some of the errors cancel out, resulting in a more accurate prediction than would have been otherwise obtained.

The key to ensemble methods is that the different models must have some variability in their predictions. If the predictions from the different models are highly correlated, then using ensemble techniques will not be beneficial. If the predictions from the different models have very low correlations, then the average will be far more accurate as it gains the strengths of each model. The following code gives an example using simulated data. This small example illustrates the point with just three models:

```
## simulated data
set.seed(1234)
d <- data.frame(
  x = rnorm(400))
d$y <- with(d, rnorm(400, 2 + ifelse(x < 0, x + x^2, x + x^2.5), 1))
d.train <- d[1:200, ]
d.test <- d[201:400, ]

## three different models
m1 <- lm(y ~ x, data = d.train)
m2 <- lm(y ~ I(x^2), data = d.train)
m3 <- lm(y ~ pmax(x, 0) + pmin(x, 0), data = d.train)

## In sample R2
cbind(M1=summary(m1)$r.squared,
```

```
M2=summary(m2)$r.squared,M3=summary(m3)$r.squared)
      M1   M2    M3
[1,] 0.33 0.6 0.76
```

We can see that the predictive value of each model, at least in the training data, varies quite a bit. Evaluating the correlations among fitted values in the training data can also help to indicate how much overlap there is among the model predictions:

```
cor(cbind(M1=fitted(m1),
  M2=fitted(m2),M3=fitted(m3)))
      M1   M2   M3
M1 1.00 0.11 0.65
M2 0.11 1.00 0.78
M3 0.65 0.78 1.00
```

Next, we generate predicted values for the testing data, the average of the predicted values, and again correlate the predictions along with reality in the testing data:

```
## generate predictions and the average prediction
d.test$yhat1 <- predict(m1, newdata = d.test)
d.test$yhat2 <- predict(m2, newdata = d.test)
d.test$yhat3 <- predict(m3, newdata = d.test)
d.test$yhatavg <- rowMeans(d.test[, paste0("yhat", 1:3)])

## correlation in the testing data
cor(d.test)
               x      y  yhat1  yhat2 yhat3 yhatavg
x          1.000   0.44  1.000 -0.098  0.60    0.55
y          0.442   1.00  0.442  0.753  0.87    0.91
yhat1      1.000   0.44  1.000 -0.098  0.60    0.55
yhat2     -0.098   0.75 -0.098  1.000  0.69    0.76
yhat3      0.596   0.87  0.596  0.687  1.00    0.98
yhatavg    0.552   0.91  0.552  0.765  0.98    1.00
```

From the results, we can see that the average of the three models' predictions performs better than any of the models individually. However, this is not always the case; one good model may have better predictions than the average predictions. In general, it is good to check that the models being averaged perform similarly, at least in the training data. The second lesson is that, given models with similar performance, it is desirable to have lower correlations between model predictions, as this will result in the best performing average.

There are other forms of ensemble methods that are included in other machine learning algorithms, for example, bagging and boosting. Bagging is used in random forests, where many models are generated, each having different samples of the data. The models are deliberately designed to be small, incomplete models. By averaging the predictions of lots of undertrained models that use only a portion of the data, we should get a more powerful model. An example of boosting includes gradient-boosted models (GBMs), which also use multiple models, but this time each model focuses on the instances that were incorrectly predicted in the previous model. Both random forests and GBMs have proven to be very successful with structured data because they reduce variance, that is, avoid overfitting the data.

Bagging and model-averaging are not used as frequently in deep neural networks because the computational cost of training each model can be quite high, and thus repeating the process many times becomes prohibitively expensive in terms of time and compute resources. Nevertheless, it is still possible to use model averaging in the context of deep neural networks, even if perhaps it is on only a handful of models rather than hundreds, as is common in random forests and some other approaches.

Use case – improving out-of-sample model performance using dropout

Dropout is a novel approach to regularization that is particularly valuable for large and complex deep neural networks. For a much more detailed exploration of dropout in deep neural networks, see Srivastava, N., Hinton, G., Krizhevsky, A., Sutskever, I., and Salakhutdinav, R. (2014). The concept behind dropout is actually quite straightforward. During the training of the model, units (for example, input and hidden neurons) are probabilistically dropped along with all connections to and from them.

For example, the following diagram is an example of what might happen at each step of training for a model where hidden neurons and their connections are dropped with a probability of 1/3 for each epoch. Once a node is dropped, its connections to the next layer are also dropped. In the the following diagram, the grayed-out nodes and dashed connections are the ones that were dropped. It is important to note that the choice of nodes that are dropped changes for each epoch:

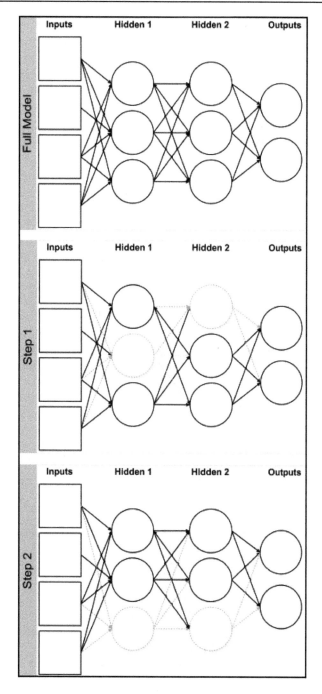

Figure 3.12: Dropout applied to a layer for different epochs

One way to think about dropout is that it forces models to be more robust to perturbations. Although many neurons are included in the full model, during training they are not all simultaneously present, and so neurons must operate somewhat more independently than they would otherwise. Another way of viewing dropout is that, if you have a large model with N weights between hidden neurons, but 50% are dropped during training, although all N weights will be used during some stages of training, you have effectively halved the total model complexity as the average number of weights will be halved. This reduces model complexity, and hence helps to prevent the overfitting of the data. Because of this feature, if the proportion of dropout is p, Srivastava, N., Hinton, G., Krizhevsky, A., Sutskever, I., and Salakhutdinov, R. (2014) recommend scaling up the target model complexity by 1/p in order to end up with a roughly equally complex model.

During model testing/scoring, neurons are not usually dropped because it is computationally inconvenient. Instead, we can use an approximate average based on scaling the weights from a single neural network based on each weight's probability of being included (that is, 1/p). This is usually taken care of by the deep learning library.

In addition to working well, this approximate weight re-scaling is a fairly trivial calculation. Thus, the primary computational cost of dropout comes from the fact that a model with more neurons and weights must be used because so many (a commonly recommended value is around 50% for hidden neurons) are dropped during each training update.

Although dropout is easy to implement, a larger model may be required to compensate. To speed up training, a higher learning rate can be used so that fewer epochs are required. One potential downside of combining these approaches is that, with fewer neurons and a faster learning rate, some weights may become quite large. Fortunately, it is possible to use dropout along with other forms of regularization, such as the L1 or L2 penalty. Taken together, the result is a larger model that that can quickly (a faster Learning rate) explore a broader parameter space, but is regularized through dropout and a penalty to keep the weights in check.

To show the use of dropout in a neural network, we will return to the **Modified National Institute of Standards and Technology (MNIST)** dataset (which we downloaded in Chapter 2, *Training a Prediction Model*) we worked with previously. We will use the nn.train() function from the deepnet package, as it allows for dropout. As in the previous chapter, we will run the four models in parallel to reduce the time it takes. Specifically, we compare four models, two with and two without dropout regularization and with either 40 or 80 hidden neurons. For dropout, we specify the proportion to dropout separately for the hidden and visible units. Based on the rule of thumb that about 50% of hidden units (and 80% of observed units) should be kept, we specify the dropout proportions at 0.5 and 0.2, respectively:

```
## Fit Models
nn.models <- foreach(i = 1:4, .combine = 'c') %dopar% {
set.seed(1234)
  list(nn.train(
     x = as.matrix(digits.X),
     y = model.matrix(~ 0 + digits.y),
     hidden = c(40, 80, 40, 80)[i],
     activationfun = "tanh",
     learningrate = 0.8,
     momentum = 0.5,
     numepochs = 150,
     output = "softmax",
     hidden_dropout = c(0, 0, .5, .5)[i],
     visible_dropout = c(0, 0, .2, .2)[i]))
}
```

Next, we can loop through the models to obtain predicted values and get the overall model performance:

```
nn.yhat <- lapply(nn.models, function(obj) {
  encodeClassLabels(nn.predict(obj, as.matrix(digits.X)))
 })
perf.train <- do.call(cbind, lapply(nn.yhat, function(yhat) {
  caret::confusionMatrix(xtabs(~ I(yhat - 1) + digits.y))$overall
 }))
colnames(perf.train) <- c("N40", "N80", "N40_Reg", "N80_Reg")
options(digits = 4)
perf.train
```

	N40	N80	N40_Reg	N80_Reg
Accuracy	0.9478	0.9622	0.9278	0.9400
Kappa	0.9420	0.9580	0.9197	0.9333
AccuracyLower	0.9413	0.9565	0.9203	0.9331
AccuracyUpper	0.9538	0.9673	0.9348	0.9464
AccuracyNull	0.1126	0.1126	0.1126	0.1126

```
AccuracyPValue  0.0000  0.0000  0.0000  0.0000
McnemarPValue      NaN     NaN     NaN     NaN
```

When evaluating the models in the in-sample training data, it seems those without regularization perform better those with regularization. Of course, the real test comes with the testing or holdout data:

```
nn.yhat.test <- lapply(nn.models, function(obj) {
  encodeClassLabels(nn.predict(obj, as.matrix(test.X)))
  })

perf.test <- do.call(cbind, lapply(nn.yhat.test, function(yhat) {
  caret::confusionMatrix(xtabs(~ I(yhat - 1) + test.y))$overall
  }))
colnames(perf.test) <- c("N40", "N80", "N40_Reg", "N80_Reg")

perf.test
                   N40      N80 N40_Reg N80_Reg
Accuracy        0.8890   0.8520  0.8980  0.9030
Kappa           0.8765   0.8352  0.8864  0.8920
AccuracyLower   0.8679   0.8285  0.8776  0.8830
AccuracyUpper   0.9078   0.8734  0.9161  0.9206
AccuracyNull    0.1180   0.1180  0.1180  0.1180
AccuracyPValue  0.0000   0.0000  0.0000  0.0000
McnemarPValue      NaN      NaN     NaN     NaN
```

The testing data highlights that the in-sample performance was overly optimistic (accuracy = 0.9622 versus accuracy = 0.8520 for the 80-neuron, non-regularized model in the training and testing data, respectively). We can see the advantage of the regularized models for both the 40- and the 80-neuron models. Although both still perform worse in the testing data than they did in the training data, they perform on a par with, or better than, the equivalent non-regularized models in the testing data. This difference is particularly important for the 80-neuron model as the best performing model on the test data is the regularized model.

Although these numbers are by no means record-setting, they do show the value of using dropout, or regularization more generally, and how one might go about trying to tune the model and dropout parameters to improve the ultimate testing performance.

Summary

This chapter began by showing you how to program a neural network from scratch. We demonstrated the neural network in a web application created by just using R code. We delved into how the neural network actually worked, showing how to code forward-propagation, `cost` functions, and backpropagation. Then we looked at how the parameters for our neural network apply to modern deep learning libraries by looking at the `mx.model.FeedForward.create` function from the `mxnet` deep learning library.

Then we covered overfitting, demonstrating several approaches to preventing overfitting, including common penalties, the L1 penalty and L2 penalty, ensembles of simpler models, and dropout, where variables and/or cases are dropped to make the model noisy. We examined the role of penalties in regression problems and neural networks. In the next chapter, we will move into deep learning and deep neural networks, and see how to push the accuracy and performance of our predictive models even further.

4
Training Deep Prediction Models

The previous chapters covered a bit of the theory behind neural networks and used some neural network packages in R. Now it is time to dive in and look at training deep learning models. In this chapter, we will explore how to train and build feedforward neural networks, which are the most common type of deep learning model. We will use MXNet to build deep learning models to perform classification and regression using a retail dataset.

This chapter will cover the following topics:

- Getting started with deep feedforward neural networks
- Common activation functions – rectifiers, hyperbolic tangent, and maxout
- Introduction to the MXNet deep learning library
- Use case – Using MXNet for classification and regression

Getting started with deep feedforward neural networks

A deep feedforward neural network is designed to approximate a function, $f()$, that maps some set of input variables, x, to an output variable, y. They are called feedforward neural networks because information flows from the input through each successive layer as far as the output, and there are no feedback or recursive loops (models including both forward and backward connections are referred to as recurrent neural networks).

Deep feedforward neural networks are applicable to a wide range of problems, and are particularly useful for applications such as image classification. More generally, feedforward neural networks are useful for prediction and classification where there is a clearly defined outcome (what digit an image contains, whether someone is walking upstairs or walking on a flat surface, the presence/absence of disease, and so on).

Deep feedforward neural networks can be constructed by chaining layers or functions together. For example, a network with four hidden layers is shown in the following diagram:

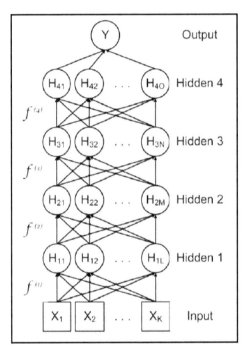

Figure 4.1: A deep feedforward neural network

This diagram of the model is a directed acyclic graph. Represented as a function, the overall mapping from the input, X, to the output, Y, is a multilayered function. The first hidden layer is $H_1 = f^{(1)}(X, w_1 a_1)$, the second hidden layer is $H_2 = f^{(2)}(H_1, w_2 a_2)$, and so on. These multiple layers can allow complex functions and transformations to be built up from relatively simple ones.

If sufficient hidden neurons are included in a layer, it can approximate to the desired degree of precision with many different types of functions. Feedforward neural networks can approximate non-linear functions by applying non-linear transformations between layers. These non-linear functions are known as activation functions, which we will cover in the next section.

The weights for each layer will be learned as the model is trained through forward- and backward-propagation. Another key piece of the model that must be determined is the cost, or loss, function. The two most commonly used cost functions are cross-entropy, which is used for classification tasks, and **mean squared error** (**MSE**), which is used for regression tasks.

Activation functions

The activation function determines the mapping between input and a hidden layer. It defines the functional form for how a neuron gets activated. For example, a linear activation function could be defined as: $f(x) = x$, in which case the value for the neuron would be the raw input, x. A linear activation function is shown in the top panel of *Figure 4.2*. Linear activation functions are rarely used because in practice deep learning models would find it difficult to learn non-linear functional forms using linear activation functions. In previous chapters, we used the hyperbolic tangent as an activation function, namely $f(x) = tanh(x)$. Hyperbolic tangent can work well in some cases, but a potential limitation is that at either low or high values, it saturates, as shown in the middle panel of the figure 4.2.

Perhaps the most popular activation function currently, and a good first choice (Nair, V., and Hinton, G. E. (2010)), is known as a *rectifier*. There are different kinds of rectifiers, but the most common is defined by the $f(x) = max(0, x)$ function, which is known as **relu**. The relu activation is flat below zero and linear above zero; an example is shown in Figure 4.2.

The final type of activation function we will discuss is maxout (Goodfellow, Warde-Farley, Mirza, Courville, and Bengio (2013)). A maxout unit takes the maximum value of its input, although as usual, this is after weighting so it is not the case that the input variable with the highest value will always win. Maxout activation functions seem to work particularly well with dropout.

The relu activation is the most commonly-used activation function and it is the default option for the deep learning models in the rest of this book. The following graphs for some of the activation functions we have discussed:

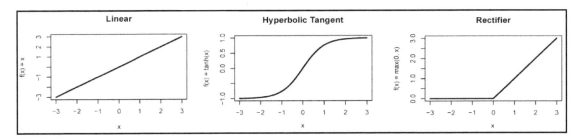

Figure 4.2: Common activation functions

Introduction to the MXNet deep learning library

The deep learning libraries we will use in this book are MXNet, Keras, and TensorFlow. Keras is a frontend API, which means it is not a standalone library as it requires a lower-level library in the backend, usually TensorFlow. The advantage of using Keras rather than TensorFlow is that it has a simpler interface. We will use Keras in later chapters in this book.

Both MXNet and TensorFlow are multipurpose numerical computation libraries that can use GPUs for mass parallel matrix operations. As such, multi-dimensional matrices are central to both libraries. In R, we are familiar with the vector, which is a one-dimensional array of values of the same type. The R data frame is a two-dimensional array of values, where each column can have different types. The R matrix is a two-dimensional array of values with the same type. Some machine learning algorithms in R require a matrix as input. We saw an example of this in Chapter 2, *Training a Prediction Model*, with the RSNSS package.

In R, it is unusual to use data structures with more than two dimensions, but deep learning uses them extensively. For example, if you have a 32 x 32 color image, you could store the pixel values in a 32 x 32 x 3 matrix, where the first two dimensions are the width and height, and the last dimension is for the red, green, and blue colors. This can be extended further by adding another dimension for a collection of images. This is called a batch and allows the processor (CPU/GPU) to process multiple images concurrently. The batch size is a hyper-parameter and the value selected depends on the size of the input data and memory capacity. If our batch size were 64, our matrix would be a 4-dimensional matrix of size 32 x 32 x 3 x 64 where the first 2 dimensions are the width and height, the third dimension is the colors, and the last dimension is the batch size, 64. The important thing to realize is that this is just another way of representing data. In R, we would store the same data as a 2-dimensional matrix (or dataframe) with 64 rows and 32 x 32 x 3 = 3,072 columns. All we are doing is reshaping the data, we are not changing it.

These n-dimensional matrices, which contain elements of the same type, are the cornerstone of using MXNet and TensorFlow. In MXNet, they are referred to as NDArrays. In TensorFlow, they are known as **tensors**. These n-dimensional matrices are important because they mean that we can feed the data into GPUs more efficiently; GPUs can process data in batches more efficiently than processing single rows of data. In the preceding example, we use 64 images in a batch, so the deep learning library will process input data in chunks of 32 x 32 x 3 x 64.

This chapter will use the MXNet deep learning library. MXNet originated at Carnegie Mellon University and is heavily supported by Amazon, they choose it as their default Deep Learning library in 2016. In 2017, MXNet was accepted as an Apache Incubator project, ensuring that it would remain as open source software. Here is a very simple example of an NDArray (matrix) operation in MXNet in R. If you have not already installed the MXNet package for R, go back to `Chapter 1, Getting Started with Deep Learning,` for instructions, or use this link: `https://mxnet.apache.org/install/index.html`:

```
library(mxnet) # 1
ctx = mx.cpu() # 2
a <- mx.nd.ones(c(2,3),ctx=ctx) # 3
b <- a * 2 + 1 # 4
typeof(b) # 5
[1] "externalptr"
class(b) # 6
[1] "MXNDArray"
b # 7
     [,1] [,2] [,3]
[1,]    3    3    3
[2,]    3    3    3
```

We can break down this code line by line:

- Line 1 loads the MXNet package.
- Line 2 sets the CPU context. This tells MXNet where to process your computations, either on the CPU or on a GPU, if one is available.
- Line 3 creates a 2-dimensional NDArray of size 2 x 3 where each value is 1.
- Line 4 creates another 2-dimensional NDArray of size 2 x 3. Each value will be 3 because we perform element-wise multiplication and add 1.
- Line 5 shows that b is an external pointer.
- Line 6 shows that the class of b is MXNDArray.
- Line 7 displays the results.

We can perform mathematical operations, such as multiplication and addition, on the b variable. However, it is important to realize that, while this behaves similarly to an R matrix, it is not a native R object. We can see this when we output the type and class of this variable.

When developing deep learning models, there are usually two distinct steps. First you create the model architecture and then you train the model. The main reason for this is because most deep learning libraries employ symbolic programming rather than the imperative programming you are used to. Most of the code you have previously written in R is an imperative program, which executes code sequentially. For mathematical optimization tasks, such as deep learning, this may not be the most efficient method of execution. Most deep learning libraries, including MXNet and TensorFlow, use symbolic programming. For symbolic programming, a computation graph for the program execution is designed first. This graph is then compiled and executed. When the computation graph is generated, the input, output, and graph operations are already defined, meaning that the code can be optimized. This means that for deep learning, symbolic programs are usually more efficient than imperative programs.

Here is a simple example of the type of optimization using symbolic programs:

$M = (M1 * M2) + (M3 * M4)$

An imperative program would calculate this as follows:

$Mtemp1 = (M1 * M2)$

$Mtemp2 = (M3 * M4)$

$M = Mtemp1 + Mtemp2$

A symbolic program would first create a computation graph, which might look like the following:

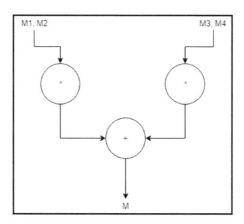

Figure 4.3: Example of a computation graph

M1, *M2*, *M3*, and *M4* are symbols that need to be operated on. The graph shows the dependencies for operations; the + operation requires the two preceding multiplication operations to be done before it can execute. But there is no dependency between the two multiplication steps, so these can be executed in parallel. This type of optimization means the code can execute much faster.

From a coding point of view, this means is that you have two steps in creating a deep learning model – first you define the architecture of the model and then you train the model. You create *layers* for your deep learning model and each layer has symbols that are placeholders. So for example, the first layer is usually:

```
data <- mx.symbol.Variable("data")
```

`data` is a placeholder for the input, which we will insert later. The output of each layer feeds into the next layer as input. This might be a convolutional layer, a dense layer, an activation layer a dropout layer, and so on. The following code example shows how the layers continue to feed into each other; this is taken from a full example later in this chapter. Notice how the symbol for each layer is used as input in the next layer, this is how the model is built layer after layer. The `data1` symbol is passed into the first call to `mx.symbol.FullyConnected`, the `fc1` symbol is passed into the first call to `mx.symbol.Activation`, and so on.

```
data <- mx.symbol.Variable("data")
fc1 <- mx.symbol.FullyConnected(data, name="fc1", num_hidden=64)
act1 <- mx.symbol.Activation(fc1, name="activ1", act_type=activ)
```

```
drop1 <- mx.symbol.Dropout(data=act1,p=0.2)
fc2 <- mx.symbol.FullyConnected(drop1, name="fc2", num_hidden=32)
act2 <- mx.symbol.Activation(fc2, name="activ2", act_type=activ)

.....
softmax <- mx.symbol.SoftmaxOutput(fc4, name="sm")
```

When you execute this code, it runs instantly as nothing is executed at this stage. Eventually, you pass the last layer into a function to train the model. In MXNet, this is the `mx.model.FeedForward.create` function. At this stage, the computation graph is computed and the model begins to be trained:

```
softmax <- mx.symbol.SoftmaxOutput(fc4, name="sm")
model <- mx.model.FeedForward.create(softmax, X = train_X, y = train_Y,
                                     ctx = devices,num.round = num_epochs,
                      ...............
```

This is when the deep learning model is created and trained. More information on the MXNet architecture is available online; the following links will get you started:

- `https://mxnet.apache.org/tutorials/basic/symbol.html`
- `https://mxnet.incubator.apache.org/architecture/program_model.html`

Deep learning layers

In the earlier code snippets, we saw some layers for a deep learning model, including `mx.symbol.FullyConnected`, `mx.symbol.Activation`, and `mx.symbol.Dropout`. Layers are how models are constructed; they are computational transformations of data. For example, `mx.symbol.FullyConnected` is the first type of layer operation we matrix operation we introduced in Chapter 1, *Getting Started with Deep Learning*. It is *fully connected* because all input values are connected to all nodes in the layer. In other deep learning libraries, such as Keras, it is called a **dense** layer.

The `mx.symbol.Activation` layer performs an activation function on the output of the previous layer. The `mx.symbol.Dropout` layer performs dropout on the output from the previous layer. Other common layer types in MXNet are:

- `mxnet.symbol.Convolution`: Performs a convolutional operation that matches patterns across the data. It is mostly used in computer vision tasks, which we will see in Chapter 5, *Image Classification Using Convolutional Neural Networks*. They can also be used for Natural Language Processing, which we will see in Chapter 6, *Natural Language Processing Using Deep Learning*.

- `mx.symbol.Pooling`: Performs pooling on the output from the previous layer. Pooling reduces the number of elements by taking the average, or max value, from sections of the input. These are commonly used with convolutional layers.
- `mx.symbol.BatchNorm`: Used to normalize the weights from the previous layer. This is done for the same reason you normalize input data before model-building: it helps the model to train better. It also prevents vanishing and exploding gradients where gradients get very, very small or very, very large during training. This can cause the model to fail to converge, that is, training will fail.
- `mx.symbol.SoftmaxOutput`: Calculates a softmax result from the output from the previous layer.

There are recognized patterns for using these layers, for example, an activation layer normally follows a fully-connected layer. A dropout layer is usually applied after the activation function, but can be between the fully connected layer and the activation function. Convolutional layers and pooling layers are often used together in image tasks in that order. At this stage, there is no need to try to memorize when to use these layers; you will encounter plenty of examples in the rest of this book!

 If all this seems confusing, take some comfort in knowing that a lot of the difficult work in applying these layers is abstracted away from you. In the previous chapter, when we built a neural network, we had to manage all the input output from the layers. This meant ensuring that the matrix dimensions were correct so that the operations worked. Deep Learning libraries, such as MXNet and TensorFlow, take care of this for you.

Building a deep learning model

Now that we have covered the basics, let's look at building our first true deep learning model! We will use the UHI HAR dataset that we used in `Chapter 2`, *Training a Prediction Model*. The following code does some data preparation: it loads the data and selects only the columns that store mean values (those that have the word `mean` in the column name). The `y` variables are from 1 to 6; we will subtract one so that the range is 0 to 5. The code for this section is in `Chapter4/uci_har.R`. It requires the UHI HAR dataset to be in the data folder; download it from `https://archive.ics.uci.edu/ml/datasets/human+activity+recognition+using+smartphones` and unzip it into the data folder:

```
train.x <- read.table("../data/UCI HAR Dataset/train/X_train.txt")
train.y <- read.table("../data/UCI HAR Dataset/train/y_train.txt")[[1]]
test.x <- read.table("../data/UCI HAR Dataset/test/X_test.txt")
test.y <- read.table("../data/UCI HAR Dataset/test/y_test.txt")[[1]]
```

```
features <- read.table("../data/UCI HAR Dataset/features.txt")
meanSD <- grep("mean\\(\\)|std\\(\\)", features[, 2])
train.y <- train.y-1
test.y <- test.y-1
```

Next, we will transpose the data and convert it into a matrix. MXNet expects the data to be width x height rather than height x width:

```
train.x <- t(train.x[,meanSD])
test.x <- t(test.x[,meanSD])
train.x <- data.matrix(train.x)
test.x <- data.matrix(test.x)
```

The next step is to define the computation graph. We create a placeholder for the data and create two fully connected (or dense) layers followed by relu activations. The first layer has 64 nodes and the second layer has 32 nodes. We create a final fully-connected layer with six nodes – the number of distinct classes in our y variable. We use a softmax activation to convert the numbers from the last six nodes into probabilities for each class:

```
data <- mx.symbol.Variable("data")
fc1 <- mx.symbol.FullyConnected(data, name="fc1", num_hidden=64)
act1 <- mx.symbol.Activation(fc1, name="relu1", act_type="relu")
fc2 <- mx.symbol.FullyConnected(act1, name="fc2", num_hidden=32)
act2 <- mx.symbol.Activation(fc2, name="relu2", act_type="relu")
fc3 <- mx.symbol.FullyConnected(act2, name="fc3", num_hidden=6)
softmax <- mx.symbol.SoftmaxOutput(fc3, name="sm")
```

When you run the previous code, nothing actually executes. To train the model, we create a `devices` object to indicate where the code should be run, CPU or GPU. Then you pass the symbol for last layer (softmax) into the `mx.model.FeedForward.create` function. This function has other parameters, which are more properly known as hyper-parameters. These include the epochs (`num.round`), which control how many times we pass through the data, the learning rate (`learning.rate`), which controls how much the gradients are updated during each pass, momentum (`momentum`), which is a hyper-parameter that can help the model to train faster, and the weights initializer (`initializer`), which controls how the weights and biases for nodes are initially set. We also pass in the evaluation metric (`eval.metric`),which is how the model is to be evaluated, and a callback function (`epoch.end.callback`), which is used to output progress information. When we run the function, it trains the model and outputs the progress as per the value we used for the `epoch.end.callback` parameter, namely every epoch:

```
devices <- mx.cpu()
mx.set.seed(0)
tic <- proc.time()
model <- mx.model.FeedForward.create(softmax, X = train.x, y = train.y,
```

```
                                    ctx = devices,num.round = 20,
                                    learning.rate = 0.08, momentum = 0.9,
                                    eval.metric = mx.metric.accuracy,
                                    initializer = mx.init.uniform(0.01),
                                    epoch.end.callback =
                                       mx.callback.log.train.metric(1))

Start training with 1 devices
[1]  Train-accuracy=0.185581140350877
[2]  Train-accuracy=0.26104525862069
[3]  Train-accuracy=0.555091594827586
[4]  Train-accuracy=0.519127155172414
[5]  Train-accuracy=0.646551724137931
[6]  Train-accuracy=0.733836206896552
[7]  Train-accuracy=0.819100215517241
[8]  Train-accuracy=0.881869612068966
[9]  Train-accuracy=0.892780172413793
[10]  Train-accuracy=0.908674568965517
[11]  Train-accuracy=0.898572198275862
[12]  Train-accuracy=0.896821120689655
[13]  Train-accuracy=0.915544181034483
[14]  Train-accuracy=0.928879310344828
[15]  Train-accuracy=0.926993534482759
[16]  Train-accuracy=0.934401939655172
[17]  Train-accuracy=0.933728448275862
[18]  Train-accuracy=0.934132543103448
[19]  Train-accuracy=0.933324353448276
[20]  Train-accuracy=0.934132543103448
print(proc.time() - tic)
   user system elapsed
   7.31 3.03 4.31
```

Now that we have trained our model, let's see how it does on the test set:

```
preds1 <- predict(model, test.x)
pred.label <- max.col(t(preds1)) - 1
t <- table(data.frame(cbind(test.y,pred.label)),
           dnn=c("Actual", "Predicted"))
acc<-round(100.0*sum(diag(t))/length(test.y),2)
print(t)
      Predicted
Actual   0   1   2   3   4   5
    0  477  15   4   0   0   0
    1  108 359   4   0   0   0
    2   13  42 365   0   0   0
    3    0   0   0 454  37   0
    4    0   0   0 141 391   0
    5    0   0   0  16   0 521
print(sprintf(" Deep Learning Model accuracy = %1.2f%%",acc))
```

```
[1] " Deep Learning Model accuracy = 87.11%"
```

Not bad! We have achieved an accuracy of 87.11% on our test set.

 Wait, where are the backward propagation, derivatives, and so on, that we covered in previous chapters? The answer to that is deep learning libraries largely manage this automatically for you. In MXNet, automatic differentiation is included in a package called the autograd package, which differentiates a graph of operations with the chain rule. It is one less thing to worry about when building deep learning models. For more information, go to https://mxnet.incubator.apache.org/tutorials/gluon/autograd.html.

Use case – using MXNet for classification and regression

In this section, we will use a new dataset to create a binary classification task. The dataset we will use here is a transactional dataset that is available at https://www.dunnhumby.com/sourcefiles. This dataset has been made available from dunnhumby, which is perhaps best known for its link to the Tesco (a British grocery store) club-card, which is one of the largest retail loyalty systems in the world. I recommend the following book, which describes how dunnhumby helped Tesco to become the number one retailer by applying analytics to their retail loyalty program: *Humby, Clive, Terry Hunt, and Tim Phillips. Scoring points. Kogan Page Publishers, 2008.* Even though this book is relatively old, it remains one of the best use cases to describe how to roll out a business-transformation program based on data analytics.

Data download and exploration

When you go to the preceding link, there are a few different data options; the one we will use is called **Let's Get Sort-of-Real**. This dataset is data for over two years for a fictional retail loyalty scheme. The data consists of purchases that are linked by basket ID and customer code, that is, we can track transactions by customers over time. There are a number of options here, including the full dataset, which is 4.3 GB zipped and over 40 GB unzipped. For our first models, we will use the smallest dataset, and will download the data titled **All transactions for a randomly selected sample of 5,000 customers**; this is 1/100th the size of the full database.

I wish to thank dunnhumby for releasing this dataset and for allowing us permission to use it. One of the problems in deep learning and machine learning in general is the lack of large scale real-life datasets that people can practice their skills on. When a company makes the effort to release such a dataset, we should appreciate the effort and not use the dataset outside the terms and conditions specified. Please take the time to read the terms and conditions and use the dataset for personal learning purposes only. Remember that any misuse of this dataset (or datasets released by other companies) means that companies will be more reluctant to make other datasets available in the future.

Once you have read the terms and conditions and downloaded the dataset to your computer, unzip it into a directory called `dunnhumby/in` under the `code` folder. Ensure the files are unzipped directly under this folder, and not a sub-directory, or you may have to copy them after unzipping the data. The data files are in **comma-delimited (CSV)** format, with a separate file for each week of data. The files can be opened and viewed using a text editor. We will use some of the fields in *Table 4.1* for our analysis:

Field name	Description	Format
BASKET_ID	Basket ID, or transaction ID. All items in a basket share the same `basket_id` value.	Numeric
CUST_CODE	Customer Code. This links the transactions/visits to a customer.	Char
SHOP_DATE	Date when shopping occurred. Date is specified in the yyyymmdd format.	Char
STORE_CODE	Store code.	Char
QUANTITY	Number of items of the same product bought in this basket.	Numeric
SPEND	Spend associated to the items bought.	Numeric
PROD_CODE	Product Code.	Char
PROD_CODE_10	Product Hierarchy Level 10 Code.	Char
PROD_CODE_20	Product Hierarchy Level 20 Code.	Char
PROD_CODE_30	Product Hierarchy Level 30 Code.	Char
PROD_CODE_40	Product Hierarchy Level 40 Code.	Char

Table 4.1: Partial data dictionary for transactional dataset

The data stores details of customer transactions. Every unique item that a person purchases in a shopping transaction is represented by one line, and items in a transaction will have the same `BASKET_ID` field. A transaction can also be linked to a customer using the `CUST_CODE` field. A PDF is included in the ZIP files if you want more information on the field types.

We are going to use this dataset for a churn prediction task. A churn prediction task is where we predict which customers will return in the next x days. Churn prediction is used to find customers who are in danger of leaving your program. It is used by companies in shopping loyalty schemes, mobile phone subscriptions, TV subscriptions, and so on to ensure they maintain enough customers. For most companies that rely on revenue from recurring subscriptions, it is more effective to spend resources on maintaining their existing customer base than trying to acquire new customers. This is because of the high cost of acquiring new customers. Also, as time progresses after a customer has left, it is harder to win them back, so there is a small window of time in which to send them special offers that may entice them to stay.

As well as binary classification, we will build a regression model. This will predict the amount that a person will spend in the next 14 days. Fortunately, we can build a dataset that is suitable for both prediction tasks.

The data was supplied as 117 CSV files (ignore `time.csv`, which is a lookup file). The first step is to perform some basic data exploration to verify that the data was downloaded successfully and then perform some basic data quality checks. This is an important first step in any analysis: especially when you are using an external dataset, you should run some validation checks on the data before creating any machine learning models. The `Chapter4/0_Explore.Rmd` script creates a summary file and does some exploratory analysis of the data. This is an RMD file, so it needs to be run from RStudio. For brevity, and because this book is about deep learning and not data processing, I will include just some of the output and plots from this script rather than reproducing all the code. You should also run the code in this file to ensure the data was imported correctly, although it may take a few minutes the first time it runs. Here are some summaries on the data from that script:

```
Number of weeks we have data: 117.
Number of transaction lines: 2541019.
Number of transactions (baskets): 390320.
Number of unique Customers: 5000.
Number of unique Products: 4997.
Number of unique Stores: 761.
```

If we compare this to the website and the PDF, it looks in order. We have over 2.5 million records, and data for 5,000 customers across 761 stores. The data-exploration script also creates some plots to give us a feel for the data. *Figure 4.3* shows the sales over the 117 weeks; we see the variety in the data (it is not a flat line indicating that each day is different) and there are no gaps indicating missing data. There are seasonal patterns, with large peaks toward the end of the calendar year, namely the holiday season:

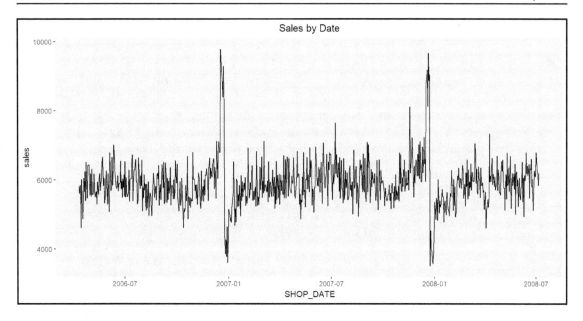

Figure 4.3: Sales plotted over time.

The plot in figure 4.3 shows that the data has been imported successfully. The data looks consistent and is what we expect for a retail transaction file, we do not see any gaps and there is seasonality.

For each item a person purchases, there is a product code (PROD_CODE) and four department codes (PROD_CODE_10, PROD_CODE_20, PROD_CODE_30, PROD_CODE_40). We will use these department codes in our analysis; the code in Chapter4/0_Explore.Rmd creates a summary for them. We want to see how many unique values there are for each department code, whether the codes represent a hierarchy (each code has at most one parent), and whether there are repeated codes:

```
PROD_CODE: Number of unique codes: 4997. Number of repeated codes: 0.
PROD_CODE_10: Number of unique codes:250. Number of repeated codes: 0.
PROD_CODE_20: Number of unique codes:90. Number of repeated codes: 0.
PROD_CODE_30: Number of unique codes:31. Number of repeated codes: 0.
PROD_CODE_40: Number of unique codes:9.
```

We have 4,997 unique product codes with 4 department codes. Our department codes go from PROD_CODE_10, which has 250 unique codes, to PROD_CODE_40, which has 9 unique codes. This is a product department code hierarchy, where PROD_CODE_40 is the primary category and PROD_CODE_10 is the lowest department code in the hierarchy. Each code in PROD_CODE_10, PROD_CODE_20, and PROD_CODE_30 has only one parent; for example, there are no repeating codes, that is, a department code belongs in only one super-category. We are not given a lookup file to say what these codes represent, but an example of a product code hierarchy for a product might be something similar to this:

```
PROD_CODE_40 : Chilled goods
  PROD_CODE_30 : Dairy
    PROD_CODE_20 : Fresh Milk
      PROD_CODE_10 : Full-fat Milk
        PROD_CODE : Brand x Full-fat Milk
```

To get a sense of these department codes, we can also plot the sales data over time by the number of unique product department codes in *Figure 4.4*. This plot is also created in Chapter4/0_Explore.Rmd:

Figure 4.4: Unique product codes purchased by date

Note that for this graph, the *y* axis is unique product codes, not sales. This data also looks consistent; there are some peaks and dips in the data, but they are not as pronounced as in *Figure 4.3*, which is as expected.

Preparing the data for our models

Now that we have downloaded and validated the data, we can use it to create a dataset for our binary classification and regression model tasks. We want to be able to predict which customers will visit the shop in the next two weeks for the binary classification task, and how much they will spend in the next two weeks for the regression task. The Chapter4/prepare_data.R script transforms the raw transactional data into a format suitable for machine learning. You need to run the code to create the dataset for the models, but you do not have to understand exactly how it works. Feel free to skip ahead if you want to focus on the deep learning model building.

We need to transform our data into a suitable format for prediction tasks. This should be a single row for each instance we want to predict. The columns will include some fields that are features (X variables) and another field that is our predictor value (Y variable). We want to predict whether a customer returns or not and their spend, so our dataset will have a single row per customer with features and predictor variables.

The first step is to find the cut-off date that separates the variables used to predict (X) and the variable we will predict for (Y). The code looks at the data, finds the last transaction date; and then subtracts 13 days from that date. This is a cut-off date, we want to predict which customers will spend in our shops *on or after* the cut-off date; based on what happens *before* the cut-off date. The data before the cut-off date will be used to make our X, or feature variables, and sales data on or after the cut-off date will be used to make our Y, or predictor variables. The following is that part of the code:

```
library(readr)
library(reshape2)
library(dplyr)

source("import.R")

# step 1, merge files
import_data(data_directory,bExploreData=0)

# step 2, group and pivot data
fileName <- paste(data_directory,"all.csv",sep="")
fileOut <- paste(data_directory,"predict.csv",sep="")
df <- read_csv(fileName,col_types = cols(.default = col_character()))
```

```
# convert spend to numeric field
df$SPEND<-as.numeric(df$SPEND)

# group sales by date. we have not converted the SHOP_DATE to date
# but since it is in yyyymmdd format,
# then ordering alphabetically will preserve date order
sumSalesByDate<-df %>%
    group_by(SHOP_WEEK,SHOP_DATE) %>%
    summarise(sales = sum(SPEND)
    )

# we want to get the cut-off date to create our data model
# this is the last date and go back 13 days beforehand
# therefore our X data only looks at everything from start to max date - 13
days
# and our Y data only looks at everything from max date - 13 days to end
(i.e. 14 days)
max(sumSalesByDate$SHOP_DATE)
[1] "20080706"
sumSalesByDate2 <- sumSalesByDate[order(sumSalesByDate$SHOP_DATE),]
datCutOff <-
as.character(sumSalesByDate2[(nrow(sumSalesByDate2)-13),]$SHOP_DATE)
datCutOff
[1] "20080623"
rm(sumSalesByDate,sumSalesByDate2)
```

If this code does not run, the most probable reason is that the source data was not saved in the correct location. The dataset must be unzipped into a directory called dunnhumby/in under the code folder, that is, at the same level as the chapter folders.

The last date in our data is 20080706, which July 7th, 2008, and the cut-off date is June 23rd, 2008. Although we have data going back to 2006, we will only use sales data from 2008. Any data that is older than six months is unlikely to influence a future customer sale. The task is to predict whether a customer will return between June 23rd, 2008 - July 7th, 2008 based on their activity before June 23rd, 2008.

We now need to create features from our data; so that we can use the spend broken down by department code, we will use the PROD_CODE_40 field. We could just group the sales on this department code, but that would give equal weighting to spends in Jan 2008 as to spends in June 2008. We would like to incorporate some time factor in our predictor columns. Instead, we will create features on a combination of the department code and the week. This will allow our models to place more importance on recent activities. First, we group by customer code, week, and department code, and create the fieldName column. We then pivot this data to create our features (X) dataset. The cell values in this dataset are the sales for that customer (row) and that week-department code (column). Here is an example of how the data is transformed for two customers. *Table 4.2* shows the sales spend by week and the PROD_CODE_40 field. *Table 4.3* then uses a pivot to create a dataset that has a single row per customer and the aggregate fields are now columns with the spend as values:

CUST_CODE	PROD_CODE_40	SHOP_WEEK	fieldName	Sales
cust_001	D00001	200801	D00001_200801	10.00
cust_002	D00001	200801	D00001_200801	12.00
cust_001	D00015	200815	D00015_200815	15.00
cust_001	D00020	200815	D00020_200815	20.00
cust_002	D00030	200815	D00030_200815	25.00

Table 4.2: Summary of sales by customer code, department code, and week

CUST_CODE	D00001_200801	D00015_200815	D00020_200815	D00030_200815
cust_001	10.00	15.00	20.00	
cust_002	12.00			25.00

Table 4.3: Data from Table 4.2 after transformation

Here is the code that does this transformation:

```
# we are going to limit our data here from year 2008 only
# group data and then pivot it
sumTemp <- df %>%
    filter((SHOP_DATE < datCutOff) & (SHOP_WEEK>="200801")) %>%
    group_by(CUST_CODE,SHOP_WEEK,PROD_CODE_40) %>%
    summarise(sales = sum(SPEND)
    )
sumTemp$fieldName <- paste(sumTemp$PROD_CODE_40,sumTemp$SHOP_WEEK,sep="_")
df_X <- dcast(sumTemp,CUST_CODE ~ fieldName, value.var="sales")
df_X[is.na(df_X)] <- 0
```

The predictor (Y) variable is a flag as to whether the customer visited the site on the weeks from 200818 to 200819. We perform a grouping on the data after the cut-off date and group the sales by customer, these form the basis of our Y values. We join the X and Y datasets, ensuring that we keep all rows on the X side by doing a left-join. Finally we create a 1/0 flag for our binary classification task. When we are done, we see that we have 3933 records in our dataset : 1560 customers who did not return and 2373 customers who did. We finish by saving our file for the model-building. The following code shows these steps:

```
# y data just needs a group to get sales after cut-off date
df_Y <- df %>%
    filter(SHOP_DATE >= datCutOff) %>%
    group_by(CUST_CODE) %>%
    summarise(sales = sum(SPEND)
    )
colnames(df_Y)[2] <- "Y_numeric"

# use left join on X and Y data, need to include all values from X
# even if there is no Y value
dfModelData <- merge(df_X,df_Y,by="CUST_CODE", all.x=TRUE)
# set binary flag
dfModelData$Y_categ <- 0
dfModelData[!is.na(dfModelData$Y_numeric),]$Y_categ <- 1
dfModelData[is.na(dfModelData$Y_numeric),]$Y_numeric <- 0
rm(df,df_X,df_Y,sumTemp)

nrow(dfModelData)
[1] 3933
table(dfModelData$Y_categ)
    0    1
1560 2373

# shuffle data
dfModelData <- dfModelData[sample(nrow(dfModelData)),]

write_csv(dfModelData,fileOut)
```

We use the sales data to create our predictor fields, but there were some customer attributes that we ignored for this task. These fields included `Customers Price Sensitivity` and `Customers Lifestage`. The main reason we did not use these fields was to avoid data-leakage. Data-leakage can occur when building prediction models; it occurs when some of your fields have values that will not be available or different when creating datasets in production. These fields could cause data-leakage because we do not know when they were set; it could have been when a customer signs up, or it could be a process that runs nightly. If these were created after our cut-off date, this would mean that these fields could unfairly predict our Y variables.

For example, `Customers Price Sensitivity` has values for `Less Affluent`, `Mid Market`, and `Up Market`, which probably are derived from what the customer purchases. Therefore, using these fields in a churn-prediction task would result in data-leakage if these fields were updated after the cut-off date used to create our dataset for our prediction models. A value of `Up Market` for `Customers Price Sensitivity` could be strongly linked to return spend, but this value is actually a summary of the value it is predicting. Data-leakage is one of the main causes of data models performing worse in production as the model was trained with data that is linked to the Y variable and can never exist in reality. You should always check for data-leakage for time-series tasks and ask yourself whether any field (especially lookup attributes) could have been modified after the date used to create the model data.

The binary classification model

The code from the previous section creates a new file called `predict.csv` in the `dunnhumby` folder. This dataset has a single row for each customer with a 0/1 field indicating whether they visited in the last two weeks and predictor variables based on sales data before those two weeks. Now we can proceed to build some machine learning models. The `Chapter4/binary_predict.R` file contains the code for our first prediction task, binary classification. The first part of the code loads the data and creates an array of predictor variables by including all columns except the customer ID, the binary classification predictor variable, and the regression predictor variable. The feature columns are all numeric fields that are heavily right-skewed distributed, so we apply a log transformation to those fields. We add `0.01` first to avoid getting a non-numeric result from attempting to get a log of a zero value *(log(0)= -Inf)*.

The following plot shows the data before transformation, on the left, and the data after transformation, on the right:

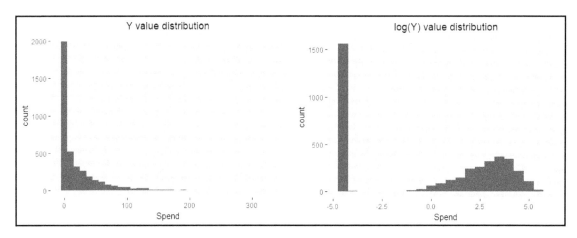

Figure 4.5: Distribution of a feature variable before and after transformation.

The large bar on the left in the second plot is where the original field was zero *(log(0+0.01) = -4.6)*. The following code loads the data, performs the log transformation, and creates the previous plot:

```
set.seed(42)
fileName <- "../dunnhumby/predict.csv"
dfData <- read_csv(fileName,
                   col_types = cols(
                      .default = col_double(),
                      CUST_CODE = col_character(),
                      Y_categ = col_integer())
                   )
nobs <- nrow(dfData)
train <- sample(nobs, 0.9*nobs)
test <- setdiff(seq_len(nobs), train)
predictorCols <- colnames(dfData)[!(colnames(dfData) %in%
c("CUST_CODE","Y_numeric","Y_categ"))]

# data is right-skewed, apply log transformation
qplot(dfData$Y_numeric, geom="histogram",binwidth=10,
      main="Y value distribution",xlab="Spend")+theme(plot.title =
element_text(hjust = 0.5))
dfData[, c("Y_numeric",predictorCols)] <- log(0.01+dfData[,
c("Y_numeric",predictorCols)])
qplot(dfData$Y_numeric, geom="histogram",binwidth=0.5,
      main="log(Y) value distribution",xlab="Spend")+theme(plot.title =
element_text(hjust = 0.5))
```

```
trainData <- dfData[train, c(predictorCols)]
testData <- dfData[test, c(predictorCols)]
trainData$Y_categ <- dfData[train, "Y_categ"]$Y_categ
testData$Y_categ <- dfData[test, "Y_categ"]$Y_categ
```

Before we train a deep learning model, we train three machine learning models – a logistic regression model, a `Random Forest` model, and an `XGBoost` model – on the data as a benchmark. This code section contains the data load, transformation, and three models:

```
#Logistic Regression Model
logReg=glm(Y_categ ~ .,data=trainData,family=binomial(link="logit"))
pr <- as.vector(ifelse(predict(logReg, type="response",
                               testData) > 0.5, "1", "0"))
# Generate the confusion matrix showing counts.
t<-table(dfData[test, c(predictorCols, "Y_categ")]$"Y_categ", pr,
         dnn=c("Actual", "Predicted"))
acc<-round(100.0*sum(diag(t))/length(test),2)
print(t)
       Predicted
Actual    0    1
     0  130   42
     1   48  174
print(sprintf(" Logistic regression accuracy = %1.2f%%",acc))
[1] " Logistic regression accuracy = 77.16%"
rm(t,pr,acc)


rf <- randomForest::randomForest(as.factor(Y_categ) ~ .,
                                 data=trainData,
                                 na.action=randomForest::na.roughfix)
pr <- predict(rf, newdata=testData, type="class")
# Generate the confusion matrix showing counts.
t<-table(dfData[test, c(predictorCols, "Y_categ")]$Y_categ, pr,
         dnn=c("Actual", "Predicted"))
acc<-round(100.0*sum(diag(t))/length(test),2)
print(t)
       Predicted
Actual    0    1
     0  124   48
     1   30  192
print(sprintf(" Random Forest accuracy = %1.2f%%",acc))
[1] " Random Forest accuracy = 80.20%"
rm(t,pr,acc)


xgb <- xgboost(data=data.matrix(trainData[,predictorCols]),
label=trainData[,"Y_categ"]$Y_categ,
               nrounds=75, objective="binary:logistic")
pr <- as.vector(ifelse(
   predict(xgb, data.matrix(testData[, predictorCols])) > 0.5, "1", "0"))
```

```
t<-table(dfData[test, c(predictorCols, "Y_categ")]$"Y_categ", pr,
         dnn=c("Actual", "Predicted"))
acc<-round(100.0*sum(diag(t))/length(test),2)
print(t)
       Predicted
Actual   0    1
       0 125   47
       1  44  178
print(sprintf(" XGBoost accuracy = %1.2f%%",acc))
[1] " XGBoost accuracy = 76.90%"
rm(t,pr,acc)
```

We create logistic regression, `Random Forest`, and `XGBoost` models for a number of reasons. Firstly, most of the work is already done in preparing the data, so it is trivial to do so. Secondly, it gives us a benchmark to compare our deep learning model to. Thirdly, if there were a problem in the data-preparation tasks, these machine learning algorithms would highlight these problems more rapidly because they will be quicker than training a deep learning model. In this case, we only have a few thousand records, so these machine learning algorithms will easily run on this data. If the data were too large for these algorithms, I would consider taking a smaller sample and running our benchmark tasks on that smaller sample. There are many machine learning algorithms to choose from, but I used these algorithms as benchmarks for the following reasons:

- Logistic regression is a basic model and is always a good benchmark to use
- `Random Forest` is known to train well using the default parameters and is robust to overfitting and correlated variables (which we have here)
- `XGBoost` is consistently rated as the one of the best-performing machine learning algorithms

All three algorithms achieve a similar amount of accuracy, the highest accuracy was achieved by `Random Forest` with an 80.2% accuracy. We now know that this dataset is suitable for prediction tasks and we have a benchmark to compare against.

Now we will build a deep learning model using MXNet:

```
require(mxnet)

# MXNet expects matrices
train_X <- data.matrix(trainData[, predictorCols])
test_X <- data.matrix(testData[, predictorCols])
train_Y <- trainData$Y_categ

# hyper-parameters
num_hidden <- c(128,64,32)
drop_out <- c(0.2,0.2,0.2)
```

```
wd=0.00001
lr <- 0.03
num_epochs <- 40
activ <- "relu"

# create our model architecture
# using the hyper-parameters defined above
data <- mx.symbol.Variable("data")
fc1 <- mx.symbol.FullyConnected(data, name="fc1", num_hidden=num_hidden[1])
act1 <- mx.symbol.Activation(fc1, name="activ1", act_type=activ)

drop1 <- mx.symbol.Dropout(data=act1,p=drop_out[1])
fc2 <- mx.symbol.FullyConnected(drop1, name="fc2",
num_hidden=num_hidden[2])
act2 <- mx.symbol.Activation(fc2, name="activ2", act_type=activ)

drop2 <- mx.symbol.Dropout(data=act2,p=drop_out[2])
fc3 <- mx.symbol.FullyConnected(drop2, name="fc3",
num_hidden=num_hidden[3])
act3 <- mx.symbol.Activation(fc3, name="activ3", act_type=activ)

drop3 <- mx.symbol.Dropout(data=act3,p=drop_out[3])
fc4 <- mx.symbol.FullyConnected(drop3, name="fc4", num_hidden=2)
softmax <- mx.symbol.SoftmaxOutput(fc4, name="sm")

# run on cpu, change to 'devices <- mx.gpu()'
# if you have a suitable GPU card
devices <- mx.cpu()
mx.set.seed(0)
tic <- proc.time()
# This actually trains the model
model <- mx.model.FeedForward.create(softmax, X = train_X, y = train_Y,
                                     ctx = devices,num.round = num_epochs,
                                     learning.rate = lr, momentum = 0.9,
                                     eval.metric = mx.metric.accuracy,
                                     initializer = mx.init.uniform(0.1),
                                     wd=wd,
                                     epoch.end.callback =
mx.callback.log.train.metric(1))
print(proc.time() - tic)
   user system elapsed
   9.23 4.65 4.37

pr <- predict(model, test_X)
pred.label <- max.col(t(pr)) - 1
t <- table(data.frame(cbind(testData[, "Y_categ"]$Y_categ,pred.label)),
           dnn=c("Actual", "Predicted"))
acc<-round(100.0*sum(diag(t))/length(test),2)
```

```
print(t)
        Predicted
Actual    0    1
      0 136   36
      1  54  168
print(sprintf(" Deep Learning Model accuracy = %1.2f%%",acc))
[1] " Deep Learning Model accuracy = 77.16%"
rm(t,pr,acc)
rm(data,fc1,act1,fc2,act2,fc3,act3,fc4,softmax,model)
```

The deep learning model achieved a 77.16% accuracy on the test data, which is only beaten by the Random Forest model. This shows that a deep learning model can be competitive against the best machine learning algorithms. It also shows that deep learning models on classification tasks do not always beat other machine learning algorithms. We used these models to provide a benchmark, so that we would know that our deep learning model was getting decent results; it gives us confidence that our deep learning model is competitive.

Our deep learning model uses 20% dropout in each layer and weight decay for regularization. Without dropout, the model overtrained significantly. This was probably because the features are highly correlated, as our columns are the spend in various departments. It figures that if one column is for a type of bread, and another column is for a type of milk, then these change together, namely someone who has more transactions and spends more is likely to buy both.

The regression model

The previous section developed a deep learning model for a binary classification task, this section develops a deep learning model to predict a continuous numeric value, regression analysis. We use the same dataset that we used for the binary classification task, but we use a different target column to predict for. In that task, we wanted to predict whether a customer would return to our stores in the next 14 days. In this task, we want to predict how much a customer will spend in our stores in the next 14 days. We follow a similar process; we load and prepare our dataset by applying log transformations to the data. The code is in Chapter4/regression.R:

```
set.seed(42)
fileName <- "../dunnhumby/predict.csv"
dfData <- read_csv(fileName,
              col_types = cols(
                 .default = col_double(),
                 CUST_CODE = col_character(),
                 Y_categ = col_integer()))
  )
```

```
nobs <- nrow(dfData)
train <- sample(nobs, 0.9*nobs)
test <- setdiff(seq_len(nobs), train)
predictorCols <- colnames(dfData)[!(colnames(dfData) %in%
c("CUST_CODE","Y_numeric","Y_numeric"))]

dfData[, c("Y_numeric",predictorCols)] <- log(0.01+dfData[,
c("Y_numeric",predictorCols)])
trainData <- dfData[train, c(predictorCols,"Y_numeric")]
testData <- dfData[test, c(predictorCols,"Y_numeric")]

xtrain <- model.matrix(Y_numeric~.,trainData)
xtest <- model.matrix(Y_numeric~.,testData)
```

We then perform regression analysis on the data using `lm` to create a benchmark before creating a deep learning model:

```
# lm Regression Model
regModel1=lm(Y_numeric ~ .,data=trainData)
pr1 <- predict(regModel1,testData)
rmse <- sqrt(mean((exp(pr1)-exp(testData[,"Y_numeric"]$Y_numeric))^2))
print(sprintf(" Regression RMSE = %1.2f",rmse))
[1] " Regression RMSE = 29.30"
mae <- mean(abs(exp(pr1)-exp(testData[,"Y_numeric"]$Y_numeric)))
print(sprintf(" Regression MAE = %1.2f",mae))
[1] " Regression MAE = 13.89"
```

We output two metrics, rmse and mae, for our regression task. We covered these earlier in the chapter. Mean absolute error measures the absolute differences between the predicted value and the actual value. **Root mean squared error (rmse)** penalizes the square of the differences between the predicted value and the actual value, so one big error costs more than the sum of the small errors. Now let's look at the deep learning regression code. First we load the data and define the model:

```
require(mxnet)
Loading required package: mxnet

# MXNet expects matrices
train_X <- data.matrix(trainData[, predictorCols])
test_X <- data.matrix(testData[, predictorCols])
train_Y <- trainData$Y_numeric

set.seed(42)
# hyper-parameters
num_hidden <- c(256,128,128,64)
drop_out <- c(0.4,0.4,0.4,0.4)
wd=0.00001
```

```
lr <- 0.0002
num_epochs <- 100
activ <- "tanh"

# create our model architecture
# using the hyper-parameters defined above
data <- mx.symbol.Variable("data")
fc1 <- mx.symbol.FullyConnected(data, name="fc1", num_hidden=num_hidden[1])
act1 <- mx.symbol.Activation(fc1, name="activ1", act_type=activ)
drop1 <- mx.symbol.Dropout(data=act1,p=drop_out[1])

fc2 <- mx.symbol.FullyConnected(drop1, name="fc2",
num_hidden=num_hidden[2])
act2 <- mx.symbol.Activation(fc2, name="activ2", act_type=activ)
drop2 <- mx.symbol.Dropout(data=act2,p=drop_out[2])

fc3 <- mx.symbol.FullyConnected(drop2, name="fc3",
num_hidden=num_hidden[3])
act3 <- mx.symbol.Activation(fc3, name="activ3", act_type=activ)
drop3 <- mx.symbol.Dropout(data=act3,p=drop_out[3])

fc4 <- mx.symbol.FullyConnected(drop3, name="fc4",
num_hidden=num_hidden[4])
act4 <- mx.symbol.Activation(fc4, name="activ4", act_type=activ)
drop4 <- mx.symbol.Dropout(data=act4,p=drop_out[4])

fc5 <- mx.symbol.FullyConnected(drop4, name="fc5", num_hidden=1)
lro <- mx.symbol.LinearRegressionOutput(fc5)
```

Now we train the model; note that the first comment shows how to switch to using a GPU instead of a CPU:

```
# run on cpu, change to 'devices <- mx.gpu()'
# if you have a suitable GPU card
devices <- mx.cpu()
mx.set.seed(0)
tic <- proc.time()
# This actually trains the model
model <- mx.model.FeedForward.create(lro, X = train_X, y = train_Y,
 ctx = devices,num.round = num_epochs,
 learning.rate = lr, momentum = 0.9,
 eval.metric = mx.metric.rmse,
 initializer = mx.init.uniform(0.1),
 wd=wd,
 epoch.end.callback = mx.callback.log.train.metric(1))
print(proc.time() - tic)
 user system elapsed
 13.90 1.82 10.50
```

```
pr4 <- predict(model, test_X)[1,]
rmse <- sqrt(mean((exp(pr4)-exp(testData[,"Y_numeric"]$Y_numeric))^2))
print(sprintf(" Deep Learning Regression RMSE = %1.2f",rmse))
[1] " Deep Learning Regression RMSE = 28.92"
mae <- mean(abs(exp(pr4)-exp(testData[,"Y_numeric"]$Y_numeric)))
print(sprintf(" Deep Learning Regression MAE = %1.2f",mae))
[1] " Deep Learning Regression MAE = 14.33"
rm(data,fc1,act1,fc2,act2,fc3,act3,fc4,lro,model)
```

For regression metrics, lower is better, so our rmse metric on the deep learning model (28.92) is an improvement on the original regression model (29.30). Interestingly, the mae on the the deep learning model (14.33) is actually worse than the original regression model (13.89). Since rsme penalizes big differences between actual and predicted values more, this indicates that the errors in the deep learning model are less extreme than the regression model.

Improving the binary classification model

This section builds on the earlier binary classification task and looks to increase the accuracy for that task. The first thing we can do to improve the model is to use more data, 100 times more data in fact! We will download the entire dataset, which is over 4 GB data in zip files and 40 GB of data when the files are unzipped. Go back to the download link (`https://www.dunnhumby.com/sourcefiles`) and select **Let's Get Sort-of-Real** again and download all the files for the **Full dataset**. There are nine files to download and the CSV files should be unzipped into the `dunnhumby/in` folder. Remember to check that the CSV files are in this folder and not a subfolder. You need to run the code in `Chapter4/prepare_data.R` again. When this completes, the `predict.csv` file should have 390,000 records.

You can try to follow along here, but be aware that preparing the data and running the deep learning model are going to take a long time. You also may run into problems if you have a slow computer. I tested this code on an Intel i5 processor with 32 GB RAM, and it took the model 30 minutes to run. It also requires over 50 GB hard disk space to store the unzipped files and temporary files. If you have problems running it on your local computer, another option is to run this example in the cloud, which we will cover in a later chapter.

The code for this section is in the `Chapter4/binary_predict2.R` script. Since we have more data, we can build a more complicated model. We have 100 times more data, so our new model adds an extra layer, and more nodes to our hidden layers. We have decreased the amount of regularization and the learning rate. We have also added more epochs. Here is the the code in `Chapter4/binary_predict2.R`, which constructs and trains the deep learning model. We have not included the boilerplate code to load and prepare the data, as that has not changed from the original script:

```
# hyper-parameters
num_hidden <- c(256,128,64,32)
drop_out <- c(0.2,0.2,0.1,0.1)
wd=0.0
lr <- 0.03
num_epochs <- 50
activ <- "relu"

# create our model architecture
# using the hyper-parameters defined above
data <- mx.symbol.Variable("data")
fc1 <- mx.symbol.FullyConnected(data, name="fc1", num_hidden=num_hidden[1])
act1 <- mx.symbol.Activation(fc1, name="activ1", act_type=activ)

drop1 <- mx.symbol.Dropout(data=act1,p=drop_out[1])
fc2 <- mx.symbol.FullyConnected(drop1, name="fc2",
num_hidden=num_hidden[2])
act2 <- mx.symbol.Activation(fc2, name="activ2", act_type=activ)

drop2 <- mx.symbol.Dropout(data=act2,p=drop_out[2])
fc3 <- mx.symbol.FullyConnected(drop2, name="fc3",
num_hidden=num_hidden[3])
act3 <- mx.symbol.Activation(fc3, name="activ3", act_type=activ)

drop3 <- mx.symbol.Dropout(data=act3,p=drop_out[3])
fc4 <- mx.symbol.FullyConnected(drop3, name="fc4",
num_hidden=num_hidden[4])
act4 <- mx.symbol.Activation(fc4, name="activ4", act_type=activ)

drop4 <- mx.symbol.Dropout(data=act4,p=drop_out[4])
fc5 <- mx.symbol.FullyConnected(drop4, name="fc5", num_hidden=2)
softmax <- mx.symbol.SoftmaxOutput(fc5, name="sm")

# run on cpu, change to 'devices <- mx.gpu()'
# if you have a suitable GPU card
devices <- mx.cpu()
mx.set.seed(0)
tic <- proc.time()
# This actually trains the model
```

```
model <- mx.model.FeedForward.create(softmax, X = train_X, y = train_Y,
 ctx = devices,num.round = num_epochs,
 learning.rate = lr, momentum = 0.9,
 eval.metric = mx.metric.accuracy,
 initializer = mx.init.uniform(0.1),
 wd=wd,
 epoch.end.callback = mx.callback.log.train.metric(1))
print(proc.time() - tic)
 user system elapsed
1919.75 1124.94 871.31

pr <- predict(model, test_X)
pred.label <- max.col(t(pr)) - 1
t <- table(data.frame(cbind(testData[,"Y_categ"]$Y_categ,pred.label)),
 dnn=c("Actual", "Predicted"))
acc<-round(100.0*sum(diag(t))/length(test),2)
print(t)
       Predicted
Actual    0    1
 0     10714  4756
 1      3870 19649
print(sprintf(" Deep Learning Model accuracy = %1.2f%%",acc))
[1] " Deep Learning Model accuracy = 77.88%"
```

The accuracy has increased from 77.16% in the earlier model to 77.88% for this model. This may not seem significant, but if we consider that the large dataset has almost 390,000 rows, the increase in accuracy of 0.72% represents about 2,808 customers that are now classified correctly. If each of these customers is worth $50, that is an additional $140,000 in revenue.

In general, as you add more data, your model should become more complicated to generalize across all the patterns in the data. We will cover more of this in Chapter 6, *Tuning and Optimizing Models,* but I would encourage you to experiment with the code in Chapter4/binary_predict.R. Try changing the hyper-parameters or adding more layers. Even a small improvement of 0.1 - 0.2% in accuracy is significant. If you manage to get over 78% accuracy on this dataset, consider it a good achievement.

If you want to explore further, there are other methods to investigate. These involve making changes in how the data for the model is created. If you really want to stretch yourself, here are a few more ideas you can try:

- Our current features are a combination of department codes and weeks, we use the `PROD_CODE_40` field as the department code. This has only nine unique values, so for every week, only nine fields represent that data. If you use `PROD_CODE_30`, `PROD_CODE_20`, or `PROD_CODE_10`, you will create a lot more features.
- In a similar manner, rather than using a combination of department codes and weeks, you could try department codes and day. This might create too many features, but I would consider doing this for the last 14 days before the cut-off date.
- Experiment with different methods of preparing the data. We use log scale, which works well for our binary classification task, but is not the best method for a regression task, as it does not create data with a normal distribution. Try applying z-scaling and min-max standardization to the data. If you do this, you must ensure that it is applied correctly to the test data before evaluating the model.
- The training data uses the sales amount. You could change this to item quantities or the number of transactions an item is in.
- You could create new features. One potentially powerful example would be to create fields based on a day of the week, or a day of the month. We could create features for the spend amounts and number of visits for each day of the week.
- We could create features based on the average size of a shopping basket, how frequently a customer visits, and so on.
- We could try a different model architecture that can take advantage of time-series data.

These are all things I would try if I was given this task as a work assignment. In traditional machine learning, adding more features often leads to problems as most traditional machine learning algorithms struggle with high-dimensionality data. Deep learning models can handle these cases, so there usually is no harm in adding more features.

The unreasonable effectiveness of data

Our first deep learning models on the binary classification task had fewer than 4,000 records. We did this so you could run the example quickly. For deep learning, you really need a lot more data, so we created a more complicated model with a lot more data, which gave us an increase in accuracy. This process demonstrated the following:

- Establishing a baseline with other machine learning algorithms provides a good benchmark before using a deep learning model
- We had to create a more complex model and adjust the hyper-parameters for our bigger dataset
- The Unreasonable Effectiveness of Data

The last point here is borrowed from an article by Peter Norvig, available at `https://static.googleusercontent.com/media/research.google.com/en//pubs/archive/35179.pdf`. There is also a YouTube video with the same name. One of the main points in Norvig's article is this: invariably simple models and a lot of data trump more elaborate models based on less data.

We have increased the accuracy on our deep learning model by 0.38%. Considering that our dataset has highly correlated variables and that our domain is modelling human activities, this is not bad. People are, well predictable; so when attempting to predict what they do next, a small dataset usually works. In other domains, adding more data has much more of an effect. Consider a complex image-recognition task with color images where the image quality and format are not consistent. In that case, increasing our training data by a factor of 10 would have much more of an effect than in the earlier example. For many deep learning projects, you should include tasks to acquire more data from the very beginning of the project. This can be done by manually labeling the data, by outsourcing tasks (Amazon Turk), or by building some form of feedback mechanism in your application.

While other machine learning algorithms may also see an improvement in performance with more data, eventually adding more data will stop making a difference and performance will stagnate. This is because these algorithms were never designed for large high-dimensional data and so cannot model the complex patterns in very large datasets. However, you can build increasingly complex deep learning architectures that can model these complex patterns. This following plot illustrates how deep learning algorithms can continue to take advantage of more data and performance can still improve after performance on other machine algorithms stagnates:

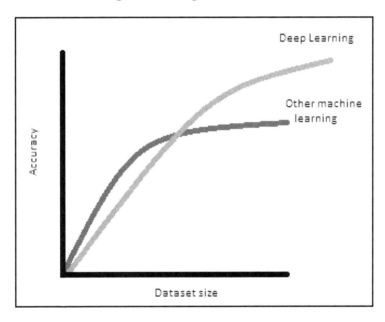

Figure 4.6: How model accuracy increases by dataset size for deep learning models versus other machine learning models

Summary

We covered a lot of ground in this chapter. We looked at activation functions and built our first true deep learning models using MXNet. Then we took a real-life dataset and created two use cases for applying a machine learning model. The first use case was to predict which customers will return in the future based on their past activity. This was a binary classification task. The second use case was to predict how much a customer will spend in the future based on their past activity. This was a regression task. We ran both models first on a small dataset and used different machine learning libraries to compare them against our deep learning model. Our deep learning model out-performed all of the algorithms.

We then took this further by using a dataset that was 100 times bigger. We built a larger deep learning model and adjusted our parameters to get an increase in our binary classification task accuracy. We finished the chapter with a brief discussion on how deep learning models out-perform traditional machine learning algorithms on large datasets.

In the next chapter, we will look at computer vision tasks, which deep learning has revolutionized.

5
Image Classification Using Convolutional Neural Networks

It is not an exaggeration to say that the huge growth of interest in deep learning can be mostly attributed to convolutional neural networks. **Convolutional neural networks (CNNs)** are the main building blocks of image classification models in deep learning, and have replaced most techniques that were previously used by specialists in the field. Deep learning models are now the de facto method to perform all large-scale image tasks, including image classification, object detection, detecting artificially generated images, and even attributing text descriptions to images. In this chapter, we will look at some of these techniques.

Why are CNNs so important? To explain why, we can look at the history of the ImageNet competition. The **ImageNet** competition is an open large-scale image classification challenge that has one thousand categories. It can be considered as the unofficial world championship for image classification. Teams, mostly fielded by academics and researchers, compete from around the world. In 2011, an error rate of around 25% was the benchmark. In 2012, a team led by Alex Krizhevsky and advised by Geoffrey Hinton achieved a huge leap by winning the competition with an error rate of 16%. Their solution consisted of 60 million parameters and 650,000 neurons, five convolutional layers, some of which are followed by max-pooling layers, and three fully-connected layers with a final 1,000-way softmax layer to do the final classification.

Other researchers built on their techniques in subsequent years, with the result that the original ImageNet competition is essentially considered *solved*. In 2017, almost all teams achieved an error rate of less than 5%. Most people consider that the 2012 ImageNet victory heralded the dawn of the new deep learning revolution.

In this chapter, we will look at image classification using CNN. We are going to start with the `MNIST` dataset, which is considered as the *Hello World* of deep learning tasks. The `MNIST` dataset consists of grayscale images of size 28 x 28 of 10 classes, the numbers 0-9. This is a much easier task than the ImageNet competition; there are 10 categories rather than 1,000, the images are in grayscale rather than color and most importantly, there are no backgrounds in the MNIST images that can potentially confuse the model. Nevertheless, the MNIST task is an important one in its own right; for example, most countries use postal codes containing digits. Every country uses automatic address routing solutions that are more complex variations of this task.

We will use the MXNet library from Amazon for this task. The MXNet library is an excellent library introduction to deep learning as it allows us to code at a higher level than other libraries such as TensorFlow, which we cover later on in this book.

The following topics will be covered in this chapter:

- What are CNNs?
- Convolutional layers
- Pooling layers
- Softmax
- Deep learning architectures
- Using MXNet for image classification

CNNs

CNNs are the cornerstone of image classification in deep learning. This section gives an introduction to them, explains the history of CNNs, and will explain why they are so powerful.

Before we begin, we will look at a simple deep learning architecture. Deep learning models are difficult to train, so using an existing architecture is often the best place to start. An architecture is an existing deep learning model that was state-of-the-art when initially released. Some examples are AlexNet, VGGNet, GoogleNet, and so on. The architecture we will look at is the original LeNet architecture for digit classification from Yann LeCun and others from the mid 1990s. This architecture was used for the `MNIST` dataset. This dataset is comprised of grayscale images of 28 x 28 size that contain the digits 0 to 9. The following diagram shows the LeNet architecture:

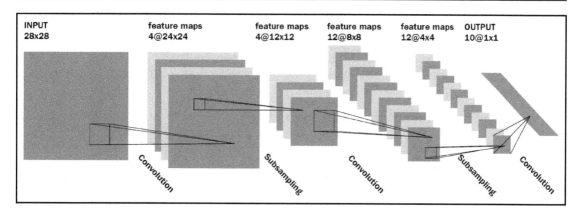

Figure 5.1: The LeNet architecture

The original images are 28 x 28 in size. We have a series of hidden layers which are convolution and pooling layers (here, they are labeled *subsampling*). Each convolutional layer changes structure; for example, when we apply the convolutions in the first hidden layer, our output size is three dimensional. Our final layer is of size 10 x 1, which is the same size as the number of categories. We can apply a `softmax` function here to convert the values in this layer to probabilities for each category. The category with the highest probability would be the category prediction for each image.

Convolutional layers

This section shows how convolutional layers work in greater depth. At a basic level, convolutional layers are nothing more than a set of filters. When you look at images while wearing glasses with a red tint, everything appears to have a red hue. Now, imagine if these glasses consisted of different tints embedded within them, maybe a red tint with one or more horizontal green tints. If you had such a pair of glasses, the effect would be to highlight certain aspects of the scene in front of you. Any part of the scene that had a green horizontal line would become more focused.

Convolutional layers apply a selection of patches (or convolutions) over the previous layer's output. For example, for a face recognition task, the first layer's patches identify basic features in the image, for example, an edge or a diagonal line. The patches are moved across the image to match different parts of the image. Here is an example of a 3 x 3 convolutional block applied across a 6 x 6 image:

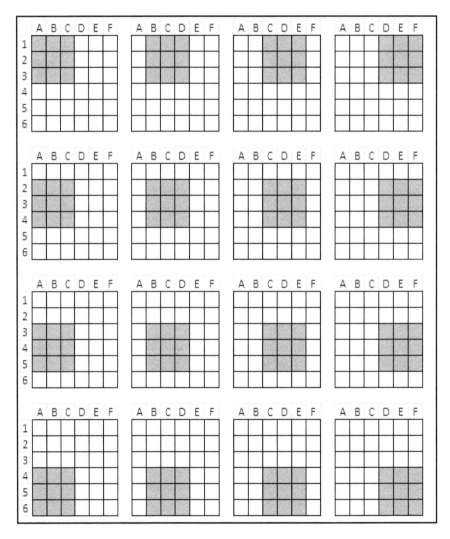

Figure 5.2: An example of a single convolution applied across an image

The values in the convolutional block are multiplied element by element (that is, not matrix multiplication), and the values are added to give a single value. Here is an example:

Input Layer						Conv. Block			Output Layer			
A	B	C	D	E	F							

	A	B	C	D	E	F								
1	0.5	0.3	0.1				3	1	1	6.3	XX	XX	XX
2	0.2	0.6	0.1				1	3	1	XX	XX	XX	XX
3	0.1	0.1	0.7				1	1	3	XX	XX	XX	XX
4				0.5	0.6	0.7				XX	XX	XX	3.6
5				0.2	0.1	0.1							
6				0.1	0.1	0.0							

Figure 5.3: An example of a convolution block applied to two parts of an input layer

In this example, our convolutional block is a diagonal pattern. The first block in the image (*A1:C3*) is also a diagonal pattern, so when we multiply the elements and sum them, we get a relatively large value of **6.3**. In comparison, the second block in the image (*D4:F6*) is a horizontal line pattern, so we get a much smaller value.

It can be difficult to visualize how convolutional layers work across the entire image, so the following R Shiny application will show it more clearly. This application is included in the code for this book in the `Chapter5/server.R` file. Open this file in **RStudio** and select **Run app**. Once the application is loaded, select **Convolutional Layers** from the left menu bar. The application loads the first 100 images from the `MNIST` dataset, which we will use later for our first deep learning image classification task. The images are grayscale images of size 28 x 28 of handwritten digits 0 to 9. Here is a screenshot of the application with the fourth image selected, which is a four:

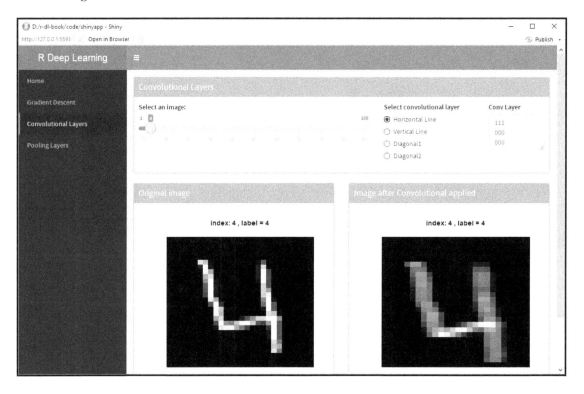

Figure 5.4: The Shiny application showing a horizontal convolutional filter

Once loaded, you can use the slider to browse through the images. In the top-right corner, there are four choices of convolutional layers to apply to the image. In the previous screenshot, a horizontal line convolutional layer is selected and we can see what this looks like in the text box in the top right corner. When we apply the convolutional filter to the input image on the left, we can see that the resulting image on the right is almost entirely grey, except for where the horizontal line was in the original image. Our convolutional filter has matched the parts in the image that have a horizontal line. If we change the convolutional filter to a vertical line, we get the following result:

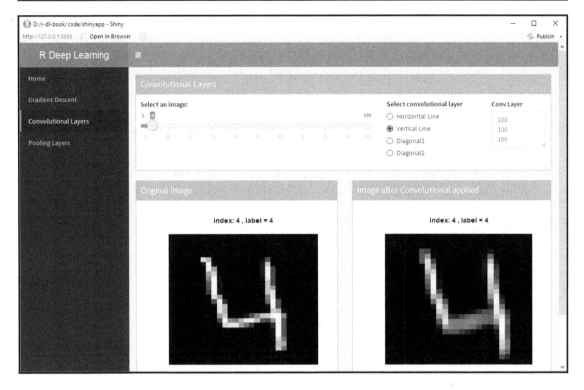

Figure 5.5: The Shiny application showing a vertical convolutional filter

Now, we can see that, after the convolution is applied, the vertical lines in the original image are highlighted in the resultant image on the right. In effect, applying these filters is a type of feature extraction. I encourage you to use the application and browse through images and see how different convolutions apply to images of the different categories.

This is the basis of convolutional filters, and while it is a simple concept, it becomes powerful when you start doing two things:

- Combining many convolutional filters to create convolutional layers
- Applying another set of convolutional filters (that is, a convolutional layer) to the output of a previous convolutional layer

This may take some time to get your head around. If I apply a filter to an image and then apply a filter to that output, what do I get? And if I then apply that a third time, that is, apply a filter to an image and then apply a filter to that output, and then apply a filter to that output, what do I get? The answer is that each subsequent layer combines identified features from the previous layers to find even more complicated patterns, for example, corners, arcs, and so on. Later layers find even richer features such as a circle with an arc over it, indicating the eye of a person.

There are two parameters that are used to control the movement of the convolution: padding and strides. In the following diagram, we can see that the original image is of size 6 x 6, while there are 4 x 4 subgraphs. We have therefore reduced the data representation from a 6 x 6 matrix to a 4 x 4 matrix. When we apply a convolution of size c_1, c_2 to data of size n, m, the output will be $n-c_1+1$, $m-c_2+1$. If we want our output to be the same size as our input, we can pad the input by adding zeros to borders of the images. For the previous example, we add a 1-pixel border around the entire image. The following diagram shows how the first 3 x 3 convolution would be applied to the image with padding:

Figure 5.6 Padding applied before a convolution

The second parameter we can apply to convolutions is strides, which control the movement of the convolution. The default is 1, which means the convolution moves by 1 each time, first to the right and then down. In practice, this value is rarely changed, so we will not consider it further.

We now know that convolutions act like small feature generators, that they are applied across an input layer (which is image data for the first layer), and that subsequent convolution layers find even more complicated features. But how are they calculated? Do we need to carefully craft a set of convolutions manually to apply them to our model? The answer is no; these convolutions are automatically calculated for us through the magic of the gradient descent algorithm. The best patterns are found after many iterations through the training dataset.

So, how do convolutions work once we get beyond 2-3 levels of layers? The answer is that it is difficult for anyone to understand the exact mathematics of how convolutional layers work. Even the original designers of these architects may not fully understand what is happening in the hidden layers in a series of CNNs. If this worries you, then recall that the solution that won the ImageNet competition in 2012 had 60 million parameters. With the advance in computing power, deep learning architectures may have hundreds of millions of parameters. It is simply not possible for any person to fully understand what is happening in such a complicated model. This is why they are often called **black-box** models.

It might surprise you at first. How can deep learning achieve human-level performance in image classification and how can we build deep learning models if we do not fully understand how they work? This question has divided the deep learning community, largely along the demarcation between industry and academia. Many (but not all) researchers believe that we should get a more fundamental understanding of how deep learning models work. Some researchers also believe that we can only develop the next generation of artificial intelligence applications by getting a better understanding of how current architectures work. At a recent NIPS conference (one of the oldest and most notable conferences for deep learning), deep learning was unfavorably compared to alchemy. Meanwhile, practitioners in the industry are not concerned with how deep learning works. They are more focused on building ever more complex deep learning architectures to maximize accuracy or performance.

Of course, this is a crude representation of the state of the industry; not all academics are inward looking and not all practitioners are just tweaking models to get small improvements. Deep learning is still relatively new (although the foundation blocks of neural networks have been known about for decades). But this tension does exist and has been around for awhile – for example, a popular deep learning architecture introduced *Inception* modules, which were named after the *Inception* movie. In the film, Leonardo DiCaprio leads a team that alter people's thoughts and opinions by embedding themselves within people's dreams. Initially, they go one layer deep, but then go deeper, in effect going to dreams within dreams. As they go deeper, the worlds get more complicated and the outcomes less certain. We will not go into detail here about what *Inception modules* are, but they combine convolutional and max pooling layers in parallel. The authors of the paper acknowledged the memory and computational cost of the model within the paper, but by naming the key component as an *Inception module,* they were subtly suggesting which side of the argument they were on.

After the breakthrough performance of the winner of the 2012 ImageNet competition, two researchers were unsatisfied that there was no insight into how the model worked. They decided to reverse-engineer the algorithm, attempting to show the input pattern that caused a given activation in the feature maps. This was a non-trivial task, as some layers used in the original model (for example, pooling layers) discarded information. Their paper showed the top 9 activations for each layer. Here is the feature visualization for the first layer:

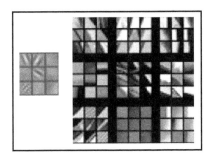

Figure 5.7: Feature visualization for the first layer in a CNN Source: https://cs.nyu.edu/~fergus/papers/zeilerECCV2014.pdf

The image is in two parts; on the left we can see the convolution (the paper only highlights 9 convolutions for each layer). On the right, we can see examples of patterns within images that match that convolution. For example, the convolution in the top-left corner is a diagonal edge detector. Here is the feature visualization for the second layer:

Figure 5.8: Feature visualization for the second layer in a CNN Source: https://cs.nyu.edu/~fergus/papers/zeilerECCV2014.pdf

Again, the image on the left is an interpretation of the convolution, while the image on the right shows examples of image patches that activate for that convolution. Here, we are starting to see some combinatorial patterns. For example, in the top-left, we can see patterns with stripes. Even more interesting is the example in the second row and second column. Here, we see circle shapes, which can indicate an eyeball in a person or an animal. Now, let's move on to feature visualization for the third layer:

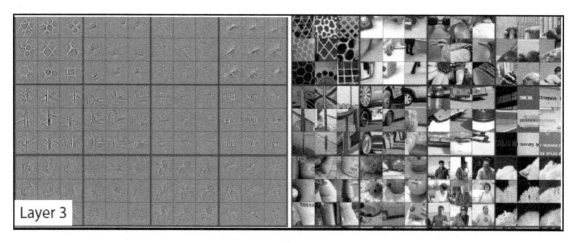

Figure 5.9: Feature visualization for the third layer in a CNN Source: https://cs.nyu.edu/~fergus/papers/zeilerECCV2014.pdf

In the third layer, we are seeing some really interesting patterns. In the second row and second column, we have identified parts of a car (wheels). In the third row and third column, we have begun to identify peoples' faces. In the second row and fourth column, we are identifying text within the images.

In the paper, the authors show examples for more layers. I encourage you to read the paper to get further insight into how convolutional layers work.

It is important to note that, while deep learning models can achieve human-level performance on image classification, they do not interpret images as humans do. They have no concept of what a cat is or what a dog is. They can only match the patterns given. In the paper, the authors highlight an example where the matched patterns have little in common; the model is matching features in the background (grass) instead of foreground objects.

In another image classification task, the model failed to work in practice. The task was to classify wolves versus dogs. The model failed in practice because the model was trained with data which had wolves in their natural habitat, that is, snow. Therefore, the model assumed its task was to differentiate between *snow* and *dog*. Any image of a wolf in another setting was wrongly classified.

 The lesson from this is that your training data should be varied and closely related to the data that the model will be expected to predict against. This may sound obvious in theory, but it is not always easy to do so in practice. We will discuss this further in the next chapter.

Pooling layers

Pooling layers are used in CNNs to reduce the number of parameters in the model and therefore they reduce overfitting. They can be thought of as a type of dimensionality reduction. Similar to convolutional layers, a pooling layer moves over the previous layer but the operation and return value are different. It returns a single value and the operation is usually the maximum value of the cells in that patch, hence the name max-pooling. You can also perform other operations, for example, average pooling, but this is less common. Here is an example of max-pooling using a 2 x 2 block. The first block has the values 7, 0, 6, 6 and the maximum value of these is 7, so the output is 7. Note that padding is not normally used with max-pooling and that it usually applies a stride parameter to move the block. Here, the stride is 2, so once we get the max of the first block, we move across, 2 cells to the right:

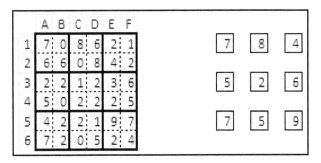

Figure 5.10: Max-Pooling applied to a matrix

We can see that max-pooling reduces the output by a factor of 4; the input was 6 x 6 and the output is 3 x 3. If you have not seen this before, your first reaction is probably disbelief. Why are we throwing away data? Why do we use max-pooling at all? There are three parts to this answer:

- **Pooling**: It is normally applied after a convolutional layer, so instead of executing over pixels, we execute over matched patterns. Downsizing after convolutional layers does not discard 75% of the input data; there is still enough signal there to find the pattern if it exists.
- **Regularization**: If you have studied machine learning, you will know that many models have problems with correlated features and that you are generally advised to remove correlated features. In image data, features are highly correlated with the spatial pattern around them. Applying max-pooling reduces the data while maintaining the features.
- **Execution speed**: When we consider the two earlier reasons, we can see that max-pooling greatly reduces the size of the network without removing too much of the signal. This makes training the model much quicker.

It is important to note the difference in the parameters used in the convolutional layer compared to the pooling layer. In general, a convolutional block is bigger (3 x 3) than the pooling block (2 x 2) and they should not overlap. For example, do not use a 4 x 4 convolutional block and a 2 x 2 pooling block. If they did overlap, the pooling block would just operate over the same convolutional blocks and the model would not train correctly.

Dropout

Dropout is a form of regularization which aims to prevent a model from overfitting. Overfitting is when the model is memorizing parts of the training dataset, but is not as accurate on unseen test data. When you build a model, you can check if overfitting is a problem by looking at the gap between the accuracy on the training set against the accuracy on the test set. If performance is much better on the training dataset, then the model is overfitting. Dropout refers to removing nodes randomly from a network temporarily during training. It is usually only applied to hidden layers, and not input layers. Here is an example of dropout applied to a neural network:

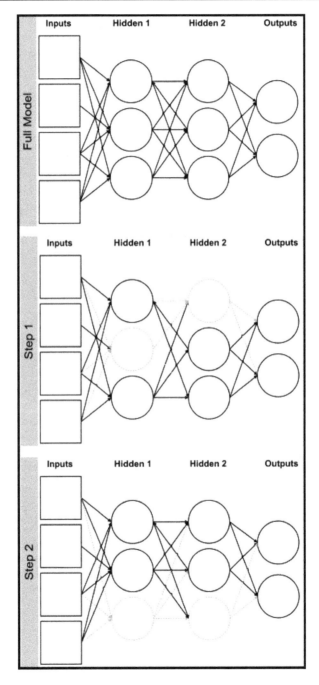

Figure 5.11: An example of dropout in a deep learning model

For each forward pass, a different set of nodes is removed, and therefore the network is different each time. In the original paper, dropout is compared to ensemble techniques, and in a way it is. There are some similarities to how dropout works and how random forest selects a random selection of features for each tree.

Another way to look at dropout is that each node in a layer must learn to work with all the nodes in that layer and the inputs it gets from the previous layer. It prevents one or a small number of nodes in a layer from getting large weights and dominating the outputs from that layer. This means that each node in a layer will work as a group and prevent some nodes from being too lazy and other nodes from being too dominant.

Flatten layers, dense layers, and softmax

After applying multiple convolutional layers, the resulting data structure is a multi-dimensional matrix (or tensor). We must transform this into a matrix that is in the shape of the required output. For example, if our classification task has 10 classes (for example, 10 for the `MNIST` example), we need the output of the model to be a 1 x 10 matrix. We do this by taking the results of our convolutional and max-pooling layers and using a Flatten layer to reshape the data. The last layer should have the same number of nodes as the number of classes we wish to predict for. If our task is binary classification, the `activation` function in our last layer will be sigmoid. If our task is binary classification, the `activation` function in our last layer will be softmax.

Before applying the softmax/sigmoid activation, we may optionally apply a number of dense layers. A dense layer is just a normal hidden layer, as we saw in `Chapter 1`, *Getting Started with Deep Learning*.

We need a softmax layer because the values in the last layer are numeric but range from -infinity to + infinity. We must convert these series of input values into a series of probabilities that says how likely the instance is for each category. The function to transform these numeric values to a series of probabilities must have the following characteristics:

- Each output value must be between 0.0 to 1.0
- The sum of the output values should be exactly 1.0

One way to do this is to just rescale the values by dividing each input value by the sum of the absolute input values. That approach has two problems:

- It does not handle negative values correctly
- Rescaling the input values may give us probabilities that are too close to each other

These two issues can be solved by first applying e^x (where e is 2.71828) to each input value and then rescaling those values. This transforms any negative number to a small positive number, and it also causes the probabilities to be more polarized. This can be demonstrated with an example; here, we can see the result from our dense layers. The values for categories 5 and 6 are quite close at 17.2 and 15.8, respectively. However, when we apply the softmax function, the probability value for category 5 is 4 times the probability value for category 6. The softmax function tends to result in probabilities that emphasize one category over all others, which is exactly what we want:

Category	Output from Dense Layer (x)	e^x	Output Probability
0	-1.3	0.27	0.00
1	5.2	181.27	0.00
2	8.3	4,023.87	0.00
3	11.2	73,130.44	0.00
4	10.1	24,343.01	0.00
5	17.2	29,502,925.92	0.78
6	15.8	7,275,331.96	0.19
7	5.2	181.27	0.00
8	3.1	22.20	0.00
9	13.5	729,416.37	0.02
		37,609,556.58	

Figure 5.12 Example of the softmax function

Image classification using the MXNet library

The MXNet package was introduced in Chapter 1, *Getting Started with Deep Learning*, so go back to that chapter for instructions on how to install the package if you have not already done so. We will demonstrate how to get almost 100% accuracy on a classification task for image data. We will use the MNIST dataset that we introduced in Chapter 2, *Image Classification Using Convolutional Neural Networks*. This dataset contains images of handwritten digits (0-9), and all images are of size 28 x 28. It is the *Hello World!* equivalent in deep learning. There's a long-term competition on Kaggle that uses this dataset. The script Chapter5/explore.Rmd is an R markdown file that explores this dataset.

1. First, we will check if the data has already been downloaded, and if it has not, we will download it. If the data is not available at this link, see the code in Chapter2/chapter2.R for an alternative way to get the data:

```
dataDirectory <- "../data"
if (!file.exists(paste(dataDirectory,'/train.csv',sep="")))
{
  link <-
'https://apache-mxnet.s3-accelerate.dualstack.amazonaws.com/R/data/
mnist_csv.zip'
  if (!file.exists(paste(dataDirectory,'/mnist_csv.zip',sep="")))
    download.file(link, destfile =
paste(dataDirectory,'/mnist_csv.zip',sep=""))
  unzip(paste(dataDirectory,'/mnist_csv.zip',sep=""), exdir =
dataDirectory)
  if (file.exists(paste(dataDirectory,'/test.csv',sep="")))
    file.remove(paste(dataDirectory,'/test.csv',sep=""))
}
```

2. Next we read the data into R and check it:

```
train <- read.csv(paste(dataDirectory,'/train.csv',sep=""),
header=TRUE, nrows=20)
```

We have 20 rows and 785 columns. Here, we will look at the rows at the tail of the dataset and look at the first 6 columns and the last 6 columns:

```
tail(train[,1:6])
    label pixel0 pixel1 pixel2 pixel3 pixel4
15      3      0      0      0      0      0
16      1      0      0      0      0      0
17      2      0      0      0      0      0
18      0      0      0      0      0      0
19      7      0      0      0      0      0
```

```
20      5      0      0      0      0      0
```

```
tail(train[,(ncol(train)-5):ncol(train)])
    pixel778 pixel779 pixel780 pixel781 pixel782 pixel783
15         0        0        0        0        0        0
16         0        0        0        0        0        0
17         0        0        0        0        0        0
18         0        0        0        0        0        0
19         0        0        0        0        0        0
20         0        0        0        0        0        0
```

We have 785 columns. The first column is the data label, and then we have 784 columns named pixel0, ..., pixel783 with the pixel values. Our images are *28 x 28 = 784*, so everything looks OK.

Before we start building models, it is always a good idea to ensure that your data is in the correct format and that your features and labels are aligned correctly. Let's plot the first 9 instances with their data labels.

3. To do this, we will create a helper function called plotInstance that takes in the pixel values and outputs the image with an optional header:

```
plotInstance <-function (row,title="")
  {
  mat <- matrix(row,nrow=28,byrow=TRUE)
  mat <- t(apply(mat, 2, rev))
   image(mat, main = title,axes = FALSE, col = grey(seq(0, 1, length
= 256)))
  }
  par(mfrow = c(3, 3))
  par(mar=c(2,2,2,2))
  for (i in 1:9)
  {
   row <- as.numeric(train[i,2:ncol(train)])
   plotInstance(row, paste("index:",i,", label =",train[i,1]))
  }
```

The output of this code shows the first 9 images and their classification:

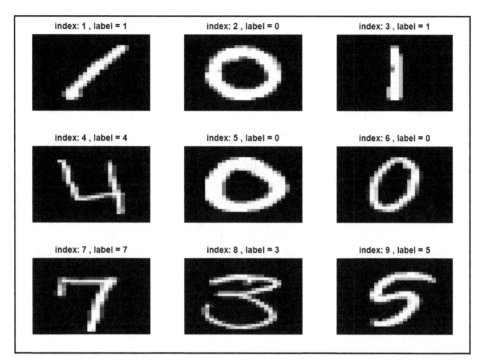

Figure 5.13: The first 9 images in the MNIST dataset

This completes our data exploration. Now, we can move on to creating some deep learning models using the MXNet library. We will create two models—the first is a standard neural network which we will use as a baseline. The second deep learning model is based on an architecture called **LeNet**. This is an old architecture, but is suitable in this case because our images are low resolution and do not contain backgrounds. Another advantage of LeNet is that it is possible to train quickly, even on CPUs, because it does not have many layers.

The code for this section is in `Chapter5/mnist.Rmd`. We must read data into R and convert it into matrices. We will split the training data into a train set and test set to get an unbiased estimate of accuracy. Because we have a large number of rows, we can use a split ratio of 90/10:

```
require(mxnet)
options(scipen=999)

dfMnist <- read.csv("../data/train.csv", header=TRUE)
yvars <- dfMnist$label
dfMnist$label <- NULL
```

```
set.seed(42)
train <- sample(nrow(dfMnist),0.9*nrow(dfMnist))
test <- setdiff(seq_len(nrow(dfMnist)),train)
train.y <- yvars[train]
test.y <- yvars[test]
train <- data.matrix(dfMnist[train,])
test <- data.matrix(dfMnist[test,])

rm(dfMnist,yvars)
```

Each image is represented as row of 784 (28 x 28) pixel values. The value of each pixel is in the range 0-255, we linearly transform it into 0-1 by dividing by 255. We also transpose the input matrix to because column major format in order to use it in `mxnet`.

```
train <- t(train / 255.0)
test <- t(test / 255.0)
```

Before creating a model, we should check that our dataset is balanced, i.e. the number of instances for each digit is reasonably even:

```
table(train.y)
## train.y
##    0    1    2    3    4    5    6    7    8    9
## 3716 4229 3736 3914 3672 3413 3700 3998 3640 3782
```

This looks ok, we can now move on to creating some deep learning models.

Base model (no convolutional layers)

Now that we have explored the data and we are satisfied that it looks OK, the next step is to create our first deep learning model. This is similar to the example we saw in the previous chapter. The code for this is in `Chapter5/mnist.Rmd`:

```
data <- mx.symbol.Variable("data")
fullconnect1 <- mx.symbol.FullyConnected(data, name="fullconnect1",
num_hidden=256)
activation1 <- mx.symbol.Activation(fullconnect1, name="activation1",
act_type="relu")
fullconnect2 <- mx.symbol.FullyConnected(activation1, name="fullconnect2",
num_hidden=128)
activation2 <- mx.symbol.Activation(fullconnect2, name="activation2",
act_type="relu")
fullconnect3 <- mx.symbol.FullyConnected(activation2, name="fullconnect3",
num_hidden=10)
softmax <- mx.symbol.SoftmaxOutput(fullconnect3, name="softmax")
```

Let's look at this code in detail:

1. In `mxnet`, we use its own data type symbol to configure the network.
2. We create the first hidden layer (`fullconnect1 <- ....`). This parameters are the data as input, the layer's name and the number of neurons in the layer.
3. We apply an activation function to the `fullconnect` layer (`activation1 <- ....`). The `mx.symbol.Activation` function takes the output from the first hidden layer, `fullconnect1`.
4. The second hidden layer (`fullconnect1 <- ....`) takes `activation1` as the input.
5. The second activation is similar to `activation1`.
6. The `fullconnect3` is the output layer. This layer has 10 neurons because this is a multi-classification problem and there are 10 classes.
7. Finally, we use a softmax activation to get a probabilistic prediction for each class.

Now, let's train the base model. I have a GPU installed, so I can use that. You may need to change the line to `devices <- mx.cpu()`:

```
devices <- mx.gpu()
mx.set.seed(0)
model <- mx.model.FeedForward.create(softmax, X=train, y=train.y,
                                    ctx=devices,array.batch.size=128,
                                    num.round=10,
                                    learning.rate=0.05, momentum=0.9,
                                    eval.metric=mx.metric.accuracy,
epoch.end.callback=mx.callback.log.train.metric(1))
```

To make a prediction, we will call the `predict` function. We can then create a confusion matrix and calculate our accuracy level on test data:

```
preds1 <- predict(model, test)
pred.label1 <- max.col(t(preds1)) - 1
res1 <- data.frame(cbind(test.y,pred.label1))
table(res1)
##        pred.label1
## test.y   0   1   2   3   4   5   6   7   8   9
##       0 405   0   0   1   1   2   1   1   0   5
##       1   0 449   1   0   0   0   0   4   0   1
##       2   0   0 436   0   0   0   0   3   1   1
##       3   0   0   6 420   0   1   0   2   8   0
##       4   0   1   1   0 388   0   2   0   1   7
##       5   2   0   0   6   1 363   3   0   2   5
##       6   3   1   3   0   2   1 427   0   0   0
```

```
##      7   0   2   3   0   1   0   0 394   0   3
##      8   0   4   2   4   0   2   1   1 403   6
##      9   1   0   1   2   7   0   1   1   0 393

accuracy1 <- sum(res1$test.y == res1$pred.label1) / nrow(res1)
accuracy1
## 0.971
```

The accuracy of our base model is 0.971. Not bad, but let's see if we can improve on it.

LeNet

Now, we can create a model based on the LeNet architecture. This is a very simple model; we have two sets of convolutional and pooling layers and then a Flatten layer, and finally two dense layers. The code for this is in Chapter5/mnist.Rmd. First let's define the model:

```
data <- mx.symbol.Variable('data')
# first convolution layer
convolution1 <- mx.symbol.Convolution(data=data, kernel=c(5,5),
num_filter=64)
activation1 <- mx.symbol.Activation(data=convolution1, act_type="tanh")
pool1 <- mx.symbol.Pooling(data=activation1, pool_type="max",
                           kernel=c(2,2), stride=c(2,2))

# second convolution layer
convolution2 <- mx.symbol.Convolution(data=pool1, kernel=c(5,5),
num_filter=32)
activation2 <- mx.symbol.Activation(data=convolution2, act_type="relu")
pool2 <- mx.symbol.Pooling(data=activation2, pool_type="max",
                           kernel=c(2,2), stride=c(2,2))

# flatten layer and then fully connected layers
flatten <- mx.symbol.Flatten(data=pool2)
fullconnect1 <- mx.symbol.FullyConnected(data=flatten, num_hidden=512)
activation3 <- mx.symbol.Activation(data=fullconnect1, act_type="relu")
fullconnect2 <- mx.symbol.FullyConnected(data=activation3, num_hidden=10)
# final softmax layer
softmax <- mx.symbol.SoftmaxOutput(data=fullconnect2)
```

Now, let's reshape the data so that it can be used in MXNet:

```
train.array <- train
dim(train.array) <- c(28,28,1,ncol(train))
test.array <- test
dim(test.array) <- c(28,28,1,ncol(test))
```

Finally, we can build the model:

```
devices <- mx.gpu()
mx.set.seed(0)
model2 <- mx.model.FeedForward.create(softmax, X=train.array, y=train.y,
                                ctx=devices,array.batch.size=128,
                                num.round=10,
                                learning.rate=0.05, momentum=0.9,
wd=0.00001,
                                eval.metric=mx.metric.accuracy,
epoch.end.callback=mx.callback.log.train.metric(1))
```

Finally, let's evaluate the model:

```
preds2 <- predict(model2, test.array)
pred.label2 <- max.col(t(preds2)) - 1
res2 <- data.frame(cbind(test.y,pred.label2))
table(res2)
## pred.label2
## test.y   0   1   2   3   4   5   6   7   8   9
##      0 412   0   0   0   0   1   1   1   0   1
##      1   0 447   1   1   1   0   0   4   1   0
##      2   0   0 438   0   0   0   0   3   0   0
##      3   0   0   6 427   0   1   0   1   2   0
##      4   0   0   0   0 395   0   0   1   0   4
##      5   1   0   0   5   0 369   2   0   1   4
##      6   2   0   0   0   1   1 432   0   1   0
##      7   0   0   2   0   0   0   0 399   0   2
##      8   1   0   1   0   1   1   1   1 414   3
##      9   2   0   0   0   4   0   0   1   1 398
```

```
accuracy2
## 0.9835714
```

The accuracy of our CNN model is `0.9835714`, which is quite an improvement over the accuracy of our base model, which was `0.971`.

Finally, we can visualize our model in R:

```
graph.viz(model2$symbol)
```

This produces the following plot, which shows the architecture of the deep learning model:

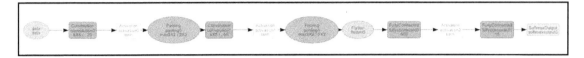

Figure 5.14: Convolutional deep learning model (LeNet)

Congratulations! You have built a deep learning model that is over 98% accurate!

We saw the architecture of LeNet in *Figure 5.1* and we have programmed it using the MXNet library. Let's analyze the LeNet architecture in more detail. Essentially, we have two convolutional groups and two fully connected layers. Our convolutional groups have a convolutional layer, followed by an `activation` function and then a pooling layer. This combination of layers is very common across many deep learning image classification tasks. The first convolution layer has 64 blocks of 5 x 5 size with no padding. This will possibly miss some features at the edges of the images, but if we look back at our sample images in *Figure 5.15*, we can see that most images do not have any data around the borders. We use pooling layers with `pool_type=max`. Other types are possible; average pooling was commonly used but has fallen out of favor recently. It is another hyper-parameter to try. We calculate our pools in 2 x 2 and then stride ("jump") by 2. Therefore, each input value is only used once in the max pool layer.

We use `tanh` as an `activation` function for our first convolutional block, and then use `relu` for subsequent layers. If you wish, you can try to change these and see what effect they have. Once we have executed our convolutional layers, we can use Flatten to restructure the data into a format that can be used by a fully connected layer. A fully connected layer is just a collection of nodes in a layer, that is, similar to the layers in the base model in the previous code. We have two layers, one with 512 nodes and the other with 10 nodes. We select 10 nodes in our last layer as this is the number of categories in our problem. Finally, we use a softmax to convert the numeric quantities in this layer into a set of probabilities for each category. We have achieved 98.35% accuracy, which is quite an improvement on a *normal* deep learning model, but there is still room for improvement. Some models can get 99.5% accuracy on this dataset, that is, 5 wrongly classified records in 1,000. Next, we will look at a different dataset that, while similar to MNIST, is harder than MNIST. This is the Fashion `MNIST` dataset, which has grayscale images of the same size as MNIST and also has 10 categories.

Classification using the fashion MNIST dataset

This dataset is in the same structure as MNIST, so we can just change our dataset and use the existing boilerplate code we have for loading the data. The script Chapter5/explore_Fashion.Rmd is an R markdown file that explores this dataset; it is almost identical to the explore.Rmd that we used for the MNIST dataset, so we will not repeat it. The only change to the explore.Rmd is to output the labels. We will look at 16 examples because this is a new dataset. Here are some sample images from this dataset that are created using the same boilerplate code we used to create the example for the MNIST dataset:

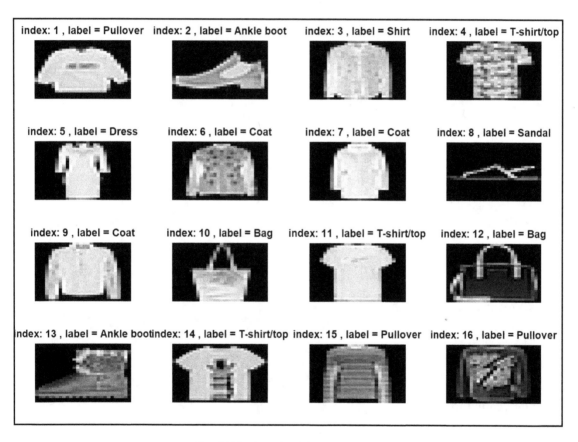

Figure 5.15: Some images from the Fashion MNIST dataset

An interesting fact about this dataset is that the company that released it also created a GitHub repository where they tested machine learning libraries against this dataset. The benchmarks are available at `http://fashion-mnist.s3-website.eu-central-1.amazonaws.com/`. If we look through these results, none of the machine libraries they tried achieved over 90% accuracy (they did not try deep learning). This is the target we want to beat with a deep learning classifier. The deep learning model code is in `Chapter5/fmnist.R` and achieves over 91% accuracy on this dataset. There are some small, but significant differences to the model architecture above. Try to spot them without peeking at the explanation.

First, let's define the model architecture.

```
data <- mx.symbol.Variable('data')
# first convolution layer
convolution1 <- mx.symbol.Convolution(data=data, kernel=c(5,5),
                                      stride=c(1,1), pad=c(2,2),
num_filter=64)
activation1 <- mx.symbol.Activation(data=convolution1, act_type=act_type1)
pool1 <- mx.symbol.Pooling(data=activation1, pool_type="max",
                    kernel=c(2,2), stride=c(2,2))


# second convolution layer
convolution2 <- mx.symbol.Convolution(data=pool1, kernel=c(5,5),
                                      stride=c(1,1), pad=c(2,2),
num_filter=32)
activation2 <- mx.symbol.Activation(data=convolution2, act_type=act_type1)
pool2 <- mx.symbol.Pooling(data=activation2, pool_type="max",
                    kernel=c(2,2), stride=c(2,2))


# flatten layer and then fully connected layers with activation and dropout
flatten <- mx.symbol.Flatten(data=pool2)
fullconnect1 <- mx.symbol.FullyConnected(data=flatten, num_hidden=512)
activation3 <- mx.symbol.Activation(data=fullconnect1, act_type=act_type1)
drop1 <- mx.symbol.Dropout(data=activation3,p=0.4)
fullconnect2 <- mx.symbol.FullyConnected(data=drop1, num_hidden=10)
# final softmax layer
softmax <- mx.symbol.SoftmaxOutput(data=fullconnect2)
```

Now let's train the model:

```
logger <- mx.metric.logger$new()
model2 <- mx.model.FeedForward.create(softmax, X=train.array, y=train.y,
                              ctx=devices, num.round=20,
                              array.batch.size=64,
                              learning.rate=0.05, momentum=0.9,
                              wd=0.00001,
                              eval.metric=mx.metric.accuracy,
```

```
eval.data=list(data=test.array,labels=test.y),
epoch.end.callback=mx.callback.log.train.metric(100,logger))
```

The first change is that we switch to use `relu` as an `Activation` function for all layers. Another change was that we use padding for the convolutional layers, which we did to capture the features at the borders of the image. We increased the number of nodes in each layer to add depth to the model. We also added a dropout layer to prevent the model from overfitting. We also added logging to our model, which outputs the train and validation metrics for each epoch. We used these to check how our model performs and to decide if it is overfitting.

Here are the accuracy results and the diagnostic plot for this model:

```
preds2 <- predict(model2, test.array)
pred.label2 <- max.col(t(preds2)) - 1
res2 <- data.frame(cbind(test.y,pred.label2))
table(res2)
          pred.label2
test.y    0    1    2    3    4    5    6    7    8    9
     0  489    0   12   10    0    0   53    0    3    0
     1    0  586    1    6    1    0    1    0    0    0
     2    8    1  513    7   56    0   31    0    0    0
     3   13    0    3  502   16    0   26    1    1    0
     4    1    1   27   13  517    0   32    0    2    0
     5    1    0    0    0    0  604    0    9    0    3
     6   63    0   47    9   28    0  454    0    3    0
     7    0    0    0    1    0   10    0  575    1   11
     8    0    0    1    0    1    2    1    0  618    0
     9    0    0    0    0    0    1    0   17    1  606
accuracy2 <- sum(res2$test.y == res2$pred.label2) / nrow(res2)
accuracy2
# 0.9106667
```

One thing to note is that we are using the same validation/test set for showing metrics during training and to evaluate the final model. This is not a good practice, but it is acceptable here because we are not using validation metrics to tune the hyperparameters of the model. The accuracy of our CNN model is `0.9106667`.

Let's plot the accuracy of the train and validation sets as the model is trained. The deep learning model code has a `callback` function which saves the metrics as the model is trained. We can use this to plot the training and validation metrics for each epoch:

```
# use the log data collected during model training
dfLogger<-as.data.frame(round(logger$train,3))
dfLogger2<-as.data.frame(round(logger$eval,3))
dfLogger$eval<-dfLogger2[,1]
```

```
colnames(dfLogger)<-c("train","eval")
dfLogger$epoch<-as.numeric(row.names(dfLogger))

data_long <- melt(dfLogger, id="epoch")

ggplot(data=data_long,
       aes(x=epoch, y=value, colour=variable,label=value)) +
  ggtitle("Model Accuracy") +
  ylab("accuracy") +
  geom_line()+geom_point() +
  geom_text(aes(label=value),size=3,hjust=0, vjust=1) +
  theme(legend.title=element_blank()) +
  theme(plot.title = element_text(hjust = 0.5)) +
  scale_x_discrete(limits= 1:nrow(dfLogger))
```

This shows us how our model is performing after each epoch (or training run). This produces the following screenshot:

Figure 5.16: Training and validation accuracy by epoch

The two main points to be taken from this graph are that:

- The model is overfitting. We can see a clear gap between performance on the training set at **0.95xxx** and the validation set at **0.91xxx**.
- We could have probably stopped the model training after 8 epochs, as performance did not improve after this point.

As we have discussed in previous chapters, deep learning models will almost always overfit by default, but there are methods to negate this. The second issue is related to *early stopping*, and it is vital that you know how to do this so that you do not waste hours in continuing to train a model which is no longer improving. This is especially relevant if you are building the model using cloud resources. We will look at these and more issues related to building deep learning models in the next chapter.

References/further reading

These papers are classical deep learning papers in this domain. Some of them document winning approaches to ImageNet competitions. I encourage you to download and read all of them. You may not understand them at first, but their importance will become more evident as you continue on your journey in deep learning.

- Krizhevsky, Alex, Ilya Sutskever, and Geoffrey E. Hinton. *ImageNet Classification with Deep Convolutional Neural Networks*. Advances in neural information processing systems. 2012.
- Szegedy, Christian, et al. *Going Deeper with Convolutions*. Cvpr, 2015.
- LeCun, Yann, et al. *Learning Algorithms for Classification: A Comparison on Handwritten Digit Recognition*. Neural networks: the statistical mechanics perspective 261 (1995): 276.
- Zeiler, Matthew D., and Rob Fergus. *Visualizing and Understanding Convolutional Networks*. European conference on computer vision. Springer, Cham, 2014.
- Srivastava, Nitish, et al. *Dropout: A Simple Way to Prevent Neural Networks from Overfitting*. The Journal of Machine Learning Research 15.1 (2014): 1929-1958.

Summary

In this chapter, we used deep learning for image classification. We discussed the different layer types that are used in image classification: convolutional layers, pooling layers, dropout, dense layers, and the softmax activation function. We saw an R-Shiny application that shows how convolutional layers perform feature engineering on image data.

We used the MXNet deep learning library in R to create a base deep learning model which got 97.1% accuracy. We then developed a CNN deep learning model based on the LeNet architecture, which achieved over 98.3% accuracy on test data. We also used a slightly harder dataset (Fashion MNIST) and created a new model that achieved over 91% accuracy. This accuracy score was better than all of the other scores that used non-deep learning algorithms. In the next chapter, we will build on what we have covered and show you how we can take advantage of pre-trained models for classification and as building blocks for new deep learning models.

In the next chapter, we are going to discuss important topics in deep learning concerning tuning and optimizing your models. This includes how to use the limited data you may have, data pre-processing, data augmentation, and hyperparameter selection.

Tuning and Optimizing Models

6

In the last two chapters, we trained deep learning models for classification, regression, and image recognition tasks. In this chapter, we will discuss some important issues in regard to managing deep learning projects. While this chapter may seem somewhat theoretical, if any of the issues discussed are not correctly managed, it can derail your deep learning project. We will look at how to choose evaluation metrics and how to create an estimate of how well a deep learning model will perform before you begin modeling. Next, we will move onto data distribution and the mistakes often made in splitting data into correct partitions for training. Many machine learning projects fail in production use because the data distribution is different to what the model was trained with. We will look at data augmentation, a valuable method to enhance your model's accuracy. Finally, we will discuss hyperparameters and learn how to tune them.

In this chapter, we will be looking at the following topics:

- Evaluation metrics and evaluating performance
- Data preparation
- Data pre-processing
- Data augmentation
- Tuning hyperparameters
- Use case—interpretability

Evaluation metrics and evaluating performance

This section will discuss how to set up a deep learning project and what evaluation metrics to select. We will look at how to select evaluation criteria and how to decide when the model is approaching optimal performance. We will also discuss how all deep learning models tend to overfit and how to manage the bias/variance tradeoff. This will give guidelines on what to do when models have low accuracy.

Types of evaluation metric

Different evaluation metrics are used for categorization and regression tasks. For categorization, accuracy is the most commonly used evaluation metric. However, accuracy is only valid if the cost of errors is the same for all classes, which is not always the case. For example, in medical diagnosis, the cost of a false negative will be much higher than the cost of a false positive. A false negative in this case says that the person is not sick when they are, and a delay in diagnosis can have serious, perhaps fatal, consequences. On the other hand, a false positive is saying that the person is sick when they are not, which is upsetting for that person but is not life threatening.

This issue is compounded when you have imbalanced datasets, that is, when one class is much more common than the other. Going back to our medical diagnosis example, if only 1% of people who get tested actually have the disease, then a machine learning algorithm can get 99% accuracy by just declaring that nobody has the disease. In this case, you can look at other metrics rather than accuracy. One such metric that is useful for imbalanced datasets is the F1 evaluation metric, which is a weighted average of precision and recall. The formula for the F1 score is as follows:

F1 = 2 * (precision * recall) / (precision + recall)

The formulas for precision and recall are as follows:

precision = true_positives / (true_positives + false_positives)
recall = true_positives / (true_positives + false_negatives)

For regression, you have a choice of evaluation metrics: MAE, MSE, and RMSE. **MAE**, or **Mean Absolute Error**, is the simplest; it is just the average of the absolute difference between the actual value and the predicted value. The advantage of MAE is that it is easily understood; if MAE is 3.5, then the difference between the predicted value and the actual value is 3.5 on average. **MSE**, or **Mean Squared Error**, is the average of the squared error, that is, it takes the difference between the actual value and the predicted value, squares it, and then takes the average of those values. The advantage of using MSE over MAE is that it penalizes errors according to their severity. If the difference between the actual value and the predicted value for two rows was 2 and 5, then the MSE would put more weight on the second example because the error is larger. **RMSE**, or **Root Mean Squared Error**, is the square root of MSE. The advantage of using MSE is that it puts the error term back into units that are comparable to the actual values. For regression tasks, RMSE is usually the preferred metric.

For more information on metrics in MXNet, see `https://mxnet.incubator.apache.org/api/python/metric/metric.html`.

For more information on metrics in Keras, see `https://keras.io/metrics/`.

Evaluating performance

We have explored a few deep learning models in earlier chapters. We got an accuracy rate of 98.36% in our image classification task on the `MNIST` dataset in `Chapter 5`, *Image Classification Using Convolutional Neural Networks*. For the binary classification task (predicting which customers will return in the next 14 days) in `Chapter 4`, *Training Deep Prediction Models*, we got an accuracy rate of 77.88%. But what does this actually mean and how do we evaluate the performance of a deep learning model?

The obvious starting point in evaluating whether your deep learning model has good predictive capability is by comparing it to other models. The `MNIST` dataset is used in a lot of benchmarks for deep learning research, so we know that there are models that achieve 99.5% accuracy. Therefore, our model is OK, but not great. In the *Data augmentation* section in this chapter, we will improve our model significantly, from 98.36% accuracy to 98.95% accuracy, by augmenting our data with new images created by making changes to the existing image data. In general, for image classification tasks anything less than 95% accuracy probably indicates a problem with your deep learning model. Either the model is not designed correctly or you do not have enough data for your task.

Our binary classification model only had 77.54% accuracy, which is much less than the image classification task. So, is it a terrible model? Not really; it is still a useful model. We also have some benchmarks from other machine learning models such as random forest and xgboost that we ran on a small section of the data. We also saw that we got an increase in accuracy when we moved from a model with 3,900 rows to a deeper model with 390,000 rows. This highlights that deep learning models improve with more data.

One step you can do to evaluate your model's performance is to see if more data will increase accuracy significantly. The data can be acquired from more training data, or from data augmentation, which we will see later. You can use learning curves to evaluate if this will help with performance. To create a learning curve, you train a series of machine learning models with increasing sizes, for example, 10,000 rows to 200,000 rows in steps of 1,000 rows. For each step, run 5 different machine learning models to smooth the results and plot average accuracy by the sample size. Here is the pseudocode to perform this task:

```
For k=10000 to 200000 step 1000
    For n=1 to 5
        [sample] = Take k rows from dataset
        Split [sample] into train (80%) / test (20%)
        Run ML (DT) algorithm
        Calculate Accuracy on test
        Save accuracy value
Plot k, avg(Accuracy)
```

Here is an example of a learning curve plot for similar task to the churn problem:

Figure 6.1: An example of a learning curve which plots accuracy by data size

In this case, accuracy is in a very narrow range and stabilizes as the # instances increase. Therefore, for this algorithm and hyperparameter choice, adding more data will not increase accuracy significantly.

If we get a learning curve that is flat like in this example, then adding more data to the existing model will not increase accuracy. We could try to improve our performance by either changing the model architecture or by adding more features. We discussed some options for this in Chapter 5, *Image Classification Using Convolutional Neural Networks*.

Going back to our binary classification model, let's consider how we could we use it in production. Recall that this model is trying to predict if customers will return in the next x days. Here is the confusion matrix from that model again:

```
          Predicted
  Actual     0      1
     0     10714   4756
     1      3870  19649
```

If we look at how the model performs for each class, we get a different accuracy rates:

- For Actual=0, we get *10714 / (10714 + 4756) = 69.3%* values correct. This is called specificity or the true negative rate.
- For Actual=1, we get *19649 / (3466 + 19649) = 85.0%* values correct. This is called sensitivity or the true positive rate.

For this use case, sensitivity is probably more of a concern than specificity. If I were a senior manager, I would be more interested in knowing which customers were predicted to return but did not. This group could be sent offers to entice them back. Here is how a senior manager might use this model, assuming that the model is built to predict whether a person comes in from September 1 to September 14. On September 15, we get the preceding confusion matrix. How should a manager allocate his/her limited marketing budget?

- I can see that I got 4,756 customers who were predicted not to return but actually did. This is good, but I cannot really act on this. I can attempt to send offers to the 10,135 who did not return, but since my model already predicted that they would not return, I would expect the response rate to be low.
- The 3,870 customers who were predicted to return but did not are more interesting. These people should be sent offers to entice them back before their change in behavior becomes permanent. This represents only 9.9% of my customer base, so by only sending offers to these customers, I am not diluting my budget by sending offers to a large contingent of my customers.

The prediction model should not be used in isolation; other metrics should be combined with it to develop a marketing strategy. For example, **customer lifetime value** (**CLV**), which measures the expected future revenue for a customer minus the cost to re-acquire that customer, could be combined with the prediction model. By using a prediction model and CLV together, we can prioritize customers that are likely to return by their predicted future value.

To summarize this section, it is all too easy to get obsessed with optimizing evaluation metrics, especially if you are new to the field. As a data scientist, you should always remember that optimizing evaluation metrics on a machine learning task is not the ultimate goal—it is just a proxy for improving some part of the business. You must be able to link the results of your machine learning model back to a business use case. In some cases, for example, digit recognition in the MNIST dataset, there is a direct link between your evaluation metrics and your business case. But sometimes it is not so obvious, and you need help to work with the business in finding out how to use the results of your analysis to maximize the benefits to the company.

Data preparation

Machine learning is about training a model to generalize on the cases it sees so that it can make predictions on unseen data. Therefore, the data used to train the deep learning model should be similar to the data that the model sees in production. However, at an early product stage, you may have little or no data to train a model, so what can you do? For example, a mobile app could include a machine learning model that predicts the subject of image taken by the mobile camera. When the app is being written, there may not be enough data to train the model using a deep learning network. One approach would be to augment the dataset with images from other sources to train the deep learning network. However, you need to know how to manage this and how to deal with the uncertainty it introduces. Another approach is transfer learning, which we will cover in Chapter 11, *The Next Level in Deep Learning*.

Another difference between deep learning and traditional machine learning is the size of the datasets. This can affect the ratios used to split data between train/test—the recommended guidelines for splitting data into 70/30 or 80/20 splits for machine learning need to be revised for training deep learning models.

Different data distributions

In previous chapters, we used the MNIST dataset for classification tasks. While this dataset contains handwritten digits, the data is not representative of real-life data. In Chapter 5, *Image Classification Using Convolutional Neural Networks,* we visualized some of the digits, if you go back and look at these images, it is clear that these images are in a standard format:

- There are all grayscale
- The images are all 28 x 28
- The images all appear to have at border of at least 1 pixel
- The images are all of the same scale, that is, each image takes up most of the image
- There is very little distortion, since the border is black and the foreground is white
- Images are the *right way up,* that is, we do not have any major rotations

The original use case for the MNIST dataset is to recognize 5 digit postcodes on letters. Let's suppose we train a model on the 60,000 images in the MNIST dataset and wish to use it in a production environment to recognize postcodes from letters and packages. Here are the steps a production system must go through before any deep learning can be applied:

- Scan the letters
- Find the postcode section
- Split the postcode digits into 5 different regions (one per digit)

In any one of these data transformation steps, additional data bias could occur. If we used the *clean* MNIST data to train a model and then tried to predict the *biased* transformed data, then our model may not work that well. Examples of how bias could affect the production data include the following:

- Correctly locating the postcode is a difficult problem in itself
- The letters will have backgrounds and foregrounds of different colors and contrasts, and so converting them to grayscale may not be consistent depending on the type of letter and pen used on the letter / package
- The results from the scanning processes may vary because of different hardware and software being used—this is a ongoing problem in applying deep learning to medical image data
- Finally, the difficultly in splitting the postcode into 5 different regions depends on the letter and pen used, as well as the quality of the preceding steps

In this example, the distribution of the data used to train and the estimate model's performance is different from the production data. If a data scientist had promised to deliver 99% accuracy before the model is deployed, then senior managers are very likely to be disappointed when the application runs in production! When creating a new model, we split data into train and test splits, so the main purpose of the test dataset is to estimate model accuracy. But if the data in the test dataset is different to what the model will be see in production, then the evaluation metrics on the test dataset cannot give a good guide to how the model will perform in production.

If the problem is that there is little or no actual labeled dataset to begin with, then one of the first steps to consider before any model training is to investigate if more data can be acquired. Acquiring data may involve setting up a mini production environment, partnering with a client or using a combination of semi-supervised and manual labelling. In the use case we just saw, I would consider it more important to set up the process to extract the digitized images before looking at any machine learning. Once this is set up, I would look to build up some training data—it still may not be enough to build a model, but it could be used but a proper test set to create evaluation metrics that would reflect real-life performance. This may appear obvious, as over optimistic expectations based on flawed evaluation metrics are probably one of the top three problems in data science projects.

One example of a very large scale project that managed this problem very well is this use case in Airbnb: `https://medium.com/airbnb-engineering/categorizing-listing-photos-at-airbnb-f9483f3ab7e3`. They had a huge number of photos of house interiors, but these were not labeled with the room type. They took their existing labeled data and also performed quality assurance to check how accurate the labels were. It is often said in data science that creating machine learning models may only be 20% of the actual work involved—acquiring an accurate large labeled dataset that is representative of what the model will see in production is often the hardest task in a deep learning project.

Once you have a dataset in place, you need to split your data into train and test splits before modeling. If you have experience in traditional machine learning, you may start with a 70/30 split, that is, 70% for training the model and 30% for evaluating the model. However, this rule is less valid in the world of large datasets and training deep learning models. Again, the only reason to split data into train and test sets is to have a holdout set to estimate the model's performance. Therefore, you only need enough records in this dataset so that the accuracy estimate you get is reliable and has the precision you require. If you have a large dataset to begin with, then a smaller percentage might be adequate for the test dataset. Let me explain this with an example, where you want to improve on an existing machine learning model:

- A prior machine learning model has 99.0% accuracy
- There is a labeled dataset with 1,000,000 records

If a new machine learning model is to be trained, then it should get at least 99.1% accuracy for you to be confident that it is an improvement on the existing model. How many records do you need when evaluating the existing model? You only need enough records so that you are fairly sure that the accuracy on the new model is accurate to 0.1%. Therefore 50,000 records in the test set, which is 5% of the dataset, would be sufficient to evaluate your model. If the accuracy on these 50,000 records was 99.1%, that would be 49,550 records. This represents 50 more correctly classified records than the benchmark model, which would strongly suggest that the second model is a better model—it would be unlikely that the difference would be simply down to chance.

You may get resistance to the suggestion you use only 5% of data for model evaluation. However, the idea of splitting data into 70/30 splits goes back to the days of small datasets, such as the iris dataset with 150 records. We previously saw the following graph in `Chapter 4`, *Training Deep Prediction Models*, which showed how accuracy on machine learning algorithms tends to stagnate as the data size increases. Therefore, there was less of an incentive to maximize the amount of data that was available for training. Deep learning models can take advantage of more data, so if we can use less data for the test set, we should get a better model overall:

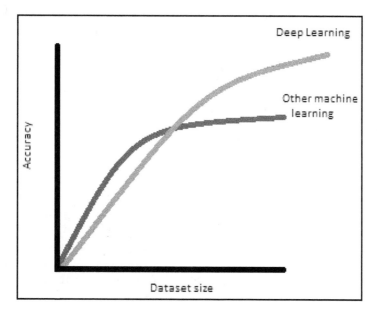

Figure 6.2: How model accuracy increases by dataset size for deep learning models versus other machine learning models

Data partition between training, test, and validation sets

The previous section highlighted the importance of acquiring some data at an early stage in the project. But if you do not have enough data to train a deep learning model, it is possible to train on other data and apply it to your data. For example, you can use a model trained on ImageNet data for image classification tasks. In this scenario, you need to use the real data that has been collected wisely. This section discusses some good practices on that subject.

 If you have ever wondered why big companies such as Google, Apple, Facebook, Amazon, and so on have such a head start in AI, this is the reason why. While they have some of the best AI people in the world working for them, their chief advantage is that they have access to tons of *labeled* data that they can use to build their machine learning models.

In the previous section, we said that the sole purpose of a test set is to evaluate the model. But if that data is not from the same distribution as the data the model will see in prediction tasks, then the evaluation will be misleading. One of the most important project priorities should be to acquire labeled data that is as similar to real-life data as soon as possible. Once you have that data, you need to be clever on how you use this valuable asset. The best use of this data, in order of priority, would be as follows:

- Can I use some of this data to create more training data? This could be through augmentation, or implementing an early prototype that users can interact with.
- If you are building several models (which you should be), use some of the data in the validation set to tune the model.
- Use the data in the test set to evaluate the model.
- Use the data in the train set.

Some of these suggestions may be contentious—especially when suggesting that you should use the data for the validation set before the test set. Remember that the sole purpose of a test set is that it should only be used once to evaluate the model, so you only get one shot at using this data. If I have only a small amount of realistic data, then I prefer to use it to tune the model and have a less precise evaluation metric than having a poorly performing model with a very precise evaluation metric.

This approach is risky, and ideally you want your validation dataset and your test dataset to be from the same distribution and be representative of the data that the model will see in production. Unfortunately, when you are at the early stages in machine learning projects with limited real-life data, then you have to make decisions on how best to use this data, and in this case it is better to use the limited data in the validation dataset rather than the test dataset.

Standardization

Another important step in data preparation is standardizing data. In the previous chapter, for the MNIST data, all pixel values were divided by 255 so that the input data was between 0.0 and 1.0. In our case, we applied min-max normalization, which transforms the data linearly using the following function:

xnew = (x-min(x))/(max(x)-min(x))

Since we already know that *min(x) = 0* and *max(x)=255*, this reduces to the following:

xnew = x / 255.0

The other most popular form of standardization scales the feature so that the mean is 0 and the standard deviation from the mean is 1. This is also known as **z-scores**, and the formula for it is as follows:

xnew = (x - mean(x)) / std.dev(x)

There are three reasons why we need to perform standardization:

- It is especially important to normalize our input features if the features are in different scales. A common example often cited in machine learning is predicting house prices from the number of bedrooms and the square foot. The number of bedrooms ranges from 1 to 10, while the square feet can range from 500 sq feet to 20,000 sq feet. Deep learning models expect features to be in the same range.
- Even if all of our features are already in the same range, it is still advisable to normalize the input features. Recall from `Chapter 3`, *Deep Learning Fundamentals*, that we looked at initializing the weights before model training. Any benefit from initializing weights will be cancelled if our features are not normalized. We also spoke about the problem of exploding and vanishing gradients. When features are on different scales this is more likely.
- Even if we avoid both of the preceding problem, if we do not apply normalization, the model will take longer to train.

For the churn model in `Chapter 4`, *Training Deep Prediction Models*, all of the columns were monetary spent, so are already on the same scale. When we applied the log to each of these variables, it will have shrunk them down to values between -4.6 to 11, so there was no need to scale them to values between 0 and 1. When correctly applied, standardization has no negative consequences and so should be one of first steps applied to data preparation.

Data leakage

Data leakage is where a feature used to train the model has values that could not exist if the model was used in production. It occurs most frequently in time series data. For example, in our churn use case in `Chapter 4`, *Training Deep Prediction Models*, there were a number of categorical variables in the data that indicated customer segmentation. A data modeler may assume that these are good predictor variables, but it is not known how and when these variables were set. They could be based on customer' spend, which means that if they are used in the prediction algorithm, there is a circular reference—an external process calculates the segment based on the spend and then this variable is used to predict spend!

When extracting data to build a model, you should be wary of categorical attributes and question when these variables could have been created and modified. Unfortunately, most database systems are poor at tracking the data lineage, so if in doubt you may consider omitting the variable from your model.

Another example of data leakage in image classification tasks is when attribute information within the image is used in the model. For example, if we build a model where the filenames were included as attributes, these names may hint at the class name. When the model is used in production, theses hints will not exist, so this is also seen as data leakage.

We will see an example of data leakage in practice in the the *Use case—interpretability* section later in this chapter.

Data augmentation

One approach to increasing the accuracy in a model regardless of the amount of data you have is to create artificial examples based on existing data. This is called **data augmentation**. Data augmentation can also be used at test time to improve prediction accuracy.

Using data augmentation to increase the training data

We are going to apply data augmentation to the MNIST dataset that we used in previous chapters. The code for this section is in Chapter6/explore.Rmd if you want to follow along. In Chapter 5, *Image Classification Using Convolutional Neural Networks*, we plotted some examples from the MNIST data, so we won't repeat the code again. It is included in the code file, and you can also refer back to the image in Chapter 5, *Image Classification Using Convolutional Neural Networks*:

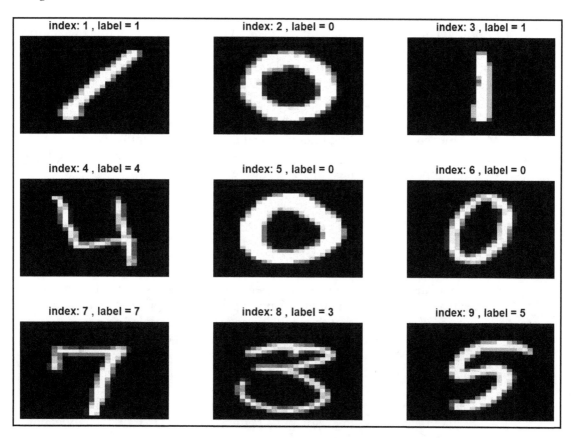

Figure 6.3: The first 9 images in the MNIST dataset

We described data augmentation as creating new data from an existing dataset. This means creating a new instance that is sufficiently different from the original instance but not so much that it no longer represents the data label. For image data, this might mean performing the following functions on the images:

- **Zooming**: By zooming into the center of the image, your model may be better able to handle images at different scales.
- **Shifting**: Moving the image up, down, left, or right can make the deep learning model more aware of examples of images taken off-center.
- **Rotation**: By rotating images, the model will be able to recognize data that is off-center.
- **Flipping**: For many objects, flipping the images 90 degrees is valid. For example, a picture of a car from the left side can be flipped to show a similar image of the car from the right side. A deep model can take advantage of this new perspective.
- **Adding noise**: Sometimes, deliberately adding noise to images can force the deep learning model to find deeper meaning.
- **Modifying color**: By adding filters to the image, you can simulate different lighting conditions. For example, you can change an image taken in bright light so that it appears to be taken in poor lighting conditions.

The goal of this task is to increase accuracy on the test dataset. However, the important rule of data augmentation is that the new data should attempt to simulate the data your model will use in production rather than trying to increase model accuracy on existing data. I cannot stress that enough. Getting 99% accuracy on a hold-out set means nothing if a model fails to work in a production environment because the data used to train and evaluate the model was not representative of real-life data. In our case, we can see that the MNIST images are grayscale and neatly centered, and so on. In a production use case, images are off-center and with different backgrounds and foregrounds (for example, with a brown background and blue writing), and so will not be classified correctly. You can attempt to pre-process the images so that you can format them to a similar manner (28 x 28 grayscale image with black background and data centered with a 2 x 2 margin), but a better solution is to train the model on typical data it will encounter in production.

If we look at the previous image, we can see that most of these data augmentation tasks are not applicable to the MNIST data. All of the images appear to be at the same zoom level already, so creating artificial examples at increased zoom will not help. Similarly, shifting is unlikely to work, since the images are already centered. Flipping images is definitely not valid, since most digits are not valid when flipped, example 7. There is no evidence of existing random noise in our data, so this will not work either.

One technique that we can try is to rotate the images. We will create two new artificial images for each existing image, the first artificial image will be rotated 15 degrees left and the second artificial image will be rotated 15 degrees right. Here are some of the artificial images after we have rotated the original images 15 degrees left:

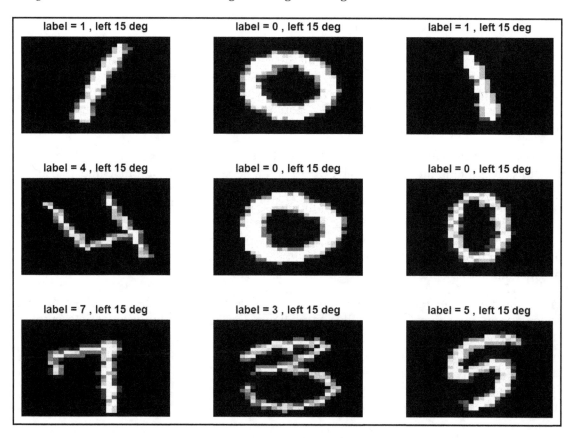

Figure 6.4: MNIST data rotated 15 degrees left

If we look at the the preceding screenshot, one strange anomaly exists. We have 10 classes, and using this approach may increase overall accuracy, but one class will not get as much uplift. The zero digit is the odd one out because rotating a zero still looks like a zero—we may still get an increase in accuracy for this class, but probably not as much as for the other classes. The function to rotate image data is in `Chapter6/img_ftns.R`. It uses the `rotateImage` function from the `OpenImageR` package:

```
rotateInstance <-function (df,degrees)
{
  mat <- as.matrix(df)
  mat2 <- rotateImage(mat, degrees, threads = 1)
  df <- data.frame(mat2)
  return (df)
}
```

There is actually two types of data augmentation that we can apply to our dataset. The first type creates new training data from existing examples. But we can also use a technique called **test time augmentation** (**TTA**), which can be used during model evaluation. It makes copies of each test row and then uses these copies and the originals to vote for the category. We will see an example of this later.

The code to create datasets for the data augmentation is in `Chapter6/augment.R`. Note that this takes a long time to run, maybe 6-10 hours depending on your machine. It also needs approx. 300 MB of free space on the drive to create the new datasets. The code is not difficult; it loads in the data, and splits it into train and test sets. For the train data, it creates two new instances: one rotated 15 degrees left and one rotated 15 degrees right. It is important that the data used to evaluate the model performance is not included in the data augmentation process, that is, split the data into a train dataset first and only apply data augmentation to the train split.

When the data augmentation is complete, there will be a new file in the data folder called `train_augment.csv`. This file should have 113,400 rows. Our original dataset for `MNIST` had 42,000 rows; we took 10% of that for test purposes (that is, to validate our model) and were left with 37,800 rows. We then made two copies of these rows, meaning that we now have 3 rows for each previous row. This means that we have *37,800 x 3* = *113,400* rows in our training data file. `augment.R` also outputs the test data (4,200 rows) as `test0.csv` and an augmented test set (`test_augment.csv`), which we will cover later.

The code to run the neural network is in `Chapter6/mnist.Rmd`. The first part which uses the augmented data for training is almost identical to the code in `Chapter 5`, *Image Classification Using Convolutional Neural Networks*. The only change is that it loads the data files created in `augment.R` (`train_augment.csv` and `test0.csv`), so we we will not repeat all of the code for the model here again. Here is the confusion matrix and the final accuracy on the test dataset:

```
## pred.label
## test.y    0    1    2    3    4    5    6    7    8    9
##      0  412    0    0    1    0    0    3    0    0    0
##      1    0  447    1    2    0    0    0    5    0    0
##      2    0    0  437    1    2    0    0    1    0    0
##      3    0    0    3  432    0    0    0    1    1    0
##      4    0    0    0    0  396    1    0    0    0    3
##      5    1    0    0    1    0  378    1    0    0    1
##      6    1    1    0    0    0    0  434    0    1    0
##      7    0    1    2    0    1    0    0  398    0    1
##      8    0    0    2    1    0    0    0    1  419    0
##      9    0    0    0    0    5    0    0    1    1  399
accuracy2 <- sum(res$test.y == res$pred.label) / nrow(res)
The accuracy of our model with augmented train data is 0.9885714.
```

This compares to an accuracy of `0.9821429` from our model in `Chapter 5`, *Image Classification Using Convolutional Neural Networks*, so this is a significant improvement. We have reduced our error rate by over 30% *(0.9885714-0.9835714) / (1.0-0.9835714)*.

Test time augmentation

We can also use data augmentation during test time. In the `augment.R` file, it created a file with the original test set of 4,200 rows (`data/test0.csv`), which was used that to evaluate the model. The `augment.R` file also created a file called `test_augment.csv`, which has the original 4,200 rows and 2 copies for each image. The copies are similar to what we did to augment the training data, that is, a row with data rotated 15 degrees left and a row with data rotated 15 degrees right. The three rows are outputted sequentially and we will use these 3 rows to *vote* for the winner. We need to take 3 records at a time from `test_augment.csv` and calculate the prediction value as the average of these three values. Here is the code that performs test time augmentation:

```
test_data <- read.csv("../data/test_augment.csv", header=TRUE)
test.y <- test_data[,1]
test <- data.matrix(test_data)
test <- test[,-1]
test <- t(test/255)
test.array <- test
```

```
dim(test.array) <- c(28, 28, 1, ncol(test))

preds3 <- predict(model2, test.array)
dfPreds3 <- as.data.frame(t(preds3))
# res is a data frame with our predictions after train data augmentation,
# i.e. 4200 rows
res$pred.label2 <- 0
for (i in 1:nrow(res))
{
    sum_r <- dfPreds3[((i-1)*3)+1,] +
            dfPreds3[((i-1)*3)+2,] + dfPreds3[(i*3),]
    res[i,"pred.label2"] <- max.col(sum_r)-1
}
accuracy3 <- sum(res$test.y == res$pred.label2) / nrow(res)
The accuracy of our CNN model with augmented train data and Test Time
Augmentation (TTA) is 0.9895238.
```

Doing this, we get predictions for 12,600 rows (*4,200 x 3*). The for loop runs through 4,200 times and takes 3 records at a time, calculating the average accuracy. The increase in accuracy over the accuracy using augmented training data is small, from 0.9885714 to 0.9895238, which is approx. 0.1% (4 rows). We can look at the effect of TTA in the following code:

```
tta_incorrect <- nrow(res[res$test.y != res$pred.label2 & res$test.y ==
res$pred.label,])
tta <- res[res$test.y == res$pred.label2 & res$test.y !=
res$pred.label,c("pred.label","pred.label2")]

Number of rows where Test Time Augmentation (TTA) changed the prediction to
the correct value 9 (nrow(tta)).
Number of rows where Test Time Augmentation (TTA) changed the prediction to
the incorrect value 5 (tta_incorrect).

tta
##      pred.label pred.label2
## 39            9           4
## 268           9           4
## 409           9           4
## 506           8           6
## 1079          2           3
## 1146          7           2
## 3163          4           9
## 3526          4           2
## 3965          2           8
```

This table shows the 9 rows where the test time augmentation was correct and the previous model was wrong. We can see three cases where the previous model (`pred.model`) predicted 9 and the test time augmentation model correctly predicted 4. Although test time augmentation did not significantly increase our accuracy in this case, it can make a difference in other computer vision tasks.

Using data augmentation in deep learning libraries

We implemented data augmentation using R packages and it took a long time to generate our augmented data. It was useful for demonstration purposes, but MXNet and Keras support data augmentation functions. In MXNet, there are a range of functions in `mx.image.*` to do this (`https://mxnet.incubator.apache.org/tutorials/python/data_augmentation.html`). In Keras, this is in `keras.preprocessing.*` (`https://keras.io/preprocessing/image/`), which applies these automatically to your models. In Chapter 11, *The Next Level in Deep Learning*, we show how to apply data augmentation using Keras.

Tuning hyperparameters

All machine learning algorithms have hyper-parameters or settings that can change how they operate. These hyper-parameters can improve the accuracy of a model or reduce the training time. We have seen some of these hyper-parameters in previous chapters, particularly Chapter 3, *Deep Learning Fundamentals*, where we looked at the hyper-parameters that can be set in the `mx.model.FeedForward.create` function. The techniques in this section can help us find better values for the hyper-parameters.

Selecting hyper-parameters is not a magic bullet; if the raw data quality is poor or if there is not enough data to support training, then tuning hyper-parameters will only get you so far. In these cases, either acquiring additional variables/features that can be used as predictors and/or additional cases may be required.

Grid search

For more information on tuning hyper-parameters, see Bengio, Y. (2012), particularly Section 3, *Hyperparameters*, which discusses the selection and characteristics of various hyper-parameters. Aside from manual trial and error, two other approaches for improving hyper-parameters are grid searches and random searches. In a grid search, several values for hyper-parameters are specified and all possible combinations are tried. This is perhaps easiest to see. In R, we can use the `expand.grid()` function to create all possible combinations of variables:

```
expand.grid(
  layers=c(1,4),
  lr=c(0.01,0.1,0.5,1.0),
  l1=c(0.1,0.5))
    layers     lr    l1
1        1   0.01   0.1
2        4   0.01   0.1
3        1   0.10   0.1
4        4   0.10   0.1
5        1   0.50   0.1
6        4   0.50   0.1
7        1   1.00   0.1
8        4   1.00   0.1
9        1   0.01   0.5
10       4   0.01   0.5
11       1   0.10   0.5
12       4   0.10   0.5
13       1   0.50   0.5
14       4   0.50   0.5
15       1   1.00   0.5
16       4   1.00   0.5
```

Grid searching is effective when there are only a few values for a few hyper-parameters. However, when there are many values for some or many hyper-parameters, it quickly becomes unfeasible. For example, even with only two values for each of eight hyper-parameters, there are $2^8 = 256$ combinations, which quickly becomes computationally impracticable. Also, if the interactions between hyper-parameters and model performance are small, then using grid search is an inefficient approach.

Random search

An alternative approach to hyper-parameter selection is searching through random sampling. Rather than pre-specifying all of the values to try and create all possible combinations, one can randomly sample values for the parameters, fit a model, store the results, and repeat. To get a very large sample size, this too would be computationally demanding, but you can specify just how many different models you are willing to run. Therefore this approach gives you a spread over the combination of hyper-parameters.

For random sampling, all that need to be specified are values to randomly sample, or distributions to randomly draw from. Typically, some limits would also be set. For example, although a model could theoretically have any integer number of layers, some reasonable number (such as 1 to 10) is used rather than sampling integers from 1 to a billion.

To perform random sampling, we will write a function that takes a seed and then randomly samples a number of hyper-parameters, stores the sampled parameters, runs the model, and returns the results. Even though we are doing a random search to try and find better values, we are not sampling from every possible hyper-parameter. Many remain fixed at values we specify or their defaults.

For some hyper-parameters, specifying how to randomly sample values can take a bit of work. For example, when using dropout for regularization, it is common to have a relatively smaller amount of dropout for early hidden layers (0%-20%) and a higher amount for later hidden layers (50-80%). Choosing the right distributions allows us to encode this prior information into our random search. The following code plots the density of two beta distributions, and the results are shown in *Figure 6.5*:

```
par(mfrow = c(2, 1))
plot(
  seq(0, .5, by = .001),
  dbeta(seq(0, .5, by = .001), 1, 12),
  type = "l", xlab = "x", ylab = "Density",
  main = "Density of a beta(1, 12)")

plot(
  seq(0, 1, by = .001)/2,
  dbeta(seq(0, 1, by = .001), 1.5, 1),
  type = "l", xlab = "x", ylab = "Density",
  main = "Density of a beta(1.5, 1) / 2")
```

By sampling from these distributions, we can ensure that our search focuses on small proportions of dropout for the early hidden layers, and in the **0** to **0.50** range for the hidden neurons with a tendency to oversample from values closer to **0.50**:

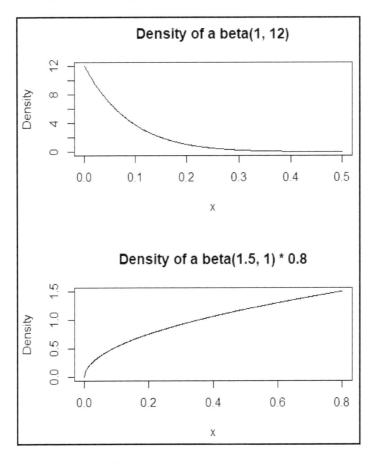

Figure 6.5: Using the beta distribution to select hyperparameters

Use case—using LIME for interpretability

Deep learning models are known to be difficult to interpret. Some approaches to model interpretability, including LIME, allow us to gain some insights into how the model came to its conclusions. Before we demonstrate LIME, I will show how different data distributions and / or data leakage can cause problems when building deep learning models. We will reuse the deep learning churn model from Chapter 4, *Training Deep Prediction Models*, but we are going to make one change to the data. We are going to introduce a bad variable that is highly correlated to the *y* value. We will only include this variable in the data used to train and evaluate the model. A separate test set from the original data will be kept to represent the data the model will see in production, this will not have the bad variable in it. The creation of this bad variable could simulate two possible scenarios we spoke about earlier:

- **Different data distributions**: The bad variable does exist in the data that the model sees in production, but it has a different distribution which means the model does not perform as expected.
- **Data leakage**: Our bad variable is used to train and evaluate the model, but when the model is used in production, this variable is not available, so we assign it a zero value, which also means the model does not perform as expected.

The code for this example is in Chapter6/binary_predict_lime.R. We will not cover the deep learning model in depth again, so go back to Chapter 4, *Training Deep Prediction Models*, if you need a refresher on how it works. We are going to make two changes to the model code:

- We will split the data into three parts: a train, validate, and test set. The train split is used to train the model, the validate set is used to evaluate the model when it is trained, and the test set represents the data that the model sees in production.
- We will create the bad_var variable, and include it in the train and validation set, but not in the test set.

Here is the code to split the data and create the bad_var variable:

```
# add feature (bad_var) that is highly correlated to the variable to be
predicted
dfData$bad_var <- 0
dfData[dfData$Y_categ==1,]$bad_var <- 1
dfData[sample(nrow(dfData), 0.02*nrow(dfData)),]$bad_var <- 0
dfData[sample(nrow(dfData), 0.02*nrow(dfData)),]$bad_var <- 1
table(dfData$Y_categ,dfData$bad_var)
       0    1
  0 1529   33
```

```
   1    46 2325
cor(dfData$Y_categ,dfData$bad_var)
[1] 0.9581345

nobs <- nrow(dfData)
train <- sample(nobs, 0.8*nobs)
validate <- sample(setdiff(seq_len(nobs), train), 0.1*nobs)
test <- setdiff(setdiff(seq_len(nobs), train),validate)
predictorCols <- colnames(dfData)[!(colnames(dfData) %in%
c("CUST_CODE","Y_numeric","Y_categ"))]

# remove columns with zero variance in train-set
predictorCols <- predictorCols[apply(dfData[train, predictorCols], 2, var,
na.rm=TRUE) != 0]

# for our test data, set the bad_var to zero
# our test dataset is not from the same distribution
# as the data used to train and evaluate the model
dfData[test,]$bad_var <- 0

# look at all our predictor variables and
# see how they correlate with the y variable
corr <- as.data.frame(cor(dfData[,c(predictorCols,"Y_categ")]))
corr <- corr[order(-corr$Y_categ),]
old.par <- par(mar=c(7,4,3,1))

barplot(corr[2:11,]$Y_categ,names.arg=row.names(corr)[2:11],
        main="Feature Correlation to target variable",cex.names=0.8,las=2)
par(old.par)
```

Our new variable is highly correlated with our y variable at 0.958. We also created a bar plot of the most highly correlated features to the y variable, and we can see that correlation between this new variable and the y variable is much higher than correlation between the other variables and the y variable. If a feature is very highly correlated to the y variable, then this is usually a sign that something is wrong in the data preparation. It also indicates that a machine learning solution is not required because a simple mathematical formula will be able to predict the outcome variable. For a real project, this variable should not be included in the model. Here is the graph with the features that are most highly correlated with the y variable, the correlation of the bad_var variable is over 0.9:

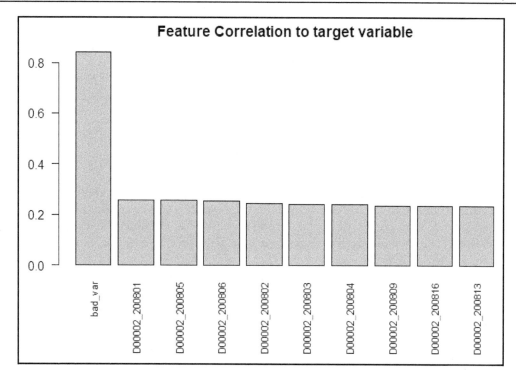

Figure 6.6: The top 10 correlations from feature to target variable

Before we go ahead and build the model, notice how we set this new feature to zero for the test set. Our test set in this example actually represents the data that the model will see when it is production, so we set it to zero to represent either a different data distribution or a data leakage problem. Here is the code that shows how the model performs on the validation set and on the test set:

```
#### Verifying the model using LIME

# compare performance on validation and test set
print(sprintf(" Deep Learning Model accuracy on validate (expected in
production) = %1.2f%%",acc_v))
[1] " Deep Learning Model accuracy on validate (expected in production) =
90.08%"
print(sprintf(" Deep Learning Model accuracy in (actual in production) =
%1.2f%%",acc_t))
[1] " Deep Learning Model accuracy in (actual in production) = 66.50%"
```

The validation set here represents the data used to evaluate the model when it is being built, while the test set represents the future production data. The accuracy on the validation set is over 90%, but the accuracy on the test set is less than 70%. This shows how different data distributions and/or data leakage problems can cause over-estimations of model accuracy.

Model interpretability with LIME

LIME stands for **Local Interpretable Model-Agnostic Explanations**. LIME can explain the predictions of any machine learning classifier, not just deep learning models. It works by making small changes to the input for each instance and trying to map the local decision boundary for that instance. By doing so, it can see which variable has the most influence for that instance. It is explained in the following paper: Ribeiro, Marco Tulio, Sameer Singh, and Carlos Guestrin. *Why should I trust you?: Explaining the predictions of any classifier. Proceedings of the 22nd ACM SIGKDD international conference on knowledge discovery and data mining. ACM, 2016.*

Let's look at using LIME to analyze the model from the previous section. We have to set up some boilerplate code to interface the MXNet and LIME structures, and then we can create LIME objects based on our training data:

```
# apply LIME to MXNet deep learning model
model_type.MXFeedForwardModel <- function(x, ...)
{return("classification")}
predict_model.MXFeedForwardModel <- function(m, newdata, ...)
{
  pred <- predict(m, as.matrix(newdata),array.layout="rowmajor")
  pred <- as.data.frame(t(pred))
  colnames(pred) <- c("No","Yes")
  return(pred)
}
explain <- lime(dfData[train, predictorCols], model, bin_continuous =
FALSE)
```

We then can pass in the first 10 records in the test set and create a plot to show feature importance:

```
val_first_10 <- validate[1:10]

explaination <- lime::explain(dfData[val_first_10,
predictorCols],explainer=explain,
                              n_labels=1,n_features=3)
plot_features(explaination) + labs(title="Churn Model - variable
explanation")
```

This will produce the following plot, which shows the features that were most influential in the model predictions:

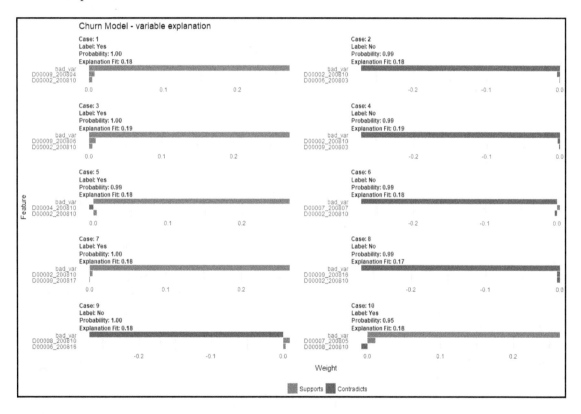

Figure 6.7: Feature importance using LIME

Note how, in each case, the `bad_var` variable is the most important variable and its scale is much larger than the other features. This matches what we saw in *Figure 6.6*. The following graph shows the heatmap visualization for feature combinations for the 10 test cases:

Figure 6.8: Feature heatmap using LIME

This example shows how to apply LIME to an existing deep learning model trained with MXNet to visualize which features were the most important for some of the predictions using the model. We can see in Figures 6.7 and 6.8 that a single feature was almost completely responsible for predicting the y variable, which is an indication that there is an issue with different data distributions and/or data leakage problems. In practice, such a variable should be excluded from the model.

As a comparison, if we train a model without this field, and plot the feature importance again, we see that one feature does not dominate:

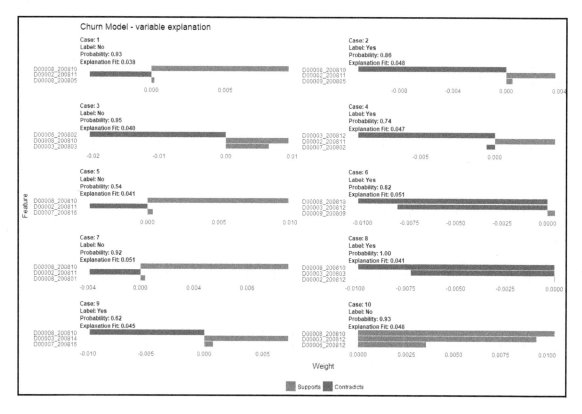

Figure 6.9: Feature importance using LIME (without the `bad_var` feature)

There is not one feature that is a number 1 feature, the explanation fit is 0.05 compared to 0.18 in *Figure 6.7,* and the significance bars for the three variables are on a similar scale. The following graph shows the feature heatmap using LIME:

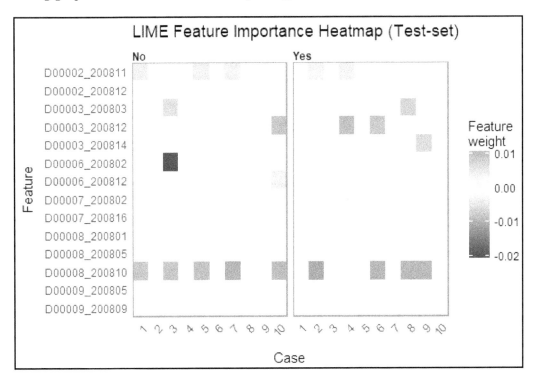

Figure 6.10: Feature heatmap using LIME (without the bad_var feature)

Again, this plot shows us that more than one feature is being used. We can see that the scale of legend for the feature weights in the preceding graph is from 0.01 - 0.02. In *Figure 6.8,* the scale of legend for the feature weights was -0.2 - 0.2, indicating that some features (just one, actually) are dominating the model.

Summary

This chapter covered topics that are critical to success in deep learning projects. These included the different types of evaluation metric that can be used to evaluate the model. We looked at some issues that can come up in data preparation, including if you only have a small amount of data to train on and how to create different splits in the data, that is, how to create proper train, test, and validation datasets. We looked at two important issues that can cause the model to perform poorly in production, different data distributions, and data leakage. We saw how data augmentation can be used to improve an existing model by creating artificial data and looked at tuning hyperparameters in order to improve the performance of a deep learning model. We closed the chapter by examining a use case where we simulated a problem with different data distributions/data leakage and used LIME to interpret an existing deep learning model.

Some of the concepts in this chapter may seem somewhat theoretical; however they are absolutely critical to the success of machine learning projects! Many books cover this material toward the end, but it is included in this book at a relatively early stage to signify its importance.

In the next chapter, we are going to look at using deep learning for **Natural Language Processing** (**NLP**), or text data. Using deep learning for text data is more efficient, simpler, and often outperforms traditional NLP approaches.

7
Natural Language Processing Using Deep Learning

This chapter will demonstrate how to use deep learning for **natural language processing** (**NLP**). NLP is the processing of human language text. NLP is a broad term for a number of different tasks involving text data, which include (but are not limited to) the following:

- **Document classification**: Classifying documents into different categories based on their subject
- **Named entity recognition**: Extracting key information from documents, for example, people, organizations, and locations
- **Sentiment analysis**: Classifying comments, tweets, or reviews as positive or negative sentiment
- **Language translation**: Translating text data from one language to another
- **Part of speech tagging**: Assigning the type to each word in a document, which is usually used in conjunction with another task

In this chapter, we will look at document classification, which is probably the most common NLP technique. This chapter follows a different structure to previous chapters, as we will be looking at a single use case (text classification) but applying multiple approaches to it. This chapter will cover:

- How to perform text classification using traditional machine learning techniques
- Word vectors
- Comparing traditional text classification and deep learning
- Advanced deep learning text classification including 1D convolutionals, RNNs, LSTMs and GRUs

Document classification

This chapter will be looking at text classification using Keras. The dataset we will use is included in the Keras library. As we have done in previous chapters, we will use traditional machine learning techniques to create a benchmark before applying a deep learning algorithm. The reason for this is to show how deep learning models perform against other techniques.

The Reuters dataset

We will use the Reuters dataset, which can be accessed through a function in the Keras library. This dataset has 11,228 records with 46 categories. To see more information about this dataset, run the following code:

```
library(keras)
?dataset_reuters
```

Although the Reuters dataset can be accessed from Keras, it is not in a format that can be used by other machine learning algorithms. Instead of the actual words, the text data is a list of word indices. We will write a short script (Chapter7/create_reuters_data.R) that downloads the data and the lookup index file and creates a data frame of the y variable and the text string. We will then save the train and test data into two separate files. Here is the first part of the code that creates the file with the train data:

```
library(keras)

# the reuters dataset is in Keras
c(c(x_train, y_train), c(x_test, y_test)) %<-% dataset_reuters()
word_index <- dataset_reuters_word_index()

# convert the word index into a dataframe
idx<-unlist(word_index)
dfWords<-as.data.frame(idx)
dfWords$word <- row.names(dfWords)
row.names(dfWords)<-NULL
dfWords <- dfWords[order(dfWords$idx),]

# create a dataframe for the train data
# for each row in the train data, we have a list of index values
# for words in the dfWords dataframe
dfTrain <- data.frame(y_train)
dfTrain$sentence <- ""
colnames(dfTrain)[1] <- "y"
for (r in 1:length(x_train))
```

```
{
  row <- x_train[r]
  line <- ""
  for (i in 1:length(row[[1]]))
  {
     index <- row[[1]][i]
     if (index >= 3)
       line <- paste(line,dfWords[index-3,]$word)
  }
  dfTrain[r,]$sentence <- line
  if ((r %% 100) == 0)
    print (r)
}
write.table(dfTrain,"../data/reuters.train.tab",sep="\t",row.names = FALSE)
```

The second part of the code is similar, it creates the file with the test data:

```
# create a dataframe for the test data
# for each row in the train data, we have a list of index values
# for words in the dfWords dataframe
dfTest <- data.frame(y_test)
dfTest$sentence <- ""
colnames(dfTest)[1] <- "y"
for (r in 1:length(x_test))
{
  row <- x_test[r]
  line <- ""
  for (i in 1:length(row[[1]]))
  {
    index <- row[[1]][i]
    if (index >= 3)
      line <- paste(line,dfWords[index-3,]$word)
  }
  dfTest[r,]$sentence <- line
  if ((r %% 100) == 0)
    print (r)
}
write.table(dfTest,"../data/reuters.test.tab",sep="\t",row.names = FALSE)
```

This creates two files called `../data/reuters.train.tab` and `../data/reuters.test.tab`. If we open the first file, this is the first data row. This sentence is a normal English sentence:

y	sentence
3	mcgrath rentcorp said as a result of its december acquisition of space co it expects earnings per share in 1987 of 1 15 to 1 30 dlrs per share up from 70 cts in 1986 the company said pretax net should rise to nine to 10 mln dlrs from six mln dlrs in 1986 and rental operation revenues to 19 to 22 mln dlrs from 12 5 mln dlrs it said cash flow per share this year should be 2 50 to three dlrs reuter 3

Now that we have the data in tabular format, we can use *traditional* NLP machine learning methods to create a classification model. When we merge the train and test sets and look at the distribution of the y variable, we can see that there are 46 classes, but that the number of instances in each class are not the same:

```
> table(y_train)
   0   1   2    3    4   5   6   7   8   9  10  11  12  13  14  15  16  17
  67 537  94 3972 2423  22  62  19 177 126 154 473  62 209  28  29 543  51

  18  19  20  21  22  23  24  25  26  27  28  29  30  31  32  33  34  35
  86 682 339 127  22  53  81 123  32  19  58  23  57  52  42  16  57  16

  36  37  38  39  40  41  42  43  44  45
  60  21  22  29  46  38  16  27  17  19
```

For our test set, we will create a binary classification problem. Our task will be to identify the news snippets where the classification is 3 from all other records. When we change the labels, our y distribution changes to the following:

```
y_train[y_train!=3] <- 0
y_train[y_train==3] <- 1
table(y_train)
   0    1
7256 3972
```

Traditional text classification

Our first NLP model will use traditional NLP techniques, that is, not deep learning. For the rest of this chapter, when we use the term traditional NLP, we mean approaches that do not use deep learning. The most used method for NLP in traditional NLP classification uses a *bag-of-words* approach.

We will also use a set of hyperparameters and machine learning algorithms to maximize accuracy:

- **Feature generation**: The features can be term frequency, tf-idf, or binary flags
- **Preprocessing**: We preprocess text data by stemming the words
- **Remove stop-words**: We treat the feature creation, stop-words, and stemming options as hyperparameters
- **Machine learning algorithm**: The script applies three machine learning algorithms to the data (Naive Bayes, SVM, neural network, and random forest)

We train 48 machine learning algorithms on the data in total, and evaluate which model is best. The script for this code is in the `Chapter7/classify_text.R` folder. The code does not contain any deep learning models, so feel free to skip it if you want. First we load in the necessary libraries and create a function that creates a set of text classification models for a combination of hyperparameters on multiple machine learning algorithms:

```
library(tm)
require(nnet)
require(kernlab)
library(randomForest)
library(e1071)
options(digits=4)

TextClassification <-function (w,stem=0,stop=0,verbose=1)
{
  df <- read.csv("../data/reuters.train.tab", sep="\t", stringsAsFactors =
FALSE)
  df2 <- read.csv("../data/reuters.test.tab", sep="\t", stringsAsFactors =
FALSE)
  df <- rbind(df,df2)

  # df <- df[df$y %in% c(3,4),]
  # df$y <- df$y-3
  df[df$y!=3,]$y<-0
  df[df$y==3,]$y<-1
  rm(df2)

  corpus <- Corpus(DataframeSource(data.frame(df[, 2])))
  corpus <- tm_map(corpus, content_transformer(tolower))
  # hyperparameters
  if (stop==1)
    corpus <- tm_map(corpus, function(x) removeWords(x,
stopwords("english")))
  if (stem==1)
    corpus <- tm_map(corpus, stemDocument)
  if (w=="tfidf")
```

```
  dtm <- DocumentTermMatrix(corpus,control=list(weighting=weightTfIdf))
else if (w=="tf")
  dtm <- DocumentTermMatrix(corpus,control=list(weighting=weightTf))
else if (w=="binary")
  dtm <- DocumentTermMatrix(corpus,control=list(weighting=weightBin))
# keep terms that cover 95% of the data
dtm2<-removeSparseTerms(dtm, 0.95)
m <- as.matrix(dtm2)
remove(dtm,dtm2,corpus)
data<-data.frame(m)
data<-cbind(df[, 1],data)
colnames(data)[1]="y"
# create train, test sets for machine learning
seed <- 42
set.seed(seed)
nobs <- nrow(data)
sample <- train <- sample(nrow(data), 0.8*nobs)
validate <- NULL
test <- setdiff(setdiff(seq_len(nrow(data)), train), validate)
```

Now that we have created a sparse data-frame, we will use 4 different machine learning algorithms on the data: Naive Bayes, SVM, a neural network model and a random forest model. We use 4 machine learning algorithms because, as you see below, the code to call a machine learning algorithm is small compared to the code needed to create the data in the previous section and the code needed to the the NLP. It is almost always a good idea to run multiple machine learning algorithms when possible because no machine learning algorithm is consistently the best.

```
# create Naive Bayes model
nb <- naiveBayes(as.factor(y) ~., data=data[sample,])
pr <- predict(nb, newdata=data[test, ])
# Generate the confusion matrix showing counts.
tab<-table(na.omit(data[test, ])$y, pr,
           dnn=c("Actual", "Predicted"))
if (verbose) print (tab)
nb_acc <- 100*sum(diag(tab))/length(test)
if (verbose) print(sprintf("Naive Bayes accuracy = %1.2f%%",nb_acc))
# create SVM model
if (verbose) print ("SVM")
if (verbose) print (Sys.time())
ksvm <- ksvm(as.factor(y) ~ .,
             data=data[sample,],
             kernel="rbfdot",
             prob.model=TRUE)
if (verbose) print (Sys.time())
pr <- predict(ksvm, newdata=na.omit(data[test, ]))
# Generate the confusion matrix showing counts.
```

```
tab<-table(na.omit(data[test, ])$y, pr,
           dnn=c("Actual", "Predicted"))
if (verbose) print (tab)
svm_acc <- 100*sum(diag(tab))/length(test)
if (verbose) print(sprintf("SVM accuracy = %1.2f%%",svm_acc))
# create Neural Network model
rm(pr,tab)
set.seed(199)
if (verbose) print ("Neural Network")
if (verbose) print (Sys.time())
nnet <- nnet(as.factor(y) ~ .,
             data=data[sample,],
             size=10, skip=TRUE, MaxNWts=10000, trace=FALSE, maxit=100)
if (verbose) print (Sys.time())
pr <- predict(nnet, newdata=data[test, ], type="class")
# Generate the confusion matrix showing counts.
tab<-table(data[test, ]$y, pr,
           dnn=c("Actual", "Predicted"))
if (verbose) print (tab)
nn_acc <- 100*sum(diag(tab))/length(test)
if (verbose) print(sprintf("Neural Network accuracy = %1.2f%%",nn_acc))
# create Random Forest model
rm(pr,tab)
if (verbose) print ("Random Forest")
if (verbose) print (Sys.time())
rf_model<-randomForest(as.factor(y) ~., data=data[sample,])
if (verbose) print (Sys.time())
pr <- predict(rf_model, newdata=data[test, ], type="class")
# Generate the confusion matrix showing counts.
tab<-table(data[test, ]$y, pr,
           dnn=c("Actual", "Predicted"))
if (verbose) print (tab)
rf_acc <- 100*sum(diag(tab))/length(test)
if (verbose) print(sprintf("Random Forest accuracy = %1.2f%%",rf_acc))
dfParams <- data.frame(w,stem,stop)
dfParams$nb_acc <- nb_acc
dfParams$svm_acc <- svm_acc
dfParams$nn_acc <- nn_acc
dfParams$rf_acc <- rf_acc
return(dfParams)
}
```

We now call the function with different hyperparameters in the following code:

```
dfResults <- TextClassification("tfidf",verbose=1) # tf-idf, no stemming
dfResults<-rbind(dfResults,TextClassification("tf",verbose=1)) # tf, no
stemming
dfResults<-rbind(dfResults,TextClassification("binary",verbose=1)) #
binary, no stemming

dfResults<-rbind(dfResults,TextClassification("tfidf",1,verbose=1)) # tf-
idf, stemming
dfResults<-rbind(dfResults,TextClassification("tf",1,verbose=1)) # tf,
stemming
dfResults<-rbind(dfResults,TextClassification("binary",1,verbose=1)) #
binary, stemming

dfResults<-rbind(dfResults,TextClassification("tfidf",0,1,verbose=1)) # tf-
idf, no stemming, remove stopwords
dfResults<-rbind(dfResults,TextClassification("tf",0,1,verbose=1)) # tf, no
stemming, remove stopwords
dfResults<-rbind(dfResults,TextClassification("binary",0,1,verbose=1)) #
binary, no stemming, remove stopwords

dfResults<-rbind(dfResults,TextClassification("tfidf",1,1,verbose=1)) # tf-
idf, stemming, remove stopwords
dfResults<-rbind(dfResults,TextClassification("tf",1,1,verbose=1)) # tf,
stemming, remove stopwords
dfResults<-rbind(dfResults,TextClassification("binary",1,1,verbose=1)) #
binary, stemming, remove stopwords

dfResults[, "best_acc"] <- apply(dfResults[,
c("nb_acc","svm_acc","nn_acc","rf_acc")], 1, max)
dfResults <- dfResults[order(-dfResults$best_acc),]
dfResults

strResult <- sprintf("Best accuracy score was %1.2f%%. Hyper-parameters:
",dfResults[1,"best_acc"])
strResult <- paste(strResult,dfResults[1,"w"],",",sep="")
strResult <- paste(strResult,
                   ifelse(dfResults[1,"stem"] == 0,"no
stemming,","stemming,"))
strResult <- paste(strResult,
                   ifelse(dfResults[1,"stop"] == 0,"no stop word
processing,","removed stop words,"))
if (dfResults[1,"best_acc"] == dfResults[1,"nb_acc"]){
  strResult <- paste(strResult,"Naive Bayes model")
} else if (dfResults[1,"best_acc"] == dfResults[1,"svm_acc"]){
  strResult <- paste(strResult,"SVM model")
} else if (dfResults[1,"best_acc"] == dfResults[1,"nn_acc"]){
```

```
    strResult <- paste(strResult,"Neural Network model")
  }else if (dfResults[1,"best_acc"] == dfResults[1,"rf_acc"]){
    strResult <- paste(strResult,"Random Forest model")
  }
```

```
print (strResult)
```

For each combination of hyperparameters, the script saves the best score from the four machine learning algorithms in the best_acc field. Once the training is complete, we can look at the results:

```
> dfResults
   w stem stop nb_acc svm_acc nn_acc rf_acc best_acc
12 binary    1    1  86.06   95.24  90.52  94.26    95.24
9  binary    0    1  87.71   95.15  90.52  93.72    95.15
10 tfidf     1    1  91.99   95.15  91.05  94.17    95.15
3  binary    0    0  85.98   95.01  90.29  93.99    95.01
6  binary    1    0  84.59   95.01  90.34  93.63    95.01
7  tfidf     0    1  91.27   94.43  94.79  93.54    94.79
11 tf        1    1  77.47   94.61  92.30  94.08    94.61
4  tfidf     1    0  92.25   94.57  90.96  93.99    94.57
5  tf        1    0  75.11   94.52  93.46  93.90    94.52
1  tfidf     0    0  91.54   94.26  91.59  93.23    94.26
2  tf        0    0  75.82   94.03  91.54  93.59    94.03
8  tf        0    1  78.14   94.03  91.63  93.68    94.03
```

```
> print (strResult)
[1] "Best accuracy score was 95.24%. Hyper-parameters: binary, stemming,
removed stop words, SVM model"
```

The results are ordered by best results, so here we can can see that our best accuracy overall was 95.24%. The reason for training so many models is that there is no right formula for traditional NLP tasks that's work for most cases, so you should try multiple combinations of preprocessing and different algorithms, as we have done here. For example, if you searched for an example online on text classification, you could find an example that would suggest to use tf-idf and naive bayes. Here, we can see that it is one of the worst performers.

Deep learning text classification

The previous code ran 48 traditional machine learning algorithms over the data across a number of different hyperparameters. Now, it is time to see if we can find a deep learning model that outperforms them. The first deep learning model is in `Chapter7/classify_keras1.R`. The first part of the code loads the data. The tokens in the reuters dataset are ranked by how often they occur (in the training set) and the `max_features` parameter controls how many distinct tokens will be used in the model. We will use all the tokens by setting this to the number of entries in the word index. The maxlen parameter controls the length of the input sequences to the model, they must all be the same length. If the sequences are longer than the maxlen variable, they are truncated, if they are shorter, then padding is added to make the length=maxlen. We set this to 250, which means our deep learning model expects 250 tokens as input per instance:

```
library(keras)

set.seed(42)
word_index <- dataset_reuters_word_index()
max_features <- length(word_index)
maxlen <- 250
skip_top = 0

reuters <- dataset_reuters(num_words = max_features,skip_top = skip_top)
c(c(x_train, y_train), c(x_test, y_test)) %<-% reuters
x_train <- pad_sequences(x_train, maxlen = maxlen)
x_test <- pad_sequences(x_test, maxlen = maxlen)
x_train <- rbind(x_train,x_test)
y_train <- c(y_train,y_test)
table(y_train)

y_train[y_train!=3] <- 0
y_train[y_train==3] <- 1
table(y_train)
```

The next section of code builds the model:

```
model <- keras_model_sequential() %>%
  layer_embedding(input_dim = max_features, output_dim = 16,input_length =
maxlen) %>%
  layer_flatten() %>%
  layer_dropout(rate = 0.25) %>%
  layer_dense(units = 16, activation = 'relu') %>%
  layer_dropout(rate = 0.5) %>%
  layer_dense(units = 16, activation = 'relu') %>%
  layer_dropout(rate = 0.5) %>%
  layer_dense(units = 1, activation = "sigmoid")
```

```
model %>% compile(
  optimizer = "rmsprop",
  loss = "binary_crossentropy",
  metrics = c("acc")
)
summary(model)
history <- model %>% fit(
  x_train, y_train,
  epochs = 5,
  batch_size = 32,
  validation_split = 0.2
)
```

The only thing in this code that we have not seen before is `layer_embedding`. This takes the input and creates an embedding layer, which is a vector of numbers for each input token. We will describe word vectors in more detail in the next section. Another thing to note is that we don't preprocess the text or create any features – we just feed in the word indices and let the deep learning algorithm make sense of it. Here is the output of the script as the model is trained:

```
Train on 8982 samples, validate on 2246 samples
Epoch 1/5
8982/8982 [==============================] - 3s 325us/step - loss: 0.4953 -
acc: 0.7674 - val_loss: 0.2332 - val_acc: 0.9274
Epoch 2/5
8982/8982 [==============================] - 3s 294us/step - loss: 0.2771 -
acc: 0.9235 - val_loss: 0.1990 - val_acc: 0.9394
Epoch 3/5
8982/8982 [==============================] - 3s 297us/step - loss: 0.2150 -
acc: 0.9414 - val_loss: 0.1975 - val_acc: 0.9497
Epoch 4/5
8982/8982 [==============================] - 3s 282us/step - loss: 0.1912 -
acc: 0.9515 - val_loss: 0.2118 - val_acc: 0.9461
Epoch 5/5
8982/8982 [==============================] - 3s 280us/step - loss: 0.1703 -
acc: 0.9584 - val_loss: 0.2490 - val_acc: 0.9466
```

Despite the simplicity of the code, we get 94.97% accuracy on the validation set after just three epochs, which is only 0.27% less than the best traditional NLP approach. Now, it is time to discuss word vectors in more detail.

Word vectors

Instead of representing our text data as a bag of words, deep learning represents them as word vectors or embeddings. A vector/embedding is nothing more than a series of numbers that represent a word. You may have already heard of popular word vectors such as Word2Vec and GloVe. The Word2vec model was invented by Google (*Mikolov, Tomas, et al. Efficient estimation of word representations in vector space. arXiv preprint arXiv:1301.3781 (2013)*). In their paper, they provide examples of how these word vectors have somewhat mysterious and magical properties. If you take the vector of the word "*King*", subtract the vector of the word "*Man*", add the vector of the word "*Man*", then you get a value close to the vector of the word "*Queen*". Other similarities also exist, for example:

- *vector('King') - vector('Man') + vector('Woman') = vector('Queen')*
- *vector('Paris') - vector('France') + vector('Italy') = vector('Rome')*

If this is the first time you have seen Word2Vec, then you are probably somewhat amazed by this. I know I was! These examples imply that word vectors *understand* language, so have we solved natural language processing? The answer is no – we are very far away from this. Vectors are learned from collections of text documents. In fact, the very first layer in our deep learning model is an embedding layer which creates a vector space for the words. Let's look at some of the code from `Chapter7/classify_keras.R` again:

```
library(keras)

word_index <- dataset_reuters_word_index()
max_features <- length(word_index)
max_features
[1] 30979
. . . . . . .

model <- keras_model_sequential() %>%
  layer_embedding(input_dim = max_features, output_dim = 16, input_length =
maxlen) %>%
. . . . . . .

summary(model)
```

```
Layer (type)              Output Shape        Param #
================================================================================
============
embedding_1 (Embedding)    (None, 150, 16)      495664
. . . . . . .
```

The value for `max_features` is `30979`, that is, we have `30979` unique features. These features are **tokens**, or words. In the traditional text classification, we had almost the same number of unique tokens (`30538`). The difference between these two numbers is not important; it is due to the different tokenization processes used between the two approaches, that is, how the documents were split into tokens. The embedding layer has `495664` parameters, which is *30,979 x 16*, that is, each unique feature/token is represented by a vector of `16` numbers. The word vectors or embeddings learned by deep learning algorithms will have some of the characteristics described earlier, for example:

- Synonyms (two words that have the same meaning) will have very similar word vectors
- Words from the same semantic collection will be clustered (for example, colors, days of the week, makes of cars, and so on)
- The vector space between related words can signify the relationship between those words (for example, gender for w(King) – w(Queen))

The embedding layer creates word vectors/embeddings based on words and their surrounding words. The word vectors end up having these characteristics because of a simple fact, which can be summarized by a quote from John Firth, an English linguist in 1957:

> *"You shall know a word by the company it keeps."*

The deep learning algorithm learns the vectors for each word by looking at surrounding words and therefore learns some of the context. When it sees the word *King*, some words near this word may indicate gender, for example, The *King* picked up *his* sword. Another sentence could be The *Queen* looked in *her* mirror. The word vectors for *King* and *Queen* have a latent gender component that is learned from the words surrounding *King* and *Queen* in the data. But it is important to realize that the deep learning algorithm has no concept of what gender is, or what type of entities it applies to. Even so, word vectors are a huge improvement over bag-of-word approaches which have no way of identifying relationships between different tokens. Using word vectors also means that we do not have to discard sparse terms. Finally, as the number of unique tokens increases, they are much more efficient to process than bag-of-words approaches.

We will look at embeddings again in `Chapter 9`, *Anomaly Detection and Recommendation Systems*, when we use them in auto-encoders. Now that we have seen some traditional machine learning and deep learning approaches for solving this problem, it is time to compare them in more detail.

Comparing traditional text classification and deep learning

The traditional text classification performed a number of preprocessing steps, including word stemming, stop-word processing, and feature generation (tf-idf, tf or binary). The deep learning text classification did not need this preprocessing. You may have heard various reasons for this previously:

- Deep learning can learn features automatically, so feature creation is not needed
- Deep learning algorithms for NLP tasks requires far less preprocessing than traditional text classification

There is some truth to this, but this does not answer why we need complex feature generation in traditional text classification. A big reason that preprocessing is needed in traditional text classification is to overcome a fundamental problem.

For some traditional NLP approaches (for example, classification), text preprocessing is not just about creating better features. It is also necessary because the bag-of-words representation creates a sparse high-dimensional dataset. Most machine learning algorithms have problems with such datasets, meaning that we have to reduce the dimensionality before applying machine learning algorithms. Proper preprocessing of the text is an essential part of this to ensure that relevant data is not thrown away.

For traditional text classification, we used an approach called **bag-of-words**. This is essentially one-hot encoding each *token* (word). Each column represents a single token, and the value of each cell is one of the following:

- A **tf-idf** (**term frequency, inverse document frequency**) for that token
- The term frequency, that is, the count of how many times that token occurs for that document/instance
- A binary flag, that is, one if the token is in that document/instance; otherwise, it is zero

You may not have heard of *tf-idf* before. It measures the importance of a token by calculating the term frequency (*tf*) of the token in the document (such as how many times it occurs in the document) divided by the log of how many times it appears in the entire corpus (*idf*). The **corpus** is the entire collection of documents. The *tf* part measures how important the token is within a single document, and the *idf* measures how unique the token is among all the documents. If the token appears many times in the document, but also many times in other documents, then it is unlikely to be useful for categorizing documents. If the token appears in only a few documents, then it is a potentially valuable feature for the classification task.

Our traditional text classification approach also used *stemming* and processed *stop-words*. Indeed, our best result in traditional text classification used both approaches. Stemming tries to reduce words to their word stem or root form, which reduces the vocabulary size. It also means that words with the same meaning but with different verb tenses or noun forms are standardized to the same token. Here is an example of stemming. Note that 6/7 of the input words have the same output value:

```
library(corpus)
text <- "love loving lovingly loved lover lovely love"
text_tokens(text, stemmer = "en") # english stemmer
[[1]]
[1] "love" "love" "love" "love" "lover" "love" "love"
```

Stop-words are common words that appear in most documents for a language. They occur so frequently in most documents that they are almost never useful for machine learning. The following example shows the list of stop-words for the English language:

```
library(tm)
> stopwords()
 [1] "i"          "me"         "my"        "myself"     "we"         "our"
 [7] "ours"       "ourselves"  "you"       "your"       "yours"      "yourself"
[13] "yourselves" "he"         "him"       "his"        "himself"    "she"
[19] "her"        "hers"       "herself"   "it"         "its"        "itself"
[25] "they"       "them"       "their"     "theirs"     "themselves" "what"
.........
```

The final piece we want to cover in traditional NLP is how it deals with sparse terms. Recall from earlier that traditional NLP uses a bag-of-words approach, where each unique token gets an individual column. For a large collection of documents, there will be thousands of unique tokens, and since most tokens will not appear in an individual document, this a very sparse representation, that is, most cells are empty. We can check this by looking at taking some of the code from `classify_text.R`, modifying it slightly, and looking at the `dtm` and `dtm2` variables:

```
library(tm)
df <- read.csv("../data/reuters.train.tab", sep="\t", stringsAsFactors =
FALSE)
df2 <- read.csv("../data/reuters.test.tab", sep="\t", stringsAsFactors =
FALSE)
df <- rbind(df,df2)

df[df$y!=3,]$y<-0
df[df$y==3,]$y<-1
rm(df2)

corpus <- Corpus(DataframeSource(data.frame(df[, 2])))
```

```
corpus <- tm_map(corpus, content_transformer(tolower))

dtm <- DocumentTermMatrix(corpus,control=list(weighting=weightBin))

# keep terms that cover 95% of the data
dtm2<-removeSparseTerms(dtm, 0.95)

dtm
<<DocumentTermMatrix (documents: 11228, terms: 30538)>>
Non-/sparse entries: 768265/342112399
Sparsity : 100%
Maximal term length: 24
Weighting : binary (bin)

dtm2
<<DocumentTermMatrix (documents: 11228, terms: 230)>>
Non-/sparse entries: 310275/2272165
Sparsity : 88%
Maximal term length: 13
Weighting : binary (bin)
```

We can see that our first document-term matrix (dtm) has 11,228 documents and 30,538 unique tokens. In this document-term matrix, only 768,265 (0.22%) cells have values. Most machine learning algorithms would struggle with such a high-dimensionality sparse data frame. If you tried using these machine learning algorithms (for example, SVM, random forest, naive bayes) on a data frame with 30,538 dimensions, they would fail to run in R (I tried!). This is a known problem in traditional NLP, so there is a function (removeSparseTerms) in the NLP libraries to remove sparse terms from the document-term matrix. This removes columns that have the most empty cells. We can see the effect of this, as the second document-term matrix has only 230 unique tokens and 310,275 (12%) cells have values. This dataset is still relatively sparse, but it is in a usable format for machine learning.

This highlights the problem with traditional NLP approaches: the *bag-of-words* approach creates a very sparse high-dimensional dataset which is not usable by machine learning algorithms. Therefore, you need to remove some of the dimensions, and this results in a number of cells with values going from 768,265 to 310,275 in our example. We threw away almost 60% of the data before applying any machine learning! This also explains why text preprocessing, such as stemming and stop-word removal, is used in traditional NLP. Stemming helps to reduce the vocabulary and standardize terms by combining variations of many words into one form.

By combining variations, it means they are more likely to survive the culling of data. We process stop-words for the opposite reason: if we don't remove stop-words, these terms will probably be kept after removing sparse terms. There are 174 terms in the `stopwords()` function in the `tm` package. If the reduced dataset had many of these terms, then they would probably not be useful as predictor variables due to their commonality throughout the documents.

It is also worth noting that this is a very small dataset in NLP terms. We only have 11,228 documents and 30,538 unique tokens. A larger *corpus* (collection of text documents) could have half a million unique tokens. In order to reduce the number of tokens to something that could be processed in R, we would have to throw away a lot more data.

When we use a deep learning approach for NLP, we represent the data as word vectors/embeddings rather than using the bag-of-words approach in traditional NLP. This is much more efficient, so do not have to preprocess data to remove common words, reduce words to a simpler form, or reduce the number of terms before applying the deep learning algorithm. The only thing we do have to do is pick an embedding size and a max length size for the number of tokens we process for each instance. This is needed because deep learning algorithms cannot use variable length sequences as inputs to a layer. When instances have more tokens than the max length, they are truncated and when instances have less tokens than the max length, they are padded.

After all of this, you may be wondering why the deep learning algorithm did not outperform the traditional NLP approach significantly, if the traditional NLP approach throws away 60% of the data. There are a few reasons for this:

- The dataset is small. If we had more data, the deep learning approach would improve at a faster rate than the traditional NLP approach.
- Certain NLP tasks such as document classification and sentiment analysis depend on a very small set of terms. For example, to differentiate between sports news and financial news, maybe 50 selected terms would be sufficient to get over 90% accuracy. Recall that the function to remove sparse terms in the traditional text classification approach – this works because it assumes (correctly) that non-sparse terms will be useful features for the machine learning algorithms.
- We ran 48 machine learning algorithms and only one deep learning approach, which was relatively simple! We will soon come across approaches that beat the traditional NLP approach.

This book has really only touched the surface of traditional NLP approaches. Entire books have been written on the subject. The purpose of looking at these approaches is to show how brittle these approaches can be. The deep learning approach is much simpler to understand and has far fewer settings. It does not involve preprocessing the text or creating features based on weightings such as tf-idf. Even so, our first deep learning approach is not very far away from the best model out of 48 models in traditional text classification.

Advanced deep learning text classification

Our basic deep learning model is much less complex than the traditional machine learning approach, but its performance is not quite as good. This section looks at some advanced techniques for text classification in deep learning. The following sections explain a number of different approaches and focus on code examples rather than heavy deep explanations. If you are interested in more detail, then look at the book *Deep Learning* by Goodfellow, Bengio, and Courville (*Goodfellow, Ian, et al. Deep learning. Vol. 1. Cambridge: MIT Press, 2016.*). Another good reference that covers NLP in deep learning is a book by Yoav Goldberg (*Goldberg, Yoav. Neural network methods for natural language processing*).

1D convolutional neural network model

We have seen that the bag-of-words approach in traditional NLP approaches ignores sentence structure. Consider applying a sentiment analysis task on the four movie reviews in the following table:

Id	sentence	Rating (1=recommended, 0=not recommended)
1	this movie is very good	1
2	this movie is not good	0
3	this movie is not very good	0
4	this movie is not bad	1

If we represent this as a bag of words with term frequency, we will get the following output:

Id	bad	good	is	movie	not	this	very
1	0	1	1	1	0	1	1
2	0	1	1	1	1	1	0
3	0	1	1	1	1	1	1
4	1	0	1	1	1	1	0

In this simple example, we can see some of the problems with a bag-of-words approach, we have lost the relationship between the negation (**not**) and the adjectives (**good, bad**). To work around this problem, traditional NLP could use bigrams, so instead of using single words as tokens, use two words as tokens. Now, for the second example, **not good** is a single token, which makes it more likely that the machine learning algorithm will pick it up. However, we still have a problem with the third example (**not very good**), where we will have tokens for **not very** and **very good**. These are still ambiguous, as **not very** implies negative sentiment, while **very good** implies positive sentiment. We could try higher order n-grams, but this further exacerbates the sparsity problem we saw in the previous section.

Word vectors or embeddings have the same problem. We need some method to handle word sequences. Fortunately, there are types of layers in deep learning algorithms that can handle sequential data. One that we have already seen is convolutional neural networks in Chapter 5, *Image Classification Using Convolutional Neural Networks*. Recall that these are 2D patches that are moved across the image to identify patterns such as a diagonal line or an edge. In a similar manner, we can apply a 1D convolutional neural network across the word vectors. Here is an example of using a 1D convolutional neural network layer for the same text classification problem. The code is in Chapter7/classify_keras2.R. We are only showing the code for the model architecture, because that is the only change from the code in Chapter7/classify_keras1.R:

```
model <- keras_model_sequential() %>%
  layer_embedding(input_dim = max_features, output_dim = 16,input_length =
maxlen) %>%
  layer_dropout(rate = 0.25) %>%
  layer_conv_1d(64,5, activation = "relu") %>%
  layer_dropout(rate = 0.25) %>%
  layer_max_pooling_1d() %>%
  layer_flatten() %>%
  layer_dense(units = 50, activation = 'relu') %>%
  layer_dropout(rate = 0.6) %>%
  layer_dense(units = 1, activation = "sigmoid")
```

We can see that this follows the same pattern that we saw in the image data; we have a convolutional layer followed by a max pooling layer. There are 64 convolutional layers with a length=5, and so these *learn* local patterns in the data. Here is the output from the model's training:

```
Train on 8982 samples, validate on 2246 samples
Epoch 1/5
8982/8982 [==============================] - 13s 1ms/step - loss: 0.3020 -
acc: 0.8965 - val_loss: 0.1909 - val_acc: 0.9470
Epoch 2/5
8982/8982 [==============================] - 13s 1ms/step - loss: 0.1980 -
acc: 0.9498 - val_loss: 0.1816 - val_acc: 0.9537
```

```
Epoch 3/5
8982/8982 [==============================] - 12s 1ms/step - loss: 0.1674 -
acc: 0.9575 - val_loss: 0.2233 - val_acc: 0.9368
Epoch 4/5
8982/8982 [==============================] - 12s 1ms/step - loss: 0.1587 -
acc: 0.9606 - val_loss: 0.1787 - val_acc: 0.9573
Epoch 5/5
8982/8982 [==============================] - 12s 1ms/step - loss: 0.1513 -
acc: 0.9628 - val_loss: 0.2186 - val_acc: 0.9408
```

This model is an improvement on our previous deep learning model; it gets 95.73% accuracy on the fourth epoch. This beats the traditional NLP approach by 0.49%, which is a significant improvement. Let's move on to other methods that also look to matching sequences. We will start with **recurrent neural networks** (**RNNs**).

Recurrent neural network model

The deep learning networks we have seen so far have no concept of memory. Every new piece of information is treated as atomic and has no relation to what has already occurred. But, sequences are important in time series and text classification, especially sentiment analysis. In the previous section, we saw how word structure and order matters, and we used CNNs to resolve this. While this approach worked, it does not resolve the problem completely as we still must pick a filter size, which limits the range of the layer. Recurrent neural networks are deep learning layers which are used to solve this problem. They are networks with feedback loops that allow information to flow and therefore are able to *remember* important features:

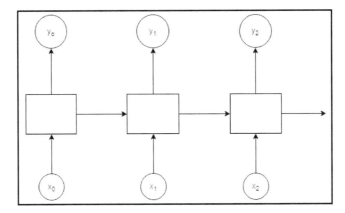

Figure 7.1: A recurrent neural network

In the preceding diagram, we can see an example of a recurrent neural network. Each piece of information (X_o, X_1, X_2) is fed into a node which predicts y variables. The predicted value is also passed to the next node as input, thus preserving some sequence information.

Our first RNN model is in Chapter7/classify_keras3.R. We have to change some of the parameters for the model: we must decrease the number of features used to 4,000, our max length to 100, and drop the most common 100 tokens. We must also increase the size of the embedding layer to 32 and run it for 10 epochs:

```
word_index <- dataset_reuters_word_index()
max_features <- length(word_index)
max_features <- 4000
maxlen <- 100
skip_top = 100


. . . . . . . .


model <- keras_model_sequential() %>%
  layer_embedding(input_dim = max_features, output_dim = 32,input_length =
maxlen) %>%
  layer_spatial_dropout_1d(rate = 0.25) %>%
  layer_simple_rnn(64,activation = "relu", dropout=0.2) %>%
  layer_dense(units = 1, activation = "sigmoid")


. . . . . . . .


history <- model %>% fit(
  x_train, y_train,
  epochs = 10,
  batch_size = 32,
  validation_split = 0.2
)
```

Here is the output from the model's training:

```
Train on 8982 samples, validate on 2246 samples
Epoch 1/10
8982/8982 [==============================] - 4s 409us/step - loss: 0.5289 -
acc: 0.7848 - val_loss: 0.3162 - val_acc: 0.9078
Epoch 2/10
8982/8982 [==============================] - 4s 391us/step - loss: 0.2875 -
acc: 0.9098 - val_loss: 0.2962 - val_acc: 0.9305
Epoch 3/10
8982/8982 [==============================] - 3s 386us/step - loss: 0.2496 -
acc: 0.9267 - val_loss: 0.2487 - val_acc: 0.9234
Epoch 4/10
8982/8982 [==============================] - 3s 386us/step - loss: 0.2395 -
```

```
acc: 0.9312 - val_loss: 0.2709 - val_acc: 0.9332
Epoch 5/10
8982/8982 [==============================] - 3s 381us/step - loss: 0.2259 -
acc: 0.9336 - val_loss: 0.2360 - val_acc: 0.9270
Epoch 6/10
8982/8982 [==============================] - 3s 381us/step - loss: 0.2182 -
acc: 0.9348 - val_loss: 0.2298 - val_acc: 0.9341
Epoch 7/10
8982/8982 [==============================] - 3s 383us/step - loss: 0.2129 -
acc: 0.9380 - val_loss: 0.2114 - val_acc: 0.9390
Epoch 8/10
8982/8982 [==============================] - 3s 382us/step - loss: 0.2128 -
acc: 0.9341 - val_loss: 0.2306 - val_acc: 0.9359
Epoch 9/10
8982/8982 [==============================] - 3s 378us/step - loss: 0.2053 -
acc: 0.9382 - val_loss: 0.2267 - val_acc: 0.9368
Epoch 10/10
8982/8982 [==============================] - 3s 385us/step - loss: 0.2031 -
acc: 0.9389 - val_loss: 0.2204 - val_acc: 0.9368
```

The best validation accuracy was after epoch 7, where we got 93.90% accuracy, which is not as good as the CNN model. One of the problems with simple RNN models is that it is difficult to maintain context as the gap grows between the different pieces of information. Let's move onto a more complex model, that is, the LSTM model.

Long short term memory model

LSTMs are designed to learn long-term dependencies. Similar to RNNs, they are chained and have four internal neural network layers. They split the state into two parts, where one part manages short-term state and the other adds long-term state. LSTMs have *gates* which control how *memories* are stored. The input gate controls which part of the input should be added to the long-term memory. The forget gate controls the part of long-term memory that should be forgotten. The final gate, the output gate, controls which part of the long-term memory should be in the output. This is a brief description of LSTMs – a good reference for more details is `http://colah.github.io/posts/2015-08-Understanding-LSTMs/`.

The code for our LSTM model is in `Chapter7/classify_keras4.R`. The parameters for the model are max length=150, the size of the embedding layer=32, and the model was trained for 10 epochs:

```
word_index <- dataset_reuters_word_index()
max_features <- length(word_index)
maxlen <- 150
```

```
skip_top = 0

.........

model <- keras_model_sequential() %>%
  layer_embedding(input_dim = max_features, output_dim = 32,input_length =
maxlen) %>%
  layer_dropout(rate = 0.25) %>%
  layer_lstm(128,dropout=0.2) %>%
  layer_dense(units = 1, activation = "sigmoid")

.........

history <- model %>% fit(
  x_train, y_train,
  epochs = 10,
  batch_size = 32,
  validation_split = 0.2
)
```

Here is the output from the model's training:

```
Train on 8982 samples, validate on 2246 samples
Epoch 1/10
8982/8982 [==============================] - 25s 3ms/step - loss: 0.3238 -
acc: 0.8917 - val_loss: 0.2135 - val_acc: 0.9394
Epoch 2/10
8982/8982 [==============================] - 26s 3ms/step - loss: 0.2465 -
acc: 0.9206 - val_loss: 0.1875 - val_acc: 0.9470
Epoch 3/10
8982/8982 [==============================] - 26s 3ms/step - loss: 0.1815 -
acc: 0.9493 - val_loss: 0.2577 - val_acc: 0.9408
Epoch 4/10
8982/8982 [==============================] - 26s 3ms/step - loss: 0.1691 -
acc: 0.9521 - val_loss: 0.1956 - val_acc: 0.9501
Epoch 5/10
8982/8982 [==============================] - 25s 3ms/step - loss: 0.1658 -
acc: 0.9507 - val_loss: 0.1850 - val_acc: 0.9537
Epoch 6/10
8982/8982 [==============================] - 25s 3ms/step - loss: 0.1658 -
acc: 0.9508 - val_loss: 0.1764 - val_acc: 0.9510
Epoch 7/10
8982/8982 [==============================] - 26s 3ms/step - loss: 0.1659 -
acc: 0.9522 - val_loss: 0.1884 - val_acc: 0.9466
Epoch 8/10
8982/8982 [==============================] - 26s 3ms/step - loss: 0.1548 -
acc: 0.9556 - val_loss: 0.1900 - val_acc: 0.9479
Epoch 9/10
```

```
8982/8982 [==============================] - 26s 3ms/step - loss: 0.1562 -
acc: 0.9548 - val_loss: 0.2035 - val_acc: 0.9461
Epoch 10/10
8982/8982 [==============================] - 26s 3ms/step - loss: 0.1508 -
acc: 0.9567 - val_loss: 0.2052 - val_acc: 0.9470
```

The best validation accuracy was after epoch 5, when we got 95.37% accuracy, which is a big improvement on the simple RNN model, although still not as good as the CNN model. We will cover GRU cells next, which are a similar concept to LSTM.

Gated Recurrent Units model

Gated recurrent units (GRUs) are similar to LSTM cells but simpler. They have one gate that combines the forget and input gates in LSTM, and there is no output gate. While GRUs are simpler than LSTMs and therefore quicker to train, it is a matter of debate on whether they are better than LSTMs, as the research is inconclusive. Therefore, it is recommended to try both, as the results of your task may vary. The code for our GRU model is in Chapter7/classify_keras5.R. The parameters for the model are max length=150, the size of the embedding layer=32, and the model was trained for 10 epochs:

```
word_index <- dataset_reuters_word_index()
max_features <- length(word_index)
maxlen <- 250
skip_top = 0

..........

model <- keras_model_sequential() %>%
  layer_embedding(input_dim = max_features, output_dim = 32,input_length =
maxlen) %>%
  layer_dropout(rate = 0.25) %>%
  layer_gru(128,dropout=0.2) %>%
  layer_dense(units = 1, activation = "sigmoid")

..........
history <- model %>% fit(
  x_train, y_train,
  epochs = 10,
  batch_size = 32,
  validation_split = 0.2
)
```

Here is the output from the model's training:

```
Train on 8982 samples, validate on 2246 samples
Epoch 1/10
8982/8982 [==============================] - 35s 4ms/step - loss: 0.3231 -
acc: 0.8867 - val_loss: 0.2068 - val_acc: 0.9372
Epoch 2/10
8982/8982 [==============================] - 35s 4ms/step - loss: 0.2084 -
acc: 0.9381 - val_loss: 0.2065 - val_acc: 0.9421
Epoch 3/10
8982/8982 [==============================] - 35s 4ms/step - loss: 0.1824 -
acc: 0.9454 - val_loss: 0.1711 - val_acc: 0.9501
Epoch 4/10
8982/8982 [==============================] - 35s 4ms/step - loss: 0.1656 -
acc: 0.9515 - val_loss: 0.1719 - val_acc: 0.9550
Epoch 5/10
8982/8982 [==============================] - 35s 4ms/step - loss: 0.1569 -
acc: 0.9551 - val_loss: 0.1668 - val_acc: 0.9541
Epoch 6/10
8982/8982 [==============================] - 35s 4ms/step - loss: 0.1477 -
acc: 0.9570 - val_loss: 0.1667 - val_acc: 0.9555
Epoch 7/10
8982/8982 [==============================] - 35s 4ms/step - loss: 0.1441 -
acc: 0.9605 - val_loss: 0.1612 - val_acc: 0.9581
Epoch 8/10
8982/8982 [==============================] - 36s 4ms/step - loss: 0.1361 -
acc: 0.9611 - val_loss: 0.1593 - val_acc: 0.9590
Epoch 9/10
8982/8982 [==============================] - 35s 4ms/step - loss: 0.1361 -
acc: 0.9620 - val_loss: 0.1646 - val_acc: 0.9568
Epoch 10/10
8982/8982 [==============================] - 35s 4ms/step - loss: 0.1306 -
acc: 0.9634 - val_loss: 0.1660 - val_acc: 0.9559
```

The best validation accuracy was after epoch 5, when we got 95.90% accuracy, which is an improvement on the 95.37% we got with LSTM. In fact, this is the best result we have seen so far. In the next section, we will look at bidirectional architectures.

Bidirectional LSTM model

We saw in *Figure 7.1* that RNNs (as well as LSTMs and GRUs) are useful because they can pass information forwards. But in NLP tasks, it is also useful to look backwards. For example, the following two strings have the same meaning:

- I went to Berlin in spring
- In spring I went to Berlin

Bidirectional LSTMs can pass information backwards as well as forwards. The code for our bidirectional LSTM model is in `Chapter7/classify_keras6.R`. The parameters for the model are max length=150, the size of the embedding layer=32, and the model was trained for 10 epochs:

```
word_index <- dataset_reuters_word_index()
max_features <- length(word_index)
maxlen <- 250
skip_top = 0


. . . . . . . . . . . . . . . . .


model <- keras_model_sequential() %>%
  layer_embedding(input_dim = max_features, output_dim = 32,input_length =
maxlen) %>%
  layer_dropout(rate = 0.25) %>%
  bidirectional(layer_lstm(units=128,dropout=0.2)) %>%
  layer_dense(units = 1, activation = "sigmoid")


. . . . . . . . . . . . . . . .
history <- model %>% fit(
  x_train, y_train,
  epochs = 10,
  batch_size = 32,
  validation_split = 0.2
)
```

Here is the output from the model's training:

```
Train on 8982 samples, validate on 2246 samples
Epoch 1/10
8982/8982 [==============================] - 82s 9ms/step - loss: 0.3312 -
acc: 0.8834 - val_loss: 0.2166 - val_acc: 0.9377
Epoch 2/10
8982/8982 [==============================] - 87s 10ms/step - loss: 0.2487 -
acc: 0.9243 - val_loss: 0.1889 - val_acc: 0.9457
Epoch 3/10
8982/8982 [==============================] - 86s 10ms/step - loss: 0.1873 -
```

```
acc: 0.9464 - val_loss: 0.1708 - val_acc: 0.9519
Epoch 4/10
8982/8982 [==============================] - 82s 9ms/step - loss: 0.1685 -
acc: 0.9537 - val_loss: 0.1786 - val_acc: 0.9577
Epoch 5/10
8982/8982 [==============================] - 83s 9ms/step - loss: 0.1634 -
acc: 0.9531 - val_loss: 0.2094 - val_acc: 0.9310
Epoch 6/10
8982/8982 [==============================] - 82s 9ms/step - loss: 0.1567 -
acc: 0.9571 - val_loss: 0.1809 - val_acc: 0.9475
Epoch 7/10
8982/8982 [==============================] - 83s 9ms/step - loss: 0.1499 -
acc: 0.9575 - val_loss: 0.1652 - val_acc: 0.9555
Epoch 8/10
8982/8982 [==============================] - 83s 9ms/step - loss: 0.1488 -
acc: 0.9586 - val_loss: 0.1795 - val_acc: 0.9510
Epoch 9/10
8982/8982 [==============================] - 83s 9ms/step - loss: 0.1513 -
acc: 0.9567 - val_loss: 0.1758 - val_acc: 0.9555
Epoch 10/10
8982/8982 [==============================] - 83s 9ms/step - loss: 0.1463 -
acc: 0.9571 - val_loss: 0.1731 - val_acc: 0.9550
```

The best validation accuracy was after epoch 4, when we got 95.77% accuracy.

Stacked bidirectional model

Bidirectional models are good at picking up information from future states that can affect the current state. Stacked bidirectional models allow us to stack multiple LSTM/GRU layers in a similar manner to how we stack multiple convolutional layers in computer vision tasks. The code for our bidirectional LSTM model is in Chapter7/classify_keras7.R. The parameters for the model are max length=150, the size of the embedding layer=32, and the model was trained for 10 epochs:

```
word_index <- dataset_reuters_word_index()
max_features <- length(word_index)
maxlen <- 250
skip_top = 0

.................

model <- keras_model_sequential() %>%
  layer_embedding(input_dim = max_features, output_dim = 32,input_length =
maxlen) %>%
  layer_dropout(rate = 0.25) %>%
  bidirectional(layer_lstm(units=32,dropout=0.2,return_sequences = TRUE))
```

```
%>%
  bidirectional(layer_lstm(units=32,dropout=0.2)) %>%
  layer_dense(units = 1, activation = "sigmoid")

..................
history <- model %>% fit(
  x_train, y_train,
  epochs = 10,
  batch_size = 32,
  validation_split = 0.2
)
```

Here is the output from the model's training:

```
Train on 8982 samples, validate on 2246 samples
Epoch 1/10
8982/8982 [==============================] - 70s 8ms/step - loss: 0.2854 -
acc: 0.9006 - val_loss: 0.1945 - val_acc: 0.9372
Epoch 2/10
8982/8982 [==============================] - 66s 7ms/step - loss: 0.1795 -
acc: 0.9511 - val_loss: 0.1791 - val_acc: 0.9484
Epoch 3/10
8982/8982 [==============================] - 69s 8ms/step - loss: 0.1586 -
acc: 0.9557 - val_loss: 0.1756 - val_acc: 0.9492
Epoch 4/10
8982/8982 [==============================] - 70s 8ms/step - loss: 0.1467 -
acc: 0.9607 - val_loss: 0.1664 - val_acc: 0.9559
Epoch 5/10
8982/8982 [==============================] - 70s 8ms/step - loss: 0.1394 -
acc: 0.9614 - val_loss: 0.1775 - val_acc: 0.9533
Epoch 6/10
8982/8982 [==============================] - 70s 8ms/step - loss: 0.1347 -
acc: 0.9636 - val_loss: 0.1667 - val_acc: 0.9519
Epoch 7/10
8982/8982 [==============================] - 70s 8ms/step - loss: 0.1344 -
acc: 0.9618 - val_loss: 0.2101 - val_acc: 0.9332
Epoch 8/10
8982/8982 [==============================] - 70s 8ms/step - loss: 0.1306 -
acc: 0.9647 - val_loss: 0.1893 - val_acc: 0.9479
Epoch 9/10
8982/8982 [==============================] - 70s 8ms/step - loss: 0.1286 -
acc: 0.9646 - val_loss: 0.1663 - val_acc: 0.9550
Epoch 10/10
8982/8982 [==============================] - 70s 8ms/step - loss: 0.1254 -
acc: 0.9669 - val_loss: 0.1687 - val_acc: 0.9492
```

The best validation accuracy was after epoch 4, when we got 95.59% accuracy, which is worse than our bidirectional model, which got 95.77% accuracy.

Bidirectional with 1D convolutional neural network model

So far, the best approaches we have seen are from the 1D convolutional neural network model which got 95.73%, and the gated recurrent units model which got 95.90% accuracy. The following code combines them! The code for our bidirectional with 1D convolutional neural network model is in `Chapter7/classify_keras8.R`.

The parameters for the model are max length=150, the size of the embedding layer=32, and the model was trained for 10 epochs:

```
word_index <- dataset_reuters_word_index()
max_features <- length(word_index)
maxlen <- 250
skip_top = 0

. . . . . . . . . . . . . . . . .

model <- keras_model_sequential() %>%
  layer_embedding(input_dim = max_features, output_dim = 32,input_length =
maxlen) %>%
  layer_spatial_dropout_1d(rate = 0.25) %>%
  layer_conv_1d(64,3, activation = "relu") %>%
  layer_max_pooling_1d() %>%
  bidirectional(layer_gru(units=64,dropout=0.2)) %>%
  layer_dense(units = 1, activation = "sigmoid")

. . . . . . . . . . . . . . . . .
history <- model %>% fit(
  x_train, y_train,
  epochs = 10,
  batch_size = 32,
  validation_split = 0.2
)
```

Here is the output from the model's training:

```
Train on 8982 samples, validate on 2246 samples
Epoch 1/10
8982/8982 [==============================] - 26s 3ms/step - loss: 0.2891 -
acc: 0.8952 - val_loss: 0.2226 - val_acc: 0.9319
Epoch 2/10
```

```
8982/8982 [==============================] - 25s 3ms/step - loss: 0.1712 -
acc: 0.9505 - val_loss: 0.1601 - val_acc: 0.9586
Epoch 3/10
8982/8982 [==============================] - 26s 3ms/step - loss: 0.1651 -
acc: 0.9548 - val_loss: 0.1639 - val_acc: 0.9541
Epoch 4/10
8982/8982 [==============================] - 26s 3ms/step - loss: 0.1466 -
acc: 0.9582 - val_loss: 0.1699 - val_acc: 0.9550
Epoch 5/10
8982/8982 [==============================] - 26s 3ms/step - loss: 0.1391 -
acc: 0.9606 - val_loss: 0.1520 - val_acc: 0.9586
Epoch 6/10
8982/8982 [==============================] - 26s 3ms/step - loss: 0.1347 -
acc: 0.9626 - val_loss: 0.1626 - val_acc: 0.9550
Epoch 7/10
8982/8982 [==============================] - 27s 3ms/step - loss: 0.1332 -
acc: 0.9638 - val_loss: 0.1572 - val_acc: 0.9604
Epoch 8/10
8982/8982 [==============================] - 26s 3ms/step - loss: 0.1317 -
acc: 0.9629 - val_loss: 0.1693 - val_acc: 0.9470
Epoch 9/10
8982/8982 [==============================] - 26s 3ms/step - loss: 0.1259 -
acc: 0.9654 - val_loss: 0.1531 - val_acc: 0.9599
Epoch 10/10
8982/8982 [==============================] - 28s 3ms/step - loss: 0.1233 -
acc: 0.9665 - val_loss: 0.1653 - val_acc: 0.9573
```

The best validation accuracy was after epoch 6, when we got 96.04% accuracy, which beats all of the previous models.

Comparing the deep learning NLP architectures

Here is a summary of all of the models in this chapter, ordered by their sequence in this chapter. We can see that the best traditional machine learning approach got 95.24%, which was beaten by many of the deep learning approaches. While the incremental changes from the best traditional machine learning to the best deep learning model may seem small at 0.80%, it reduces our misclassified examples by 17%, which is a significant relative change:

Model	Accuracy
Best traditional machine learning approach	95.24%
Simple deep learning approach	94.97%
1D convolutional neural network model	95.73%
Recurrent neural network model	93.90%

Long short term memory model	95.37%
Gated recurrent units model	95.90%
Bidirectional LSTM model	95.77%
Stacked bidirectional model	95.59%
Bidirectional with 1D convolutional neural network	96.04%

Summary

We really covered a lot in this chapter! We built a fairly complex traditional NLP example that had many hyperparameters, as well as training it on several machine learning algorithms. It achieved a reputable result of getting 95.24% accuracy. However, when we looked into traditional NLP in more detail, we found that it had some major problems: it requires non-trivial feature engineering, it creates sparse high-dimensional data frames, and it may require discarding a substantial amount of data before machine learning.

In comparison, the deep learning approach uses word vectors or embeddings, which are much more efficient and do not require preprocessing. We ran through a number of deep learning approaches, including 1D convolutional layers, Recurrent Neural Networks, GRUs, and LSTM. We finally combined the two best previous approaches into one approach in our final model to get 96.08% accuracy, compared to 95.24% by using traditional NLP.

In the next chapter, we will develop models using TensorFlow. We will look at TensorBoard, which allows us to visualize and debug complex deep learning models. We will also look at using TensorFlow estimators, an alternative option for using TensorFlow. Then, we will also look at TensorFlow Runs, which automates a lot of the steps for hyperparameter tuning. Finally, we will look at options for deploying deep learning models.

Deep Learning Models Using TensorFlow in R

8

This chapter is about using TensorFlow in R. We have already used TensorFlow quite a lot, as Keras is a high-level neural network API that uses either TensorFlow, CNTK, or Theano. In R, Keras uses TensorFlow in the background. TensorFlow is more difficult to develop deep learning models in. However, there are two interesting packages in TensorFlow that could be overlooked: TensorFlow estimators and TensorFlow runs. We will cover both of these packages in this chapter.

In this chapter, we will cover the following topics:

- Introduction to TensorFlow
- Building models using TensorFlow
- TensorFlow estimators
- TensorFlow runs packages

Introduction to the TensorFlow library

TensorFlow is not just a deep learning library, but an expressive programming language that can implement various optimization and mathematical transformations on data. While it is mainly used to implement deep learning algorithms, it can perform much more. In TensorFlow, programs are represented as computational graphs, and data in TensorFlow is stored in `tensors`. A **tensor** is an array of data that has the same data type, and the rank of a tensor is the number of dimensions. Because all the data in a tensor must have the same type, they are more similar to R matrices than data frames.

Here is an example of tensors of various ranks:

```
library(tensorflow)

> # tensor of rank-0
> var1 <- tf$constant(0.1)
> print(var1)
Tensor("Const:0", shape=(), dtype=float32)

> sess <- tf$InteractiveSession()
T:\src\github\tensorflow\tensorflow\core\common_runtime\gpu\gpu_device.cc:1
084] Created TensorFlow device
(/job:localhost/replica:0/task:0/device:GPU:0 with 3019 MB memory) ->
physical GPU (device: 0, name: GeForce GTX 1050 Ti, pci bus id:
0000:01:00.0, compute capability: 6.1)

> sess$run(tf$global_variables_initializer())
> var2 <- tf$constant(2.3)
> var3 = var1 + var2
> print(var1)
Tensor("Const:0", shape=(), dtype=float32)
 num 0.1

> print(var2)
Tensor("Const_1:0", shape=(), dtype=float32)
 num 2.3

> print(var3)
Tensor("Add:0", shape=(), dtype=float32)
 num 2.4

> # tensor of rank-1
> var4 <- tf$constant(4.5,shape=shape(5L))
> print(var4)
Tensor("Const_2:0", shape=(5,), dtype=float32)
 num [1:5(1d)] 4.5 4.5 4.5 4.5 4.5

> # tensor of rank-2
> var5 <- tf$constant(6.7,shape=shape(3L,3L))
> print(var5)
Tensor("Const_3:0", shape=(3, 3), dtype=float32)
 num [1:3, 1:3] 6.7 6.7 6.7 6.7 6.7 ...
```

A TensorFlow program has two parts. First, you have to build the computational graph, which contains the tensors and the operations on those tensors. When they have defined the graph, the second part is to create a TensorFlow session to run the graph. In the previous example, the first time we print out the value for the tensor, a, we only get the tensor definition and not the value. All we have done is define part of the computation graph. It is only when we call `tf$InteractiveSession` that we tell TensorFlow to run the operations on the tensors. A session is responsible for running the computational graph.

The TensorFlow program is referred to as a graph because the code can be structured as a graph. This might not be obvious to us as most of the deep learning models that we have built in this book have consisted of sequential operations on layers. In TensorFlow (and Keras and MXNet), it is possible to use the output of an operation multiple times and to combine inputs in one operation.

As deep learning models get larger, it is increasingly difficult to visualize and debug them. In some code blocks, we have printed a summary of the model showing the layers, or we have plotted the network. However, neither of these tools would be helpful for debugging problems in a model with 10 million+ parameters! Fortunately, there is a visualization tool included with TensorFlow to help summarize, debug, and fix TensorFlow programs. This is called TensorBoard, and we will cover this next.

Using TensorBoard to visualize deep learning networks

Computation graphs in TensorFlow can be very complex, so there is a visualization tool called **TensorBoard** to visualize these graphs and assist in debugging. TensorBoard can plot a computation graph, display metrics from training, and so on. Since Keras uses TensorFlow in the backend, it too can use TensorBoard. Here is the MNIST example from Keras with TensorBoard logging enabled. This code can be found in the `Chapter8/mnist_keras.R` folder. The first part of the code loads the data, pre-processes it, and defines the model architecture. Hopefully, this should be familiar to you at this stage:

```
library(keras)

mnist_data <- dataset_mnist()
xtrain <-
array_reshape(mnist_data$train$x,c(nrow(mnist_data$train$x),28,28,1))
ytrain <- to_categorical(mnist_data$train$y,10)
xtrain <- xtrain / 255.0
```

```
model <- keras_model_sequential()
model %>%
  layer_conv_2d(filters=32,kernel_size=c(5,5),activation='relu',
                input_shape=c(28,28,1)) %>%
  layer_max_pooling_2d(pool_size=c(2,2)) %>%
  layer_dropout(rate=0.25) %>%
  layer_conv_2d(filters=32,kernel_size=c(5,5),activation='relu') %>%
  layer_max_pooling_2d(pool_size=c(2,2)) %>%
  layer_dropout(rate=0.25) %>%
  layer_flatten() %>%
  layer_dense(units=256,activation='relu') %>%
  layer_dropout(rate=0.4) %>%
  layer_dense(units=10,activation='softmax')

model %>% compile(
  loss=loss_categorical_crossentropy,
  optimizer="rmsprop",metrics="accuracy"
)
```

To enable logging, add a `callbacks` parameter to the `model.fit` function to tell Keras/TensorFlow to log events to a directory. The following code will output log data to the `/tensorflow_logs` directory:

```
model %>% fit(
  xtrain,ytrain,
  batch_size=128,epochs=10,
  callbacks=callback_tensorboard("/tensorflow_logs",
                                 histogram_freq=1,write_images=0),
  validation_split=0.2
)
# from cmd line,run 'tensorboard --logdir /tensorflow_logs'
```

 Warning: The event logs can take up a lot of space. For 5 epochs on the `MNIST` dataset, 1.75 GB of information was created. Most of this was because of the image data that was included, so you may consider setting `write_images=0` to reduce the size of the logs.

TensorBoard is a web application, and you must start the TensorBoard program for it to run. When the model has finished training, follow these steps to start the TensorBoard web application:

1. Open up Command Prompt and enter the following:

```
$ tensorboard --logdir /tensorflow_logs
```

2. If TensorBoard starts successfully, you should get a message similar to the following at Command Prompt:

```
TensorBoard 0.4.0rc2 at http://xxxxxx:6006 (Press CTRL+C to quit)
```

3. Open a web browser to the link that was provided. The web page should be similar to the following:

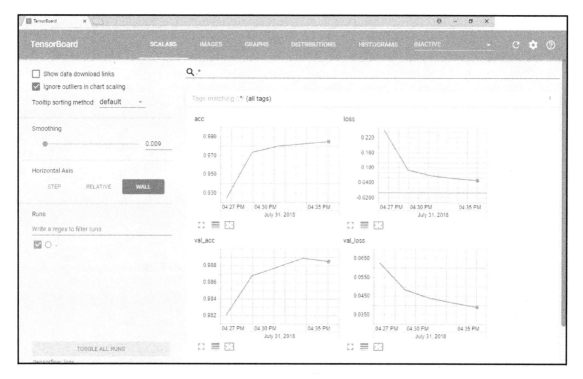

Figure 8.1: TensorBoard – model metrics

4. The preceding screenshot shows us the model metrics on the training and validation test sets – these are similar to the metrics shown in RStudio during training:

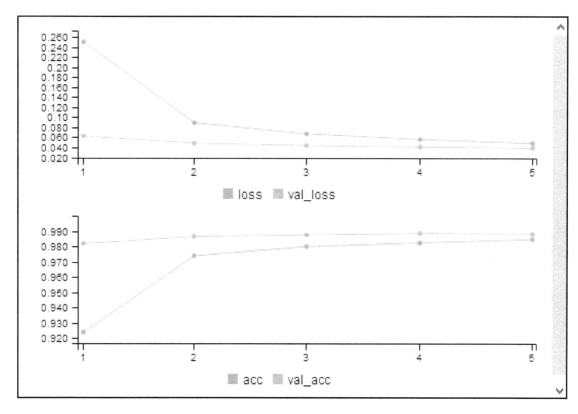

Figure 8.2: RStudio – model metrics

5. If you click on the **Images** option, you will be able to visualize the layers in the model and see how they change over epochs:

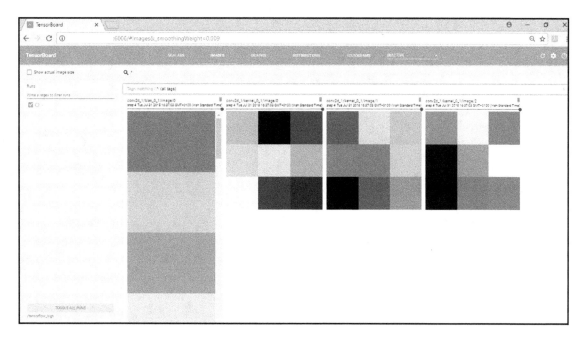

Figure 8.3: TensorBoard – visualizing the model layers

6. If you click on the **Graphs** option, it will show the computation graph for the model. You can also download it as an image file. Here is the computation graph for this model:

Figure 8.4: TensorBoard – computation graph

Some of this will seem familiar. We can see our convolutional, max pooling, flatten, dense, and dropout layers. The rest are not as obvious. As a higher-level abstraction, Keras takes care of a lot of the complexities in creating the computation graph.

7. By clicking on the **Histogram** option, you can see how the distribution of tensors changes over time:

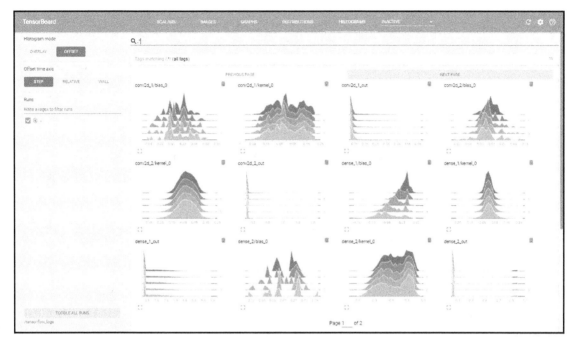

Figure 8.5: TensorBoard – histograms

It is possible to use TensorBoard to debug a model. For example, it would be possible to investigate a vanishing gradient or an exploding gradient problem to see where the weights of the model were either vanishing to zero or exploding to infinity. There is a lot more to TensorBoard, so if you are curious you can follow the online documentation on it.

In the next section, we will use TensorFlow to build a regression model and a convolutional neural network.

TensorFlow models

In this section, we will use TensorFlow to build some machine learning models. First, we will build a simple linear regression model and then a convolutional neural network model, similar to what we have seen in Chapter 5, *Image Classification Using Convolutional Neural Networks*.

The following code loads the TensorFlow library. We can confirm it loaded successfully by setting and accessing a constant string value:

```
> library(tensorflow)

# confirm that TensorFlow library has loaded
> sess=tf$Session()
> hello_world <- tf$constant('Hello world from TensorFlow')
> sess$run(hello_world)
b'Hello world from TensorFlow'
```

Linear regression using TensorFlow

In this first Tensorflow example, we will look at regression. The code for this section is in the `Chapter8/regression_tf.R` folder:

1. First, we create some fake data for an an input value, *x*, and an output value, *y*. We set *y* to be approximately equal to `0.8 + x * 1.3`. We want the application to discover the `beta0` and `beta1` values, which are `0.8` and `1.3`, respectively:

```
library(tensorflow)

set.seed(42)
# create 50000 x variable between 0 and 100
x_var <- runif(50000,min=0,max=1)
#y = approx(1.3x + 0.8)
y_var <- rnorm(50000,0.8,0.04) + x_var * rnorm(50000,1.3,0.05)

# y_pred = beta0 + beta1 * x
beta0 <- tf$Variable(tf$zeros(shape(1L)))
beta1 <- tf$Variable(tf$random_uniform(shape(1L), -1.0, 1.0))
y_pred <- beta0 + beta1*x_var
```

2. Now, we set up our `loss` function so that the gradient descent algorithm can work:

```
# create our loss value which we want to minimize
loss <- tf$reduce_mean((y_pred-y_var)^2)
# create optimizer
optimizer <- tf$train$GradientDescentOptimizer(0.6)
train <- optimizer$minimize(loss)
```

3. We then set up a TensorFlow session and initialize the variables. Finally, we can run the graph:

```
# create TensorFlow session and initialize variables
sess = tf$Session()
sess$run(tf$global_variables_initializer())

# solve the regression
for (step in 0:80) {
  if (step %% 10 == 0)
    print(sprintf("Step %1.0f:beta0=%1.4f,
beta1=%1.4f",step,sess$run(beta0), sess$run(beta1)))
  sess$run(train)
}
[1] "Step 0:beta0=0.0000, beta1=-0.3244"
[1] "Step 10:beta0=1.0146, beta1=0.8944"
[1] "Step 20:beta0=0.8942, beta1=1.1236"
[1] "Step 30:beta0=0.8410, beta1=1.2229"
[1] "Step 40:beta0=0.8178, beta1=1.2662"
[1] "Step 50:beta0=0.8077, beta1=1.2850"
[1] "Step 60:beta0=0.8033, beta1=1.2932"
[1] "Step 70:beta0=0.8014, beta1=1.2967"
[1] "Step 80:beta0=0.8006, beta1=1.2983"
```

We can see that the model manages to find the values for beta0 and beta1 that solve the function y=beta0 + beta1*x. The next section is a more more complex example, where we will build a TensorFlow model for image classification.

Convolutional neural networks using TensorFlow

In this section, we will build a TensorFlow model on the MNIST dataset. The code has similar layers and parameters to the Lenet model that we saw in Chapter 5, *Image Classification Using Convolutional Neural Networks*. However, the code to build the model in TensorFlow is more complicated than the code to build the model in Keras or in MXNet. One reason for this is that it is the programmer's job to ensure that the sizes of the layers are correctly aligned. In the Keras/MXNet models, we can just change the number of nodes in a layer in one statement. In TensorFlow, if we change the number of nodes in a layer, we must ensure that we also change the inputs in the next layer.

In some ways, programming in TensorFlow is closer to the hand-written neural network code we wrote in Chapter 3, *Deep Learning Fundamentals*. Another difference from Keras/MXNet in the training loop is that we need to manage the batches rather than just call, asking to iterate over all the data *x* times (where *x* is an epoch). The code for this example is in the Chapter8/mnist_tf.R folder. First, we load the Keras package to get the MNIST data, but we train the model using TensorFlow. Here is the first part of the code:

```
library(RSNNS) # for decodeClassLabels
library(tensorflow)
library(keras)

mnist <- dataset_mnist()
set.seed(42)

xtrain <- array_reshape(mnist$train$x,c(nrow(mnist$train$x),28*28))
ytrain <- decodeClassLabels(mnist$train$y)
xtest <- array_reshape(mnist$test$x,c(nrow(mnist$test$x),28*28))
ytest <- decodeClassLabels(mnist$test$y)
xtrain <- xtrain / 255.0
xtest <- xtest / 255.0
head(ytrain)
      0 1 2 3 4 5 6 7 8 9
[1,] 0 0 0 0 0 1 0 0 0 0
[2,] 1 0 0 0 0 0 0 0 0 0
[3,] 0 0 0 0 1 0 0 0 0 0
[4,] 0 1 0 0 0 0 0 0 0 0
[5,] 0 0 0 0 0 0 0 0 0 1
[6,] 0 0 1 0 0 0 0 0 0 0
```

We use the decodeClassLabels function from the RSNNS library because TensorFlow requires a dummy coded matrix, so each possible class is represented as a column coded as 0/1, as shown in the preceding code output.

In the next code block, we create some placeholders for our input and output values in the model. We also reshape the input data into a rank-4 tensor, that is, a 4 dimensional data structure. The first dimension (-1L) is for the records that will be processed in a batch. The next two dimensions are the dimensions of the image files, and the final dimension is the channels, which is the number of colors. Since our images are greyscale, there is only 1 channel. If the images were color images, there would be 3 channels. The following code block creates the placeholders and reshapes the data:

```
# placeholders
x <- tf$placeholder(tf$float32, shape(NULL,28*28L))
y <- tf$placeholder(tf$float32, shape(NULL,10L))
x_image <- tf$reshape(x, shape(-1L,28L,28L,1L))
```

Next, we will define the model architecture. We will create convolution blocks, just like we did previously. However, there are a lot more values that need to be set. For example, in the first convolutional layer, we must define the shape, initialize the weights, and take care of the bias variable. Here is the code for the TensorFlow model:

```
# first convolution layer
conv_weights1 <- tf$Variable(tf$random_uniform(shape(5L,5L,1L,16L), -0.4,
0.4))
conv_bias1 <- tf$constant(0.0, shape=shape(16L))
conv_activ1 <- tf$nn$tanh(tf$nn$conv2d(x_image, conv_weights1,
strides=c(1L,1L,1L,1L), padding='SAME') + conv_bias1)
pool1 <- tf$nn$max_pool(conv_activ1,
ksize=c(1L,2L,2L,1L),strides=c(1L,2L,2L,1L), padding='SAME')

# second convolution layer
conv_weights2 <- tf$Variable(tf$random_uniform(shape(5L,5L,16L,32L), -0.4,
0.4))
conv_bias2 <- tf$constant(0.0, shape=shape(32L))
conv_activ2 <- tf$nn$relu(tf$nn$conv2d(pool1, conv_weights2,
strides=c(1L,1L,1L,1L), padding='SAME') + conv_bias2)
pool2 <- tf$nn$max_pool(conv_activ2,
ksize=c(1L,2L,2L,1L),strides=c(1L,2L,2L,1L), padding='SAME')

# densely connected layer
dense_weights1 <- tf$Variable(tf$truncated_normal(shape(7L*7L*32L,512L),
stddev=0.1))
dense_bias1 <- tf$constant(0.0, shape=shape(512L))
pool2_flat <- tf$reshape(pool2, shape(-1L,7L*7L*32L))
dense1 <- tf$nn$relu(tf$matmul(pool2_flat, dense_weights1) + dense_bias1)

# dropout
keep_prob <- tf$placeholder(tf$float32)
dense1_drop <- tf$nn$dropout(dense1, keep_prob)

# softmax layer
dense_weights2 <- tf$Variable(tf$truncated_normal(shape(512L,10L),
stddev=0.1))
dense_bias2 <- tf$constant(0.0, shape=shape(10L))

yconv <- tf$nn$softmax(tf$matmul(dense1_drop, dense_weights2) +
dense_bias2)
```

Now, we have to define the loss equation, define the optimizer to use (Adam), and define the accuracy metric:

```
cross_entropy <- tf$reduce_mean(-tf$reduce_sum(y * tf$log(yconv),
reduction_indices=1L))
train_step <- tf$train$AdamOptimizer(0.0001)$minimize(cross_entropy)
correct_prediction <- tf$equal(tf$argmax(yconv, 1L), tf$argmax(y, 1L))
accuracy <- tf$reduce_mean(tf$cast(correct_prediction, tf$float32))
```

Finally, we can train the model over 10 epochs. However, one complication still exists, so we must manually manage the batches. We get the number of batches to train for and load them in turn. If we have 60,000 images in our train dataset, we have 469 batches (60,000/128 = 468.75 and round up to 469) per epoch. We feed in every batch and output metrics every 100 batches:

```
sess <- tf$InteractiveSession()
sess$run(tf$global_variables_initializer())

# if you get out of memory errors when running on gpu
# then lower the batch_size
batch_size <- 128
batches_per_epoch <- 1+nrow(xtrain) %/% batch_size
for (epoch in 1:10)
{
  for (batch_no in 0:(-1+batches_per_epoch))
  {
    nStartIndex <- 1 + batch_no*batch_size
    nEndIndex <- nStartIndex + batch_size-1
    if (nEndIndex > nrow(xtrain))
      nEndIndex <- nrow(xtrain)
    xvalues <- xtrain[nStartIndex:nEndIndex,]
    yvalues <- ytrain[nStartIndex:nEndIndex,]
    if (batch_no %% 100 == 0) {
      batch_acc <-
accuracy$eval(feed_dict=dict(x=xvalues,y=yvalues,keep_prob=1.0))
      print(sprintf("Epoch %1.0f, step %1.0f: training
accuracy=%1.4f",epoch, batch_no, batch_acc))
    }
    sess$run(train_step,feed_dict=dict(x=xvalues,y=yvalues,keep_prob=0.5))
  }
  cat("\n")
}
```

Here is the output for the first epoch:

```
[1] "Epoch 1, step 0: training accuracy=0.0625"
[1] "Epoch 1, step 100: training accuracy=0.8438"
[1] "Epoch 1, step 200: training accuracy=0.8984"
[1] "Epoch 1, step 300: training accuracy=0.9531"
[1] "Epoch 1, step 400: training accuracy=0.8750"
```

When training is complete, we can evaluate the model by calculating the accuracy on the test set. Again, we have to do this in batches to prevent out-of-memory errors:

```
# calculate test accuracy
# have to run in batches to prevent out of memory errors
batches_per_epoch <- 1+nrow(xtest) %/% batch_size
test_acc <- vector(mode="numeric", length=batches_per_epoch)
for (batch_no in 0:(-1+batches_per_epoch))
{
  nStartIndex <- 1 + batch_no*batch_size
  nEndIndex <- nStartIndex + batch_size-1
  if (nEndIndex > nrow(xtest))
    nEndIndex <- nrow(xtest)
  xvalues <- xtest[nStartIndex:nEndIndex,]
  yvalues <- ytest[nStartIndex:nEndIndex,]
  batch_acc <-
accuracy$eval(feed_dict=dict(x=xvalues,y=yvalues,keep_prob=1.0))
  test_acc[batch_no+1] <- batch_acc
}
# using the mean is not totally accurate as last batch is not a complete
batch
print(sprintf("Test accuracy=%1.4f",mean(test_acc)))
[1] "Test accuracy=0.9802"
```

We get a final accuracy of 0.9802. If we compare this code to the MNIST example in Chapter 5, *Image Classification Using Convolutional Neural Networks*, the TensorFlow code is more verbose and it is easier to make mistakes. We can really see the benefit of using a higher, level abstraction, such as MXNet or Keras (which can use TensorFlow as a backend). For most deep learning use cases, especially for building deep learning models using existing layers as building blocks, there is little to be gained in developing code in TensorFlow. For these use cases, it is simpler and more efficient to use Keras or MXNet.

After seeing this code, you may want to go back to something more familiar in Keras and MXNet. However, the next section looks at TensorFlow estimators and TensorFlow runs, which are two useful packages that you should be aware of.

TensorFlow estimators and TensorFlow runs packages

TensorFlow estimators and the TensorFlow runs packages are great packages to use for deep learning. In this section, we will use both to train a model based on our churn prediction data from `Chapter 4`, *Training Deep Prediction Models*.

TensorFlow estimators

TensorFlow estimators allow you to build TensorFlow models using a simpler API interface. In R, the `tfestimators` package allows you to call this API. There are different model types, including linear models and neural networks. The following estimators are available:

- `linear_regressor()` for linear regression
- `linear_classifier()` for linear classification
- `dnn_regressor()` for deep neural network regression
- `dnn_classifier()` for deep neural network classification
- `dnn_linear_combined_regressor()` for deep neural network linear combined regression
- `dnn_linear_combined_classifier()` for deep neural network linear combined classification

Estimators hide a lot of the detail in creating a deep learning model, including building the graph, initializing variables and layers, and they can also integrate with TensorBoard. More details are available at https://tensorflow.rstudio.com/tfestimators/. We will use dnn_classifier with the data from the binary classification task from Chapter 4, *Training Deep Prediction Models*. The following code in the Chapter8/tf_estimators.R folder demonstrates TensorFlow estimators.

1. We only include the code that is specific to TensorFlow estimators and omit the code at the start of the file that loads the data and splits it into train and test data:

```
response <- function() "Y_categ"
features <- function() predictorCols

FLAGS <- flags(
  flag_numeric("layer1", 256),
  flag_numeric("layer2", 128),
  flag_numeric("layer3", 64),
  flag_numeric("layer4", 32),
  flag_numeric("dropout", 0.2)
)
num_hidden <-
c(FLAGS$layer1,FLAGS$layer2,FLAGS$layer3,FLAGS$layer4)

classifier <- dnn_classifier(
  feature_columns = feature_columns(column_numeric(predictorCols)),
  hidden_units = num_hidden,
  activation_fn = "relu",
  dropout = FLAGS$dropout,
  n_classes = 2
)

bin_input_fn <- function(data)
{
  input_fn(data, features = features(), response = response())
}
tr <- train(classifier, input_fn = bin_input_fn(trainData))
[\] Training -- loss: 22.96, step: 2742

tr
Trained for 2,740 steps.
Final step (plot to see history):
 mean_losses: 61.91
total_losses: 61.91
```

2. Once the model is trained, the following code plots the training and validation metrics:

```
plot(tr)
```

3. This produces the following plot:

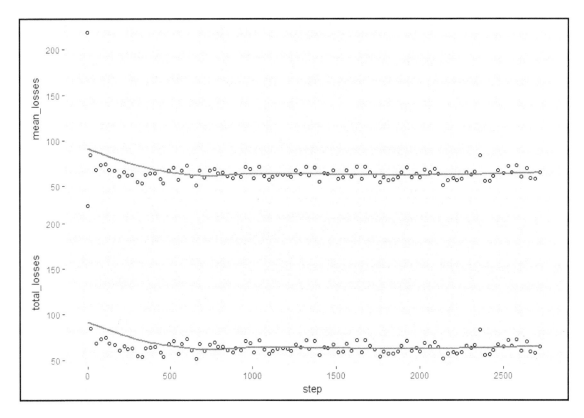

Figure 8.6: Training a loss plot for a TensorFlow estimator model

4. The next part of the code calls the `evaluate` function to produce metrics for the model:

```
# predictions <- predict(classifier, input_fn =
bin_input_fn(testData))
evaluation <- evaluate(classifier, input_fn =
bin_input_fn(testData))
[-] Evaluating -- loss: 37.77, step: 305

for (c in 1:ncol(evaluation))
 print(paste(colnames(evaluation)[c]," = ",evaluation[c],sep=""))
[1] "accuracy = 0.77573162317276"
[1] "accuracy_baseline = 0.603221416473389"
[1] "auc = 0.842994153499603"
[1] "auc_precision_recall = 0.887594640254974"
[1] "average_loss = 0.501933991909027"
[1] "label/mean = 0.603221416473389"
[1] "loss = 64.1636199951172"
[1] "precision = 0.803375601768494"
[1] "prediction/mean = 0.562777876853943"
[1] "recall = 0.831795573234558"
[1] "global_step = 2742"
```

We can see that we got an accuracy of 77.57%, which is actually almost identical to the accuracy we got on the MXNet model in Chapter 4, *Training Deep Prediction Models*, which had a similar architecture. The `dnn_classifier()` function hides a lot of the detail, so Tensorflow estimators are a good way to use the power of TensorFlow for tasks with structured data.

Models created using TensorFlow estimators can be saved onto disk and loaded later. The `model_dir()` function shows the location of where the model artifacts were saved (usually in a `temp` directory, but it can be copied elsewhere):

```
model_dir(classifier)
"C:\\Users\\xxxxxx\\AppData\\Local\\Temp\\tmpv1e_ri23"
# dnn_classifier has a model_dir parameter to load an existing model
?dnn_classifier
```

Included in the model artifacts are the event logs that can be used by TensorBoard. For example, when I load TensorBoard up and point it to the logs directory in the `temp` directory, I can see the TensorFlow graph that was created:

Figure 8.7: Graph using TensorBoard for a TensorFlow estimator model

TensorFlow runs package

The tfruns package is a set of utilities for managing different training runs for deep learning models. It can be used as a framework to build multiple deep learning models using different hyper-parameters. It can track the hyper-parameters, metrics, output, and source code for every training run and allows you to compare the best models so that you can see the differences between the training runs. This makes hyper-parameter tuning much easier and can be used with any tfestimator model or Keras model. For more details, go to https://tensorflow.rstudio.com/tools/tfruns/articles/overview.html.

The following code is in the Chapter8/hyperparams.R folder and also uses the script we used in the *TensorFlow estimators* section (Chapter8/tf_estimators.R):

```
library(tfruns)
# FLAGS <- flags(
# flag_numeric("layer1", 256),
# flag_numeric("layer2", 128),
# flag_numeric("layer3", 64),
# flag_numeric("layer4", 32),
# flag_numeric("dropout", 0.2),
# flag_string("activ","relu")
# )

training_run('tf_estimators.R')
training_run('tf_estimators.R', flags =
list(layer1=128,layer2=64,layer3=32,layer4=16))
training_run('tf_estimators.R', flags = list(dropout=0.1,activ="tanh"))
```

This will run the Chapter8/tf_estimators.R script with different hyper-parameters. The first time, we don't change any hyper-parameters, so it uses the defaults included in Chapter8/tf_estimators.R. Each time a new model is trained using the classification script, it is called a **training run**, and the details of the training run is stored in the runs folder in the current working directory.

For each training run, a new website will pop up with details on the run, as shown in the following screenshot:

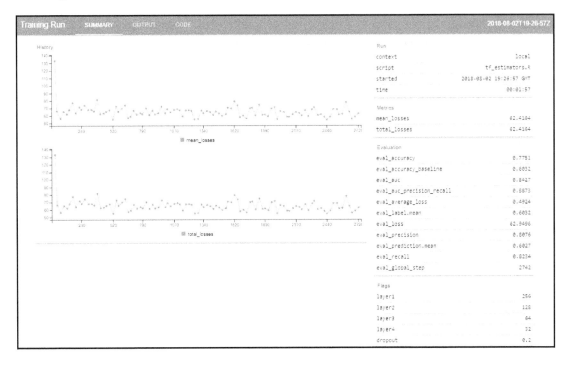

Figure 8.8: TensorFlow training run – Summary screen

We can see the progress of the training in the plots, along with the details of when the training run occurred and the evaluation metrics. We can also see in the bottom right that the **flags** (that is, hyper-parameters) used in the training run are also shown. There is another tab for the R code output, which includes all of the output from the R code in the inner file (Chapter8/tf_estimators.R), including plots.

Once all of the training runs are complete, the following code shows a summary of all the training runs:

```
ls_runs(order=eval_accuracy)
ls_runs(order=eval_accuracy)[,1:5]
Data frame: 3 x 5
                 run_dir eval_accuracy eval_accuracy_baseline eval_auc
eval_auc_precision_recall
3 runs/2018-08-02T19-50-17Z          0.7746                 0.6032   0.8431
0.8874
2 runs/2018-08-02T19-52-04Z          0.7724                 0.6032   0.8425
```

```
0.8873
1 runs/2018-08-02T19-53-39Z          0.7711              0.6032    0.8360
0.8878
```

Here, we have ordered the results by the column `eval_accuracy`. If you close the window showing the summary for the training run, you can display it again by calling the `view_run` function and passing in the folder name. For example, to show the summary for the best training run, use the following code:

```
dir1 <- ls_runs(order=eval_accuracy)[1,1]
view_run(dir1)
```

Finally, you can also compare two runs. Here, we are comparing the two best models:

```
dir1 <- ls_runs(order=eval_accuracy)[1,1]
dir2 <- ls_runs(order=eval_accuracy)[2,1]
compare_runs(runs=c(dir1,dir2))
```

This brings up a page similar to the following:

Compare Runs		2018-08-02T19-50-17Z	2018-08-02T19-52-04Z	
Run			**Run**	
context	local		context	local
script	tf_estimators.R		script	tf_estimators.R
started	2018-08-02 19:50:17 GMT		started	2018-08-02 19:52:04 GMT
time	00:01:45		time	00:01:34
Metrics			**Metrics**	
mean_losses	58.6853		mean_losses	68.7100
total_losses	58.6853		total_losses	68.7100
Evaluation			**Evaluation**	
eval_accuracy	0.7746		eval_accuracy	0.7724
eval_accuracy_baseline	0.6032		eval_accuracy_baseline	0.6032
eval_auc	0.8431		eval_auc	0.8426
eval_auc_precision_recall	0.8874		eval_auc_precision_recall	0.8873
eval_average_loss	0.4896		eval_average_loss	0.4844
eval_label.mean	0.6032		eval_label.mean	0.6032
eval_loss	62.5818		eval_loss	61.9193
eval_precision	0.8053		eval_precision	0.822
eval_prediction.mean	0.59		eval_prediction.mean	0.5918
eval_recall	0.8259		eval_recall	0.7948
eval_global_step	2742		eval_global_step	2742
FLAGS				
@@ -1,6 +1,6 @@				
- layer1: 256				
- layer2: 128				
+ layer1: 128				
- layer3: 64				
+ layer2: 64				

Figure 8.9: Comparing two TensorFlow runs

This page shows the evaluation metrics for both training runs and also displays the hyper-parameters that were used. As we can see, this makes managing the process of tuning deep learning models much easier. This approach to hyper-parameter tuning has automatic logging, traceability, and it is easy to compare different sets of hyper-parameters. You can see the metrics and the different hyper-parameters used for the training runs. There's no more comparing configuration files to try and match hyper-parameter settings to output logs! In comparison, the code I wrote for hyper-parameter selection for the NLP example in `Chapter 7`, *Natural Language Processing Using Deep Learning*, seems crude in comparison

Summary

In this chapter, we developed some TensorFlow models. We looked at TensorBoard, which is a great tool for visualizing and debugging deep learning models. We built a couple of models using TensorFlow, including a basic regression model and a Lenet model for computer vision models. From these examples, we saw that programming in TensorFlow was more complicated and error-prone than using the higher-level APIs (MXNet and Keras) that we used elsewhere in this book.

We then moved onto using TensorFlow estimators, which is a much easier interface than using TensorFlow. We then used that script in another package called **tfruns**, which stands for TensorFlow runs. This package allows us to call a TensorFlow estimators or Keras script with different flags each time. We used this for hyper-parameter selection, running, and evaluating multiple models. The TensorFlow runs have excellent integration with RStudio and we were able to view summaries for each run and compare runs to see the difference in the metrics and hyper-parameters that were used.

In the next chapter, we we will look at embeddings and auto-encoders. We have already seen embeddings in `Chapter 7`, *Natural Language Processing Using Deep Learning*, so in the next chapter we will see how embeddings can create a lower level encoding of data. We will also use train auto-encoders, which create these embeddings. We will use auto-encoders for anomaly detection and also for collaborative filtering (recommender system).

9
Anomaly Detection and Recommendation Systems

This chapter will look at auto-encoder models and recommendation systems. Although these two use cases may seem very different, they both rely on finding different representations of data. These representations are similar to the embeddings we saw in Chapter 7, *Natural Language Processing Using Deep Learning*. The first part of this chapter introduces unsupervised learning where there is no specific outcome to be predicted. The next section provides a conceptual overview of auto-encoder models in a machine learning and deep neural network context in particular. We will show you how to build and apply an auto-encoder model to identify anomalous data. Such atypical data may be bad data or outliers, but could also be instances that require further investigation, for example, fraud detection. An example of applying anomaly detection is detecting when an individual's credit card spending pattern differs from their usual behavior. Finally, this chapter closes with a use case on how to apply recommendation systems for cross-sell and up-sell opportunities using the retail dataset that was introduced in Chapter 4, *Training Deep Prediction Models*.

This chapter will cover the following topics:

- What is unsupervised learning?
- How do auto-encoders work?
- Training an auto-encoder in R
- Using auto-encoders for anomaly detection
- Use case – collaborative filtering

What is unsupervised learning?

So far, we have focused on models and techniques that broadly fall under the category of supervised learning. Supervised learning is supervised because the task is for the machine to learn the relationship between a set of variables or features and one or more outcomes. For example, in Chapter 4, *Training Deep Prediction Models*, we wanted to predict whether someone would visit a store in the next 14 days. In this chapter, we will delve into methods of unsupervised learning. In contrast with supervised learning, where there is an outcome variable(s) or labeled data is being used, unsupervised learning does not use any outcomes or labeled data. Unsupervised learning uses only input features for learning. A common example of unsupervised learning is cluster analysis, such as k-means clustering, where the machine learns hidden or latent clusters in the data to minimize a criterion (for example, the smallest variance within a cluster).

Another unsupervised learning method is to find another representation of the data, or to reduce the input data into a smaller dataset without losing too much information in the process, this is known as dimensionality reduction. The goal of dimensionality reduction is for a set of p features to find a set of latent variables, k, so that $k < p$. However, with k latent variables, p raw variables can be reasonably reproduced. We used **principal component analysis (PCA)** in the neural networks example from Chapter 2, *Training a Prediction Model*. In that example, we saw that there is a trade-off between the number of dimensions and the information loss, as shown in *Figure 2.1*. Principal component analysis uses an orthogonal transformation to go from the raw data to the principal components. In addition to being uncorrelated, the principal components are ordered from the component that explains the most variance to that which explains the least. Although all principal components can be used (in which case the dimensionality of the data is not reduced), only components that explain a sufficiently large amount of variance (for example, based on high eigenvalues) are included and components that account for relatively little variance are dropped as noise or unnecessary. In the neural networks example in Chapter 2, *Training a Prediction Model*, we had 624 inputs after eliminating the features with zero variance. When we applied PCA, we found that 50% of our variance (information) by our data could be represented in just 23 principal components.

How do auto-encoders work?

Auto-encoders are a form of dimensionality reduction technique. When they are used in this manner, they mathematically and conceptually have similarities to other dimensionality reduction techniques such as PCA. Auto-encoders consist of two parts: an encoder which creates a representation of the data, and a decoder which tries to reproduce or predict the inputs. Thus, the hidden layers and neurons are not maps between an input and some other outcome, but are self (auto)-encoding. Given sufficient complexity, auto-encoders can simply learn the identity function, and the hidden neurons will exactly mirror the raw data, resulting in no meaningful benefit. Similarly, in PCA, using all the principal components also provides no benefit. Therefore, the best auto-encoder is not necessarily the most accurate one, but one that reveals some meaningful structure or architecture in the data or one that reduces noise, identifies outliers, or anomalous data, or some other useful side-effect that is not necessarily directly related to accurate predictions of the model inputs.

Auto-encoders with a lower dimensionality than the raw data are called **undercomplete**; by using an undercomplete auto-encoder, one can force the auto-encoder to learn the most important features of the data. One common application of auto-encoders is to pre-train deep neural networks or other supervised learning models. In addition, it is possible to use the hidden features themselves. We will see this later on for anomaly detection. Using an undercomplete model is effectively a way to regularize the model. However, it is also possible to train overcomplete auto-encoders where the hidden dimensionality is greater than the raw data, so long as some other form of regularization is used.

There are broadly two parts to auto-encoders:

- First, an encoding function, $f()$, encodes the raw data, x, to the hidden neurons, H
- Second, a decoding function, $g()$, decodes H back to x

The following diagram shows an undercomplete encoder, where we have fewer nodes in the hidden layer. The output layer on the right is the decoded version of the input layer on the left. The task of the hidden layer is to store as much information as possible about the input layer (encode the input layer) so that the input layer can be re-constructed (or decoded):

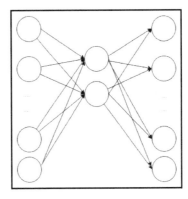

Figure 9.1: An example of an auto-encoder

Regularized auto-encoders

An undercomplete auto-encoder is a form of a regularized auto-encoder, where the regularization occurs through using a shallower (or in some other way lower) dimensional representation than the data. However, regularization can be accomplished through other means as well. These are penalized auto-encoders.

Penalized auto-encoders

As we have seen in previous chapters, one approach to preventing overfitting is to use penalties, that is, regularization. In general, our goal is to minimize the reconstruction error. If we have an objective function, F, we may optimize $F(y, f(x))$, where $f()$ encodes the raw data inputs to generate predicted or expected y values. For auto-encoders, we have $F(x, g(f(x)))$, so that the machine learns the weights and functional form of $f()$ and $g()$ to minimize the discrepancy between x and the reconstruction of x, namely $g(f(x))$. If we want to use an overcomplete auto-encoder, we need to introduce some form of regularization to force the machine to learn a representation that does not simply mirror the input. For example, we might add a function that penalizes based on complexity, so that instead of optimizing $F(x, g(f(x)))$, we optimize $F(x, g(f(x))) + P(f(x))$, where the penalty function, P, depends on the encoding or the raw inputs, $f()$.

Such penalties differ somewhat from those we have seen before, in that the penalty is designed to induce sparseness, not of the parameters but rather of the latent variables, *H*, which are the encoded representations of the raw data. The goal is to learn a latent representation that captures the essential features of the data.

Another type of penalty that can be used to provide regularization is one based on the derivative. Whereas sparse auto-encoders have a penalty that induces sparseness of the latent variables, penalizing the derivatives results in the model learning a form of *f()* that is relatively insensitive to minor perturbations of the raw input data, *x*. What we mean by this is that it forces a penalty on functions where the encoding varies greatly for changes in *x*, preferring regions where the gradient is relatively flat.

Denoising auto-encoders

Denoising auto-encoders remove noise or denoise data, and are a useful technique for learning a latent representation of raw data (*Vincent, P., Larochelle, H., Bengio, Y., and Manzagol, P. A. (2008, July); Bengio, Y.,Courville, A., and Vincent, P. (2013)*). We said that the general task of an auto-encoder was to optimize: *F(x, g(f(x)))*. However, for a denoising auto-encoder, the task is to recover *x* from a noisy or corrupted version of *x*. One application of denoising auto-encoders is to restore old images that may be blurred or corrupted.

Although denoising auto-encoders are used to try and recover the true representation from corrupted data or data with noise, this technique can also be used as a regularization tool. As a method of regularization, rather than having noisy or corrupted data and attempting to recover the truth, the raw data is purposefully corrupted. This forces the auto-encoder to do more than merely learn the identity function, as the raw inputs are no longer identical to the output. This process is shown in the following diagram:

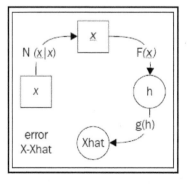

Figure 9.2: Denoising auto-encoders

The remaining choice is what the function, *N()*, which adds the noise or corrupts *x*, should be. Two choices are to add noise through a stochastic process or for any given training iteration to only include a subset of the raw *x* inputs. In the next section, we will explore how to actually train auto-encoder models in R.

Training an auto-encoder in R

In this section, we are going to train an auto-encoder in R and show you that it can be used as a dimensionality reduction technique. We will compare it with the approach we took in `Chapter 2`, *Training a Prediction Model*, where we used PCA to find the principal components in the image data. In that example, we used PCA and found that 23 factors was sufficient to explain 50% of the variance in the data. We built a neural network model using just these 23 factors to classify a dataset with either *5* or *6*. We got 97.86% accuracy in that example.

We are going to follow a similar process in this example, and we will use the `MINST` dataset again. The following code from `Chapter8/encoder.R` loads the data. We will use half the data for training an auto-encoder and the other half will be used to build a classification model to evaluate how good the auto-encoder is at dimensionality reduction. The first part of the code is similar to what we have seen in previous examples; it loads and normalizes the data so that the values are between 0.0 and 1.0:

```
library(keras)
library(corrplot)
library(neuralnet)
options(width = 70, digits = 2)
options(scipen=999)
dataDirectory <- "../data"
if (!file.exists(paste(dataDirectory,'/train.csv',sep="")))
{
  link <-
'https://apache-mxnet.s3-accelerate.dualstack.amazonaws.com/R/data/mnist_cs
v.zip'
  if (!file.exists(paste(dataDirectory,'/mnist_csv.zip',sep="")))
  download.file(link, destfile =
paste(dataDirectory,'/mnist_csv.zip',sep=""))
  unzip(paste(dataDirectory,'/mnist_csv.zip',sep=""), exdir = dataDirectory)
  if (file.exists(paste(dataDirectory,'/test.csv',sep="")))
  file.remove(paste(dataDirectory,'/test.csv',sep=""))
}

data <- read.csv("../data/train.csv", header=TRUE)
set.seed(42)
```

```
sample<-sample(nrow(data),0.5*nrow(data))
test <- setdiff(seq_len(nrow(data)),sample)
train.x <- data[sample,-1]
test.x <- data[test,-1]
train.y <- data[sample,1]
test.y <- data[test,1]
rm(data)
train.x <- train.x/255
test.x <- test.x/255
train.x <- data.matrix(train.x)
test.x <- data.matrix(test.x)
input_dim <- 28*28 #784
```

Now, we will move on to our first auto-encoder. We will use 16 hidden neurons in our auto-encoder and use tanh as the activation function. We use 20% of our data as validation to provide an unbiased estimate of how the auto-encoder performs. Here is the code. To keep it concise, we are only showing part of the output:

```
# model 1
inner_layer_dim <- 16
input_layer <- layer_input(shape=c(input_dim))
encoder <- layer_dense(units=inner_layer_dim,
activation='tanh')(input_layer)
decoder <- layer_dense(units=784)(encoder)
autoencoder <- keras_model(inputs=input_layer, outputs = decoder)
autoencoder %>% compile(optimizer='adam',
loss='mean_squared_error',metrics='accuracy')
history <- autoencoder %>% fit(train.x,train.x,
 epochs=40, batch_size=128,validation_split=0.2)

Train on 16800 samples, validate on 4200 samples
Epoch 1/40
16800/16800 [==============================] - 1s 36us/step - loss: 0.0683
- acc: 0.0065 - val_loss: 0.0536 - val_acc: 0.0052
Epoch 2/40
16800/16800 [==============================] - 1s 30us/step - loss: 0.0457
- acc: 0.0082 - val_loss: 0.0400 - val_acc: 0.0081
Epoch 3/40
16800/16800 [==============================] - 0s 29us/step - loss: 0.0367
- acc: 0.0101 - val_loss: 0.0344 - val_acc: 0.0121
...
...
Epoch 38/40
16800/16800 [==============================] - 0s 29us/step - loss: 0.0274
- acc: 0.0107 - val_loss: 0.0275 - val_acc: 0.0098
Epoch 39/40
```

```
16800/16800 [==============================] - 1s 31us/step - loss: 0.0274
- acc: 0.0111 - val_loss: 0.0275 - val_acc: 0.0093
Epoch 40/40
16800/16800 [==============================] - 1s 32us/step - loss: 0.0274
- acc: 0.0120 - val_loss: 0.0275 - val_acc: 0.0095
```

The validation loss is 0.0275, which shows that the model is performing quite well.
Another nice feature is that if you run the code in RStudio, it will show the training metrics
in graphs, which will automatically update as the model is trained. This is shown in the
following screenshot:

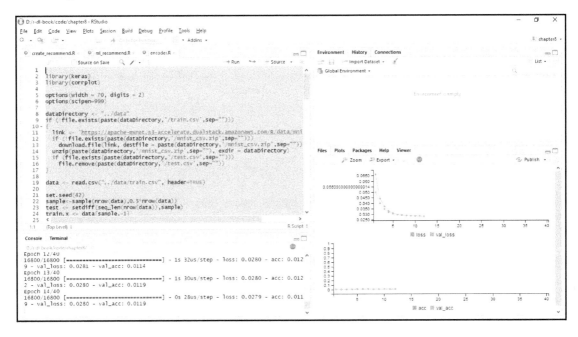

Figure 9.3: Model metrics showing in the Viewer pane in RStudio

Once the model has completed training, you can also plot the model architecture and
model metrics using the following code (the output is also included). By calling the plot
function, you can see the plots for the accuracy and the loss on the training and validation
datasets:

```
summary(autoencoder)
```

Layer (type)	Output Shape	Param #
input_1 (InputLayer)	(None, 784)	0

dense_1 (Dense)	(None, 16)	12560
dense_2 (Dense)	(None, 784)	13328

```
========================================================================
Total params: 25,888
Trainable params: 25,888
Non-trainable params: 0
```

```
plot(history)
```

This code produces the following plot:

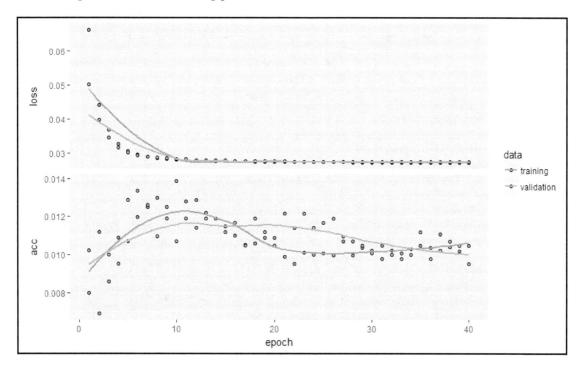

Figure 9.4: Auto-encoder model metrics

The preceding plots shows that the validation accuracy is relatively stable, but it probably peaked after epoch 20. We will now train a second model with 32 hidden nodes instead in the following code:

```
# model 2
inner_layer_dim <- 32
input_layer <- layer_input(shape=c(input_dim))
encoder <- layer_dense(units=inner_layer_dim,
```

```
activation='tanh')(input_layer)
decoder <- layer_dense(units=784)(encoder)
autoencoder <- keras_model(inputs=input_layer, outputs = decoder)
autoencoder %>% compile(optimizer='adam',
 loss='mean_squared_error',metrics='accuracy')
history <- autoencoder %>% fit(train.x,train.x,
 epochs=40, batch_size=128,validation_split=0.2)

Train on 16800 samples, validate on 4200 samples
Epoch 1/40
16800/16800 [==============================] - 1s 41us/step - loss: 0.0591
- acc: 0.0104 - val_loss: 0.0406 - val_acc: 0.0131
Epoch 2/40
16800/16800 [==============================] - 1s 34us/step - loss: 0.0339
- acc: 0.0111 - val_loss: 0.0291 - val_acc: 0.0093
Epoch 3/40
16800/16800 [==============================] - 1s 33us/step - loss: 0.0262
- acc: 0.0108 - val_loss: 0.0239 - val_acc: 0.0100
...
...
Epoch 38/40
16800/16800 [==============================] - 1s 33us/step - loss: 0.0174
- acc: 0.0130 - val_loss: 0.0175 - val_acc: 0.0095
Epoch 39/40
16800/16800 [==============================] - 1s 31us/step - loss: 0.0174
- acc: 0.0132 - val_loss: 0.0175 - val_acc: 0.0098
Epoch 40/40
16800/16800 [==============================] - 1s 34us/step - loss: 0.0174
- acc: 0.0126 - val_loss: 0.0175 - val_acc: 0.0100
```

Our validation loss has improved to 0.0175, so let's try 64 hidden nodes:

```
# model 3
inner_layer_dim <- 64
input_layer <- layer_input(shape=c(input_dim))
encoder <- layer_dense(units=inner_layer_dim,
activation='tanh')(input_layer)
decoder <- layer_dense(units=784)(encoder)
autoencoder <- keras_model(inputs=input_layer, outputs = decoder)
autoencoder %>% compile(optimizer='adam',
 loss='mean_squared_error',metrics='accuracy')
history <- autoencoder %>% fit(train.x,train.x,
 epochs=40, batch_size=128,validation_split=0.2)

Train on 16800 samples, validate on 4200 samples
Epoch 1/40
16800/16800 [==============================] - 1s 50us/step - loss: 0.0505
- acc: 0.0085 - val_loss: 0.0300 - val_acc: 0.0138
```

```
Epoch 2/40
16800/16800 [==============================] - 1s 39us/step - loss: 0.0239
- acc: 0.0110 - val_loss: 0.0197 - val_acc: 0.0090
Epoch 3/40
16800/16800 [==============================] - 1s 41us/step - loss: 0.0173
- acc: 0.0115 - val_loss: 0.0156 - val_acc: 0.0117
...
...
Epoch 38/40
16800/16800 [==============================] - 1s 41us/step - loss: 0.0094
- acc: 0.0124 - val_loss: 0.0096 - val_acc: 0.0131
Epoch 39/40
16800/16800 [==============================] - 1s 39us/step - loss: 0.0095
- acc: 0.0128 - val_loss: 0.0095 - val_acc: 0.0121
Epoch 40/40
16800/16800 [==============================] - 1s 37us/step - loss: 0.0094
- acc: 0.0126 - val_loss: 0.0098 - val_acc: 0.0133
```

Our validation loss here is `0.0098`, which again is an improvement. We have probably got to the stage where adding more hidden nodes will cause the model to overfit because we are only using `16800` rows to train the autoencoder. We could look at applying regularization, but since our first models have an accuracy of `0.01`, we are doing well enough.

Accessing the features of the auto-encoder model

We can extract the deep features from the model, that is, the values for the hidden neurons in the model. For this, we will use the model with 16 hidden nodes. We will examine the distribution of correlations using the `ggplot2` package, as shown in the following code. The results are shown in *Figure 9.5*. The deep features have small correlations, that is, usually with an absolute value of *<.20*. This is what we expect in order for the auto-encoder to work. This means that the features should not duplicate information between them:

```
encoder <- keras_model(inputs=input_layer, outputs=encoder)
encodings <- encoder %>% predict(test.x)
encodings<-as.data.frame(encodings)
M <- cor(encodings)
corrplot(M, method = "circle", sig.level = 0.1)
```

The preceding code produces the following plot:

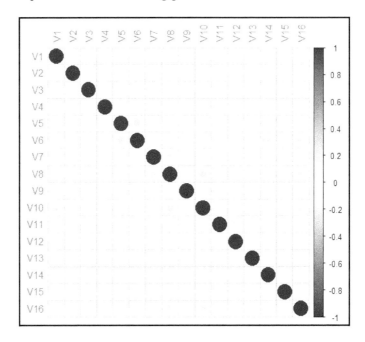

Figure 9.5: Correlation between weights in the hidden layer of the auto-encoder

In `Chapter 2`, *Training a Prediction Model*, we used PCA for dimensionality reduction and found that for a binary classification task of telling the difference between 5 and 6, we could still get 97.86% accuracy, even if we only used 23 features as input. These 23 features were the 23 **principal components** and accounted for 50% of the variance in our dataset. We will use the weights in the auto-encoder to perform the same experiment. Note that we trained the auto-encoder on 50% of the data, and that we are using the other 50% of the data for the binary classification task, that is, we do not want to try and build a classification task on data that was used to build the auto-encoder:

```
encodings$y <- test.y
encodings <- encodings[encodings$y==5 | encodings$y==6,]
encodings[encodings$y==5,]$y <- 0
encodings[encodings$y==6,]$y <- 1
table(encodings$y)
   0    1
1852 2075
nobs <- nrow(encodings)
train <- sample(nobs, 0.9*nobs)
test <- setdiff(seq_len(nobs), train)
trainData <- encodings[train,]
```

```
testData <- encodings[test,]
col_names <- names(trainData)
f <- as.formula(paste("y ~", paste(col_names[!col_names
%in%"y"],collapse="+")))
nn <- neuralnet(f,data=trainData,hidden=c(4,2),linear.output = FALSE)
preds_nn <- compute(nn,testData[,1:(-1+ncol(testData))])
preds_nn <- ifelse(preds_nn$net.result > 0.5, "1", "0")
t<-table(testData$y, preds_nn,dnn=c("Actual", "Predicted"))
acc<-round(100.0*sum(diag(t))/sum(t),2)
print(t)
        Predicted
Actual 0 1
      0 182 5
      1 3 203
print(sprintf(" accuracy = %1.2f%%",acc))
[1] " accuracy = 97.96%"
```

Our model gets 97.96% accuracy, which is a slight improvement on the 97.86% accuracy we achieved in Chapter 2, *Training a Prediction Model*. It is not really a surprise that the two models are very similar as the mathematical foundations for PCA involves matrix decomposition, while the auto-encoder uses back-propagation to set the matrix weights for the hidden layer. In fact, if we dropped the non-linear activation function, our encodings would be very similar to PCA. This demonstrates that auto-encoder models can be used effectively as a dimensionality reduction technique.

Using auto-encoders for anomaly detection

Now that we have built an auto-encoder and accessed the features of the inner layers, we will move on to an example of how auto-encoders can be used for anomaly detection. The premise here is quite simple: we take the reconstructed outputs from the decoder and see which instances have the most error, that is, which instances are the most difficult for the decoder to reconstruct. The code that is used here is in Chapter9/anomaly.R, and we will be using the UCI HAR dataset that we have already been introduced to in Chapter 2, *Training a Prediction Model*. If you have not already downloaded the data, go back to that chapter for instructions on how to do so.. The first part of the code loads the data, and we subset the features to only use the ones with mean, sd, and skewness in the feature names:

```
library(keras)
library(ggplot2)
train.x <- read.table("UCI HAR Dataset/train/X_train.txt")
train.y <- read.table("UCI HAR Dataset/train/y_train.txt")[[1]]
test.x <- read.table("UCI HAR Dataset/test/X_test.txt")
test.y <- read.table("UCI HAR Dataset/test/y_test.txt")[[1]]
```

```
use.labels <- read.table("UCI HAR Dataset/activity_labels.txt")
colnames(use.labels) <-c("y","label")

features <- read.table("UCI HAR Dataset/features.txt")
meanSD <- grep("mean\\(\\)|std\\(\\)|max\\(\\)|min\\(\\)|skewness\\(\\)",
features[, 2])

train.x <- data.matrix(train.x[,meanSD])
test.x <- data.matrix(test.x[,meanSD])
input_dim <- ncol(train.x)
```

Now, we can build our auto-encoder model. This is going to be a stacked auto-encoder with two 40 neuron hidden encoder layers and two 40-neuron hidden decoder layers. For conciseness, we have removed some of the output:

```
# model
inner_layer_dim <- 40
input_layer <- layer_input(shape=c(input_dim))
encoder <- layer_dense(units=inner_layer_dim,
activation='tanh')(input_layer)
encoder <- layer_dense(units=inner_layer_dim, activation='tanh')(encoder)
decoder <- layer_dense(units=inner_layer_dim)(encoder)
decoder <- layer_dense(units=inner_layer_dim)(decoder)
decoder <- layer_dense(units=input_dim)(decoder)

autoencoder <- keras_model(inputs=input_layer, outputs = decoder)
autoencoder %>% compile(optimizer='adam',
 loss='mean_squared_error',metrics='accuracy')
history <- autoencoder %>% fit(train.x,train.x,
 epochs=30, batch_size=128,validation_split=0.2)
Train on 5881 samples, validate on 1471 samples
Epoch 1/30
5881/5881 [==============================] - 1s 95us/step - loss: 0.2342 -
acc: 0.1047 - val_loss: 0.0500 - val_acc: 0.1013
Epoch 2/30
5881/5881 [==============================] - 0s 53us/step - loss: 0.0447 -
acc: 0.2151 - val_loss: 0.0324 - val_acc: 0.2536
Epoch 3/30
5881/5881 [==============================] - 0s 44us/step - loss: 0.0324 -
acc: 0.2772 - val_loss: 0.0261 - val_acc: 0.3413
...
...

Epoch 27/30
5881/5881 [==============================] - 0s 45us/step - loss: 0.0098 -
acc: 0.2935 - val_loss: 0.0094 - val_acc: 0.3379
Epoch 28/30
5881/5881 [==============================] - 0s 44us/step - loss: 0.0096 -
```

```
acc: 0.2908 - val_loss: 0.0092 - val_acc: 0.3215
Epoch 29/30
5881/5881 [==============================] - 0s 44us/step - loss: 0.0094 -
acc: 0.2984 - val_loss: 0.0090 - val_acc: 0.3209
Epoch 30/30
5881/5881 [==============================] - 0s 44us/step - loss: 0.0092 -
acc: 0.2955 - val_loss: 0.0088 - val_acc: 0.3209
```

We can see the layers and number of parameters for the model by calling the summary function, like so:

```
summary(autoencoder)
```

Layer (type)	Output Shape	Param #
input_4 (InputLayer)	(None, 145)	0
dense_16 (Dense)	(None, 40)	5840
dense_17 (Dense)	(None, 40)	1640
dense_18 (Dense)	(None, 40)	1640
dense_19 (Dense)	(None, 40)	1640
dense_20 (Dense)	(None, 145)	5945

```
Total params: 16,705
Trainable params: 16,705
Non-trainable params: 0
```

Our validation loss is 0.0088, which means that our model is good at encoding the data. Now, we will use the test set on the auto-encoder and get the reconstructed data. This will create a dataset with the same size as the test set. We will then select any instance where the sum of the squared error (se) between the predicted values and the test set is greater than 4.

These are the instances that the auto-encoder had the most trouble in reconstructing, and therefore they are potential anomalies. The limit value of 4 is a hyperparameter; if it is set higher, fewer potential anomalies are detected and if it is set lower, more potential anomalies are detected. This value would be different according to the dataset used.

There are 6 classes in this dataset. We want to analyze if the anomalies are spread over all of our classes or if they are specific to some classes. We will print out a table of the frequencies of our classes in our test set, and we will see that the distribution of our classes is fairly even. When printing out a table of the frequencies of our classes of our potential anomalies, we can see that most of them are in the WALKING_DOWNSTAIRS class. The potential anomalies are shown in *Figure 9.6*:

```
# anomaly detection
preds <- autoencoder %>% predict(test.x)
preds <- as.data.frame(preds)
limit <- 4
preds$se_test <- apply((test.x - preds)^2, 1, sum)
preds$y_preds <- ifelse(preds$se_test>limit,1,0)
preds$y <- test.y
preds <- merge(preds,use.labels)
table(preds$label)
LAYING SITTING STANDING WALKING WALKING_DOWNSTAIRS WALKING_UPSTAIRS
   537     491      532     496                420               471

table(preds[preds$y_preds==1,]$label)
LAYING SITTING STANDING WALKING WALKING_DOWNSTAIRS WALKING_UPSTAIRS
    18       7        1      17                 45               11
```

We can plot this with the following code:

```
ggplot(as.data.frame(table(preds[preds$y_preds==1,]$label)),aes(Var1,
Freq)) +
 ggtitle("Potential anomalies by activity") +
 geom_bar(stat = "identity") +
 xlab("") + ylab("Frequency") +
 theme_classic() +
 theme(plot.title = element_text(hjust = 0.5)) +
 theme(axis.text.x = element_text(angle = 45, hjust = 1, vjust = 1))
```

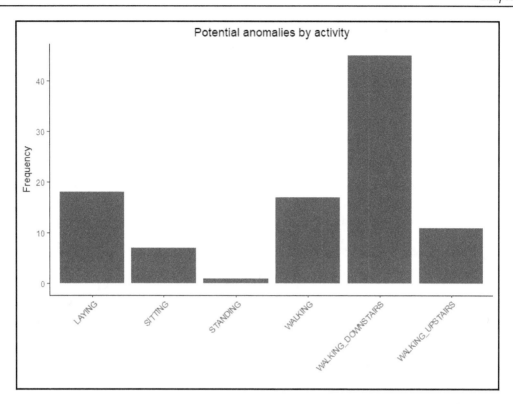

Figure 9.6: Distribution of the anomalies

In this example, we used a deep auto-encoder model to learn the features of actimetry data from smartphones. Such work can be useful for excluding unknown or unusual activities, rather than incorrectly classifying them. For example, as part of an app that classifies what activity you engaged in for how many minutes, it may be better to simply leave out a few minutes where the model is uncertain or the hidden features do not adequately reconstruct the inputs, rather than to aberrantly call an activity walking or sitting when it was actually walking downstairs.

Such work can also help to identify where the model tends to have more issues. Perhaps further sensors and additional data are needed to represent walking downstairs or more could be done to understand why walking downstairs tends to produce relatively high error rates.

These deep auto-encoders are also useful in other contexts where identifying anomalies is important, such as with financial data or credit card usage patterns. Anomalous spending patterns may indicate fraud or that a credit card has been stolen. Rather than attempt to manually search through millions of credit card transactions, one could train an auto-encoder model and use it to identify anomalies for further investigation.

Use case – collaborative filtering

This use-case is about collaborative filtering. We are going to build a recommendation system based on embeddings created from a deep learning model. To do this, we are going to use the same dataset we used in `Chapter 4`, *Training Deep Prediction Models*, which is the retail transactional database. If you have not already downloaded the database, then go to the following link, `https://www.dunnhumby.com/sourcefiles`, and select *Let's Get Sort-of-Real*. Select the option for the smallest dataset, titled *All transactions for a randomly selected sample of 5,000 customers*. Once you have read the terms and conditions and downloaded the dataset to your computer, unzip it into a directory called `dunnhumby/in` under the code folder. Ensure that the files are unzipped directly under this folder, and not a subdirectory, as you may have to copy them after unzipping the data.

The data contains details of retail transactions linked by basket IDs. Each transaction has a date and a store code, and some are also linked to customers. Here are the fields that we will use in this analysis:

Field-name	Description	Format
CUST_CODE	Customer Code. This links the transactions/visits to a customer.	Char
SPEND	Spend associated to the items bought.	Numeric
PROD_CODE	Product Code.	Char
PROD_CODE_10	Product Hierarchy Level 10 Code.	Char
PROD_CODE_20	Product Hierarchy Level 20 Code.	Char
PROD_CODE_30	Product Hierarchy Level 30 Code.	Char
PROD_CODE_40	Product Hierarchy Level 40 Code.	Char

If you want more details on the structure of the files, you can go back and re-read the use case in `Chapter 4`, *Training Deep Prediction Models*. We are going to use this dataset to create a recommendation engine. There are a family of machine learning algorithms called **Market Basket Analysis** that can be used with transactional data, but this use case is based on collaborative filtering. Collaborative filtering are recommendations based on the ratings people give to products. They are commonly used for music and film recommendations, where people rate the items, usually on a scale of 1-5. Perhaps the best known recommendation system is Netflix because of the Netflix prize (`https://en.wikipedia.org/wiki/Netflix_Prize`).

We are going to use our dataset to create implicit rankings of how much a customer *rates* an item. If you are not familiar with implicit rankings, then they are rankings that are derived from data rather than explicitly assigned by the user. We will use one of the product codes, PROD_CODE_40, and calculate the quantiles of the spend for that product code. The quantiles will divide the fields into 5 roughly equally sized groups. We will use these to assign a rating to each customer for that product based on how much they spent on that product code. The top 20% of customers will get a rating of 5, the next 20% will get a rating of 4, and so on. Each customer/product code combination that exists will have a rating from 1-5:

> There is a rich history of using quantiles in retail loyalty systems. One of the earliest segmentation approaches for retail loyalty data was called **RFM analysis**. RFM is an acronym for Recency, Frequency, and Monetary spend. It gives each customer a ranking 1 (lowest) – 5 (highest) on each of these categories, with an equal number of customers in each ranking. For *Recency*, the 20% of the customers that visited most recently would be given a 5, the next 20% would be given a 4, and so on. For *Frequency*, the top 20% of customers with the most transactions would be given a 5, the next 20% would be given a 4, and so on. Similarly for *Monetary* spend, the top 20% of the customers by revenue would be given a 5, the next 20% would be given a 4, and so on. The numbers would then be concatenated, so a customer with an RFM of 453 would be 4 for Recency, 5 for Frequency, and 3 for Monetary spend. Once the score has been calculated, it can be used for many purposes, for example, cross-sell, churn analysis, and so on. RFM analysis was very popular in the late 1990's / early 2000's with many marketing managers because it is easily implemented and well-understood. However, it is not flexible and is being replaced with machine learning techniques.

Preparing the data

The code to create our ratings is in Chapter9/create_recommend.R. The first part of the code runs through the raw transactional data. The data is in separate CSV files, so it processes each file, selects the records that have a customer linked (that is, CUST_CODE!="") to them, and then groups the sales by CUST_CODE and PROD_CODE_40. It then appends the results to a temporary file and moves on to the next input file:

```
library(magrittr)
library(dplyr)
library(readr)
library(broom)
```

```
set.seed(42)
file_list <- list.files("../dunnhumby/in/", "trans*")
temp_file <- "../dunnhumby/temp.csv"
out_file <- "../dunnhumby/recommend.csv"
if (file.exists(temp_file)) file.remove(temp_file)
if (file.exists(out_file)) file.remove(out_file)
options(readr.show_progress=FALSE)

i <- 1
for (file_name in file_list)
{
  file_name<-paste("../dunnhumby/in/",file_name,sep="")
  df<-suppressMessages(read_csv(file_name))

  df2 <- df %>%
    filter(CUST_CODE!="") %>%
    group_by(CUST_CODE,PROD_CODE_40) %>%
    summarise(sales=sum(SPEND))

  colnames(df2)<-c("cust_id","prod_id","sales")
  if (i ==1)
    write_csv(df2,temp_file)
  else
    write_csv(df2,temp_file,append=TRUE)
  print (paste("File",i,"/",length(file_list),"processed"))
  i <- i+1
}
[1] "File 1 / 117 processed"
[1] "File 2 / 117 processed"
[1] "File 3 / 117 processed"
...
...
...
[1] "File 115 / 117 processed"
[1] "File 116 / 117 processed"
[1] "File 117 / 117 processed"
rm(df,df2)
```

This section groups by customer and product code for the 117 input files. As we process each file, we rename the customer code to `cust_id` and the product department code to `prod_id`. Once we are done, the combined file will obviously have duplicate customer-product code combinations; that is, we need to group again over the combined data. We do that by opening up the temporary file and grouping over the fields again:

```
df_processed<-read_csv(temp_file)
if (file.exists(temp_file)) file.remove(temp_file)
```

```
df2 <- df_processed %>%
  group_by(cust_id,prod_id) %>%
  summarise(sales=sum(sales))
```

We could have tried to load all of the transactional data and run a group on that data, but that would have been memory and computationally expensive. By running it in two steps, we reduce the amount of data we need to process at each stage, which means it is more likely to run on machines with limited memory.

Once we have the total spend for each customer and product department code combination, we can create the ratings. Thanks to the excellent tidyr packages, it only takes a few lines to assign a rating to each row. First, we group by the prod_id field, and use the quantile function to return quantiles for the sales for each product code. These quantiles will return the sales ranges that correspond to splitting the customers into 5 equal sized groups. We then use these quantiles to assign rankings:

```
# create quantiles
dfProds <- df2 %>%
  group_by(prod_id) %>%
  do( tidy(t(quantile(.$sales, probs = seq(0, 1, 0.2)))) )
colnames(dfProds)<-c("prod_id","X0","X20","X40","X60","X80","X100")
df2<-merge(df2,dfProds)
df2$rating<-0
df2[df2$sales<=df2$X20,"rating"] <- 1
df2[(df2$sales>df2$X20) & (df2$sales<=df2$X40),"rating"] <- 2
df2[(df2$sales>df2$X40) & (df2$sales<=df2$X60),"rating"] <- 3
df2[(df2$sales>df2$X60) & (df2$sales<=df2$X80),"rating"] <- 4
df2[(df2$sales>df2$X80) & (df2$sales<=df2$X100),"rating"] <- 5
```

The only thing remaining is to save the results. Before we do, we do a couple of sanity checks to ensure that our ratings are evenly distributed from 1-5 overall. We then select a random product code and check that our ratings are evenly distributed from 1-5 for those products:

```
# sanity check, are our ratings spread out relatively evenly
df2 %>%
  group_by(rating) %>%
  summarise(recs=n())
  rating  recs
1      1 68246
2      2 62592
3      3 62162
4      4 63488
5      5 63682
df2 %>%
  filter(prod_id==df2[sample(1:nrow(df2), 1),]$prod_id) %>%
```

```
   group_by(prod_id,rating) %>%
   summarise(recs=n())
   prod_id rating recs
1 D00008        1  597
2 D00008        2  596
3 D00008        3  596
4 D00008        4  596
5 D00008        5  596

df2 <- df2[,c("cust_id","prod_id","rating")]
write_csv(df2,out_file)
```

Everything looks good here: the count for `rating=1` is higher at 68246 against 62162 to 63682 for ratings 2 to 5, but that is not really a concern as collaborative filtering models do not expect an even distribution of ratings. For the individual item (D00008), the distribution is even at 596 or 597 for each rating.

Building a collaborative filtering model

Before we jump into applying a deep learning model, we should follow the same practice as we have done in previous chapters and create a benchmark accuracy score using a standard machine learning algorithm. It is quick, easy, and will give us confidence that our deep learning model is working better than just using *normal* machine learning. Here are the 20 lines of code to do collaborative filtering in R. This code can be found in Chapter8/ml_recommend.R:

```
library(readr)
library(recommenderlab)
library(reshape2)

set.seed(42)
in_file <- "../dunnhumby/recommend.csv"
df <- read_csv(in_file)
dfPivot <-dcast(df, cust_id ~ prod_id)
m <- as.matrix(dfPivot[,2:ncol(dfPivot)])

recommend <- as(m,"realRatingMatrix")
e <- evaluationScheme(recommend,method="split",
 train=0.9,given=-1, goodRating=5)
e
Evaluation scheme using all-but-1 items
Method: 'split' with 1 run(s).
Training set proportion: 0.900
Good ratings: >=5.000000
Data set: 5000 x 9 rating matrix of class 'realRatingMatrix' with 25688
```

```
ratings.

r1 <- Recommender(getData(e,"train"),"UBCF")
r1
Recommender of type 'UBCF' for 'realRatingMatrix'
learned using 4500 users.

p1 <- predict(r1,getData(e,"known"),type="ratings")
err1<-calcPredictionAccuracy(p1,getData(e,"unknown"))
print(sprintf(" User based collaborative filtering model MSE =
%1.4f",err1[2]))
[1] " User based collaborative filtering model MSE = 0.9748"
```

This code creates a collaborative filtering model, and the MSE for the model is 0.9748. As before, we do this because most of the work for this sample is in data preparation and not model building, so it is relatively easy to use a base machine learning algorithm to compare the performance against a deep learning model. The code here uses standard R libraries to create a recommendation system, and as you can see, it is relatively simple because the data is already in the expected format. If you want more information on this collaborative filtering algorithm, then search for user based collaborative filtering in r, or go through the doc pages.

Now lets focus on creating a deep learning model.

Building a deep learning collaborative filtering model

Here, we will see if we can build a deep learning model to beat the previous approach! The following code is in Chapter9/keras_recommend.R. The first part loads the dataset and creates new IDs for the customer and product codes. This is because Keras expects the indexes to be sequential, starting at zero, and unique:

```
library(readr)
library(keras)

set.seed(42)
use_session_with_seed(42, disable_gpu = FALSE, disable_parallel_cpu =
FALSE)

df<-read_csv("recommend.csv")
custs <- as.data.frame(unique(df$cust_id))
custs$cust_id2 <- as.numeric(row.names(custs))
colnames(custs) <- c("cust_id","cust_id2")
custs$cust_id2 <- custs$cust_id2 - 1
```

```
prods <- as.data.frame(unique(df$prod_id))
prods$prod_id2 <- as.numeric(row.names(prods))
colnames(prods) <- c("prod_id","prod_id2")
prods$prod_id2 <- prods$prod_id2 - 1
df<-merge(df,custs)
df<-merge(df,prods)
n_custs = length(unique(df$cust_id2))
n_prods = length(unique(df$prod_id2))

# shuffle the data
trainData <- df[sample(nrow(df)),]
```

We have 5,000 unique customers and 9 unique product codes. This is not typical of most collaborative filtering examples; usually, the number of products is much higher than the number of customers. The next part creates the model. We will create embedding layers for the customer and the products and then calculate the dot product of those embedding layers. An embedding layer is a lower-order representation of the data and is exactly the same as the encoders in the auto-encoder examples we saw earlier. We will also have a bias term for each customer and product – this performs a sort of normalization on the data. If a particular product is very popular, or a customer has a lot of high ratings, this accounts for this. We will use 10 factors in our embedding layer for both customers and products. We will use some L2 regularization in our embeddings to prevent overfitting. The following code defines the model architecture:

```
n_factors<-10
# define the model
cust_in <- layer_input(shape = 1)
cust_embed <- layer_embedding(
 input_dim = n_custs
 ,output_dim = n_factors
 ,input_length = 1
 ,embeddings_regularizer=regularizer_l2(0.0001)
 ,name = "cust_embed"
 )(cust_in)
prod_in <- layer_input(shape = 1)
prod_embed <- layer_embedding(
 input_dim = n_prods
 ,output_dim = n_factors
 ,input_length = 1
 ,embeddings_regularizer=regularizer_l2(0.0001)
 ,name = "prod_embed"
 )(prod_in)

ub = layer_embedding(
 input_dim = n_custs,
 output_dim = 1,
```

```
 input_length = 1,
 name = "custb_embed"
 )(cust_in)
ub_flat <- layer_flatten()(ub)

mb = layer_embedding(
 input_dim = n_prods,
 output_dim = 1,
 input_length = 1,
 name = "prodb_embed"
 )(prod_in)
mb_flat <- layer_flatten()(mb)

cust_flat <- layer_flatten()(cust_embed)
prod_flat <- layer_flatten()(prod_embed)

x <- layer_dot(list(cust_flat, prod_flat), axes = 1)
x <- layer_add(list(x, ub_flat))
x <- layer_add(list(x, mb_flat))
```

Now, we are ready to build the model. We are going to hold out 10% of our data for validation:

```
model <- keras_model(list(cust_in, prod_in), x)
compile(model,optimizer="adam", loss='mse')

model.optimizer.lr=0.001
fit(model,list(trainData$cust_id2,trainData$prod_id2),trainData$rating,
 batch_size=128,epochs=40,validation_split = 0.1 )
Train on 23119 samples, validate on 2569 samples
Epoch 1/40
23119/23119 [==============================] - 1s 31us/step - loss: 10.3551
- val_loss: 9.9817
Epoch 2/40
23119/23119 [==============================] - 0s 21us/step - loss: 8.6549
- val_loss: 7.7826
Epoch 3/40
23119/23119 [==============================] - 0s 20us/step - loss: 6.0651
- val_loss: 5.2164
...
...
...
Epoch 37/40
23119/23119 [==============================] - 0s 19us/step - loss: 0.6674
- val_loss: 0.9575
Epoch 38/40
23119/23119 [==============================] - 0s 18us/step - loss: 0.6486
- val_loss: 0.9555
```

```
Epoch 39/40
23119/23119 [==============================] - 0s 19us/step - loss: 0.6271
- val_loss: 0.9547
Epoch 40/40
23119/23119 [==============================] - 0s 20us/step - loss: 0.6023
- val_loss: 0.9508
```

Our model achieved an MSE of `0.9508`, which is an improvement on the MSE of `0.9748` that we got on our machine learning model. Our deep learning model is overfitting, but one reason for this is because we have a relatively small database. I tried increasing the regularization, but this did not improve the model.

Applying the deep learning model to a business problem

Now that we have a model, how can we use it? The most typical example of using a collaborative filtering model is to recommend items to people they have not rated yet. That concept works well in domains such as music and movie recommendations where collaborative filtering models are often applied. However, we are going to use it for a different purpose. One concern of marketing managers is the **Share of wallet** they get from a customer. The definition of this (from `https://en.wikipedia.org/wiki/Share_of_wallet`) is the *percentage ('share') of a customer's expenses ('of wallet') for a product that goes to the firm selling the product.* It basically measures the value of a customer on the percentage of the potential spend they could have with us. As an example, we may have customers who visit our shop regularly and spend a considerable amount. But are they buying all of their goods from us? Maybe they buy their fresh food elsewhere, that is, they purchase their meat, fruit, vegetables, and so on, at other stores. We can use collaborative filtering to find customers where the collaborative filtering model predicts that they purchase certain products in our store, but in fact they do not. Remember that collaborative filtering works on the basis of making recommendations based on what other similar customers do. So, if customer A does not purchase meat, fruit, vegetables, and so on, at our store when other similar customers do, then we could try and entice them to spend more at our stores by sending them offers for these products.

We will look for customer-product department codes where the prediction is greater than 4, but the actual value is less than 2. These customers should be purchasing these goods from us (according to the model), so by sending them vouchers for items in these departments, we can capture a greater amount of their spending.

A collaborative filtering model should work well for this type of analysis. The basis of this algorithm is to find the recommend products based on the activity of similar customers, so it already adjusts for the scale of spend. For example, if the prediction for a customer is that their spend on fresh fruit and vegetables should be 5, that is based on the comparison with other similar customers. Here is the evaluation code, which is also in `Chapter8/kerarecommend.R`. The first part of the code generates the predictions and links it back. We output a few metrics, which look impressive, but note that they are run on all the data, including the data that the model was trained on, so these metrics are overly optimistic. We make one adjustment to the predictions – some of these values are greater than 5 or less than 1, so we change them back to valid values. This produces a very small improvement on our metrics:

```
##### model use-case, find products that customers 'should' be purchasing
######
df$preds<-predict(model,list(df$cust_id2,df$prod_id2))
# remove index variables, do not need them anymore
df$cust_id2 <- NULL
df$prod_id2 <- NULL
mse<-mean((df$rating-df$preds)^2)
rmse<-sqrt(mse)
mae<-mean(abs(df$rating-df$preds))
print (sprintf("DL Collaborative filtering model: MSE=%1.3f, RMSE=%1.3f,
MAE=%1.3f",mse,rmse,mae))
[1] "DL Collaborative filtering model: MSE=0.478, RMSE=0.691, MAE=0.501"

df <- df[order(-df$preds),]
head(df)
      prod_id         cust_id rating       preds
10017 D00003 CUST0000283274      5    5.519783
4490  D00002 CUST0000283274      5    5.476133
9060  D00002 CUST0000084449      5    5.452055
6536  D00002 CUST0000848462      5    5.447111
10294 D00003 CUST0000578851      5    5.446453
7318  D00002 CUST0000578851      5    5.442836

df[df$preds>5,]$preds <- 5
df[df$preds<1,]$preds <- 1
mse<-mean((df$rating-df$preds)^2)
rmse<-sqrt(mse)
mae<-mean(abs(df$rating-df$preds))
print (sprintf("DL Collaborative filtering model (adjusted): MSE=%1.3f,
RMSE=%1.3f, MAE=%1.3f",mse,rmse,mae))
[1] "DL Collaborative filtering model (adjusted): MSE=0.476, RMSE=0.690,
MAE=0.493"
```

Now, we can look at the customer-product department codes that have the biggest difference between predicted ratings and actual ratings:

```
df$diff <- df$preds - df$rating
df <- df[order(-df$diff),]
head(df,20)
        prod_id        cust_id rating      preds      diff
3259   D00001 CUST0000375633      1 5.000000 4.000000
12325  D00003 CUST0000038166      1 4.306837 3.306837
14859  D00004 CUST0000817991      1 4.025836 3.025836
15279  D00004 CUST0000620867      1 4.016025 3.016025
22039  D00008 CUST0000588390      1 3.989520 2.989520
3370   D00001 CUST0000530875      1 3.969685 2.969685
22470  D00008 CUST0000209037      1 3.927513 2.927513
22777  D00008 CUST0000873432      1 3.905162 2.905162
13905  D00004 CUST0000456347      1 3.877517 2.877517
18123  D00005 CUST0000026547      1 3.853488 2.853488
24208  D00008 CUST0000732836      1 3.810606 2.810606
22723  D00008 CUST0000872856      1 3.746022 2.746022
22696  D00008 CUST0000549120      1 3.718482 2.718482
15463  D00004 CUST0000035935      1 3.714494 2.714494
24090  D00008 CUST0000643072      1 3.679629 2.679629
21167  D00006 CUST0000454947      1 3.651651 2.651651
23769  D00008 CUST0000314496      1 3.649187 2.649187
14294  D00004 CUST0000127124      1 3.625893 2.625893
22534  D00008 CUST0000556279      1 3.578591 2.578591
22201  D00008 CUST0000453430      1 3.576008 2.576008
```

This gives us a list of customers and the products we should send them offers for. For example, for the second row, the actual rating is 1 and the predicted rating is 4.306837. This customer is not purchasing the items for this product code and our model *predicts* he should be purchasing these items.

We can also look at cases where the actual rating is much higher than the predicted value. These are customers who are over-spending in that department compared to other similar customers:

```
df <- df[order(df$diff),]
head(df,20)
        prod_id        cust_id rating      preds      diff
21307  D00006 CUST0000555858      5 1.318784 -3.681216
15353  D00004 CUST0000640069      5 1.324661 -3.675339
21114  D00006 CUST0000397007      5 1.729860 -3.270140
23097  D00008 CUST0000388652      5 1.771072 -3.228928
21551  D00006 CUST0000084985      5 1.804969 -3.195031
21649  D00007 CUST0000083736      5 1.979534 -3.020466
23231  D00008 CUST0000917696      5 2.036216 -2.963784
```

```
21606  D00007  CUST0000899988     5  2.050258  -2.949742
21134  D00006  CUST0000373894     5  2.071380  -2.928620
14224  D00004  CUST0000541731     5  2.081161  -2.918839
15191  D00004  CUST0000106540     5  2.162569  -2.837431
13976  D00004  CUST0000952727     5  2.174777  -2.825223
21851  D00008  CUST0000077294     5  2.202812  -2.797188
16545  D00004  CUST0000945695     5  2.209504  -2.790496
23941  D00008  CUST0000109728     5  2.224301  -2.775699
24031  D00008  CUST0000701483     5  2.239778  -2.760222
21300  D00006  CUST0000752292     5  2.240073  -2.759927
21467  D00006  CUST0000754753     5  2.240705  -2.759295
15821  D00004  CUST0000006239     5  2.264089  -2.735911
15534  D00004  CUST0000586590     5  2.272885  -2.727115
```

What can we do with these recommendations? Our model assigns a score of 1-5 based on a customers' spend in each product department, so if a customer has a high actual rating compared to the predicted value in general, they are over-spending in these departments compared to similar customers. These people are probably not spending in other departments, so they should be targeted as part of a cross-sell campaign; that is, they should be sent offers for products in other departments to tempt them to purchase there.

Summary

I hope that this chapter has shown you that deep learning is not just about computer vision and NLP problems! In this chapter, we covered using Keras to build auto-encoders and recommendation systems. We saw that auto-encoders can be used as a form of dimensionality reduction and, in their simplest forms with only one layer, they are similar to PCA. We used an auto-encoder model to create an anomaly detection system. If the reconstruction error in the auto-encoder model was over a threshold, then we marked that instance as a potential anomaly. Our second major example in this chapter built a recommendation system using Keras. We constructed a dataset of implicit ratings from transactional data and built a recommendation system. We demonstrated the practical application of this model by showing you how it could be used for cross-sell purposes.

In the next chapter, we will look at various options for training your deep learning model in the cloud. If you do not have a GPU on your local machine, cloud providers such as AWS, Azure, Google Cloud, and Paperspace allow you to access GPU instances cheaply. We will cover all of these options in the next chapter.

Running Deep Learning Models in the Cloud

10

Up till now, we have only briefly discussed the hardware requirements for training deep learning models, as almost all of the examples in this book run on any modern computer. While you do not need a **GPU (Graphical Processing Unit)** based computer to run the examples in this book, there is no getting away from the fact that training complicated deep learning models requires a computer with a GPU. Even if you have a suitable GPU on your machine, installing the necessary software to train deep learning models using GPUs is not a trivial task. This section will briefly discuss how to install the necessary software to run deep learning models on GPUs and also discusses the advantages and disadvantages of using cloud computing for deep learning. We will use various cloud providers to create virtual instances or access services that will allow us to train deep learning models in the cloud.

This chapter covers the following topics:

- Setting up a local computer for deep learning
- Using Amazon Web Services (AWS) for deep learning
- Using Azure for deep learning
- Using Google Cloud for deep learning
- Using Paperspace for deep learning

Setting up a local computer for deep learning

At the time of writing this book, it is possible to purchase a computer with a GPU card suitable for deep learning for under $1,000. The current on-demand cost of the cheapest GPU computer on AWS is $0.90 per hour, which is equivalent to using the machine constantly for 46 days. So, if you are just starting with deep learning, cloud resources are the cheapest way to begin. Once you have learned the basics, then you may decide to get a GPU-based computer, but even then you may continue using cloud resources for deep learning. You have much more flexibility in the cloud. For example, in AWS, you can get a p3.16xlarge machine with 8 Tesla V100 GPU cards for an on-demand price of $24.48 per hour. An equivalent box is the DGX-1 from NVIDIA (`https://www.nvidia.com/en-us/data-center/dgx-1/`), which has 8 Tesla V100 GPU cards and costs $149,000!

If you are considering using your own computer for deep learning, then one of the following applies to you:

- You already have a computer that you can use with a suitable GPU processor
- You will buy a computer to build deep learning models
- You will build a computer to build deep learning models

If you want to use your local computer for deep learning, you need a suitable GPU card, which must be from NVIDIA. The best way to check this is to go to the NVIDIA site and check if your graphics card is compatible with CUDA. CUDA is an application programming interface (API) that allows programs to use GPU for computing. You need to install CUDA to be able to use the GPU for deep learning. The current link to check if your graphics card is compatible with CUDA is `https://developer.nvidia.com/cuda-gpus`.

While some companies sell machines that are designed specifically for deep learning, they are very expensive. I would not advise getting one of them if you are just beginning to, learn deep learning. Instead, I would recommend looking at buying a computer that is for high-end computer games. This computer should have an appropriate GPU card for deep learning. Again, check that the card is compatible with CUDA (`https://developer.nvidia.com/cuda-gpus`) first.

A gaming computer for deep learning? It is not as strange as it seems. GPUs were developed to play high-end games on computers, not for deep learning. But a machine that is designed for games is likely to have a higher than usual specification, for example, an SSD drive, lots of (fast) RAM, and most importantly a GPU card. Early deep learning practitioners realized that the matrix operations involved in calculating 3D spaces were very similar to the matrix operations used in neural networks. NVIDIA released CUDA as an API so that other applications could use the GPU as a co-processor. Whether it was luck or foresight, NVIDIA became the de facto standard for GPU cards for deep learning and has seen its share price grow by 10 times in the past 3 years, largely because of the huge demand for GPU cards for artificial intelligence.

The third option is to build your own deep learning computer. If you are considering this option, then other than the GPU card, memory, and an SSD drive, you will also need to consider the power supply and the motherboard. You may need a bigger capacity power supply than what is in a standard computer because of the GPU card and fans. For the motherboard, you need to consider if the hardware interface between the motherboard and the GPU card may limit the data transfer – these are PCIe lanes. A GPU can use 16 PCIe lanes at full capacity. For expansion purposes, you may want a motherboard that supports 40 PCIe lanes so that you can support two GPU cards and an SSD drive simultaneously.

Before we move on to the rest of this chapter which discusses using cloud computing for deep learning, we should briefly discuss the performance of GPU cards in the cloud against what was used for this book. For this book, I used a GTX 1050 Ti which has 768 cores and 4 GB RAM. In my experience, the performance of this card is about the same as a **p2.xlarge** instance on AWS. I checked this by running two models on a local CPU (i5 processor), local GPU (GTX 1050 Ti), and AWS GPU (**p2.xlarge**). I ran the test on two models: the binary prediction task from Chapter 4, *Training Deep Prediction Models*, and the LeNet convolutional neural network from Chapter 5, *Image Classification Using Convolutional Neural Networks*. Both of these models were built using MXNet, and ran for 50 epochs:

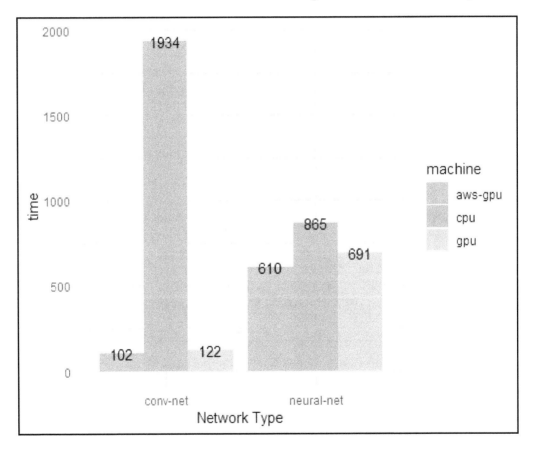

Figure 10.1: Execution time in seconds for two deep learning networks on CPU, local GPU, and AWS GPU

On my local machine, running the deep learning model for the binary prediction task on the GPU is about 20% faster than running on the CPU, and the AWS GPU machine is approximately 13% faster than the local GPU. However, there is a much bigger difference when running convolutional neural networks, training it on the local CPU is almost 16 times slower than training it on the local GPU. In turn, the AWS GPU is approximately 16% faster than the local GPU. These results are expected and mirror what I have seen in practice and other benchmarks on the web and show conclusively that for deep learning computer vision tasks, a GPU is a necessity. The GPU card on my local machine (GTX 1050 Ti) is probably the lowest specification GPU card you should use for deep learning. It currently costs under $200. As a comparison, a high-end GPU card (GTX 1080 Ti) has 3,584 cores and 11 GB of RAM, and currently costs approx $700. The GTX 1080 Ti is approximately 4-5 times faster than the GTX 1050 Ti.

Why does the previous graph just look at AWS and not Azure, Google Cloud, and Paperspace? Why did I not benchmark all of them on performance and/or cost? I decided not to do so for a few reasons. Firstly, and most importantly, any recommendation would have been out of date after a few months—deep learning is very popular and the various cloud providers are changing their offerings and prices constantly. Another reason is that the examples in this book are relatively small and we are using the cheapest GPU instances. Therefore, any comparisons to production use cases would be misleading. Finally, when you are starting out, ease of use is probably more important than raw cost. All the examples in this book should run in under 1 hour in the cloud regardless of which provider you use, so arguing that one provider costs $0.55/hour and another costs $0.45/hour is not important.

How do I know if my model is training on a GPU?

One question that many people starting in deep learning ask is, *how do I know if my model is training on a GPU?* Fortunately, whether you are using a cloud instance or your local machine, you can check if the deep learning model is being trained on the GPU or the CPU. There is a utility on the instance that shows the GPU's activity. In Linux, you can type in the following command:

```
watch -n0.5 nvidia-smi
```

In Windows, you can use the following command from a command prompt:

```
nvidia-smi -l 1
```

This will run a script that outputs diagnostic messages about the GPU on the computer. If your model is currently training on the GPU, the GPU utility will be high. In the following example, we can see that it is 75-78%. We can also see that the file called `rsession.exe` is using GPU memory. This confirms that the model is being trained on the GPU:

Figure 10.2: nvidia-smi utility showing that the GPU card is at 75-85% utilization

Using AWS for deep learning

AWS is the biggest cloud provider, and so it deserves our attention. If you know how to use AWS and especially if you are familiar with spot requests, it can be a very cost-effective method to train complex deep learning models.

A brief introduction to AWS

This section gives you a brief introduction to how AWS works. It describes EC2, AMIs, and how to create a virtual machine in the cloud. This will not be an exhaustive introduction to AWS – there are plenty of tutorials online that will guide you.

AWS is a suite of cloud resources. Another term for it is **Infrastructure as a Service** (**IaaS**), as opposed to **Software as a Service** (**SaaS**) or **Platform as a Service** (**PaaS**). In IaaS, as opposed to SaaS or PaaS, you are supplied with infrastructure (hardware), and it is up to you to use it as you wish. This includes installing software and managing security and networking, although AWS take care of some aspects of security and networking. AWS has many services, but for deep learning, the one you will use is EC2, which is a virtual computing environment so that you can launch instances (virtual computers). You can control these virtual computers either through web interfaces or by remote logging into them to run commands from the shell. When you launch an EC2 instance, you can select the operating system (Ubuntu, Linux, Windows, and so on) and the type of machine you want.

You can also select to use an **Amazon Machine Image** (**AMI**), which has software applications and libraries pre-installed on it. This is a good choice for deep learning as it means that you can start an EC2 instance with the deep learning libraries already installed and jump straight into deep learning.

One other service you should be familiar with is S3, which is a form of persistent storage. A very useful practice that I suggest you to adopt is to consider your virtual machines as temporary resources and to keep your data and interim results in S3. We will not discuss this in this chapter because it is an advanced topic.

In the previous section, we stated that the current on-demand cost of the cheapest GPU computer on AWS is $0.90 per hour. *On-demand* is one way to use a virtual machine in AWS, but there are three different ways to rent a virtual machine in AWS:

- **On-demand instances**: When you rent an instance as needed.
- **Reserved instances**: When you commit to renting the machine for a certain period of time (usually 1-3 years). This is about 50% cheaper than on-demand instances. However you are committed to paying for the resource for the period of time.
- **Spot instances**: In order to deal with fluctuating demand, Amazon has spare computing capacity most of the time. You can bid for this unused capacity and, depending on the demand for that type of machine, you can usually get it cheaper than on-demand and reserved instances. However, once you have the machine, it is not guaranteed that you will keep it as long as you need – if the demand for the computer goes up, your computer may be terminated.

Reserve instances are not useful for deep learning. The cost of renting the cheapest GPU machine for 1 year would be over $5,000, and you can buy a deep learning machine with better performance for much less. On-demand instances guarantee that you will have the resource as long as needed, but are expensive. Spot instances are an interesting and cost-effective method to use if you know how to use them correctly and plan for the chance that your computer will be terminated.

Typically, the spot price is about 30% of the on-demand price, so the savings are significant. Your bid is the maximum amount that you are willing to pay for the spot instances, the actual price depends on the market price, which is based on the demand.

Therefore, you should set your bid price higher; I recommend to set it at either 51%, 76%, or 101% of the on-demand price. The extra 1% from 50%, 75%, and 100% is because, similar to any bidding market, humans anchor their bids to round numbers, so by avoiding this with an extra 1%, it can make a difference.

The original use case for spot instances was for low-priority batch jobs. Companies used spot instances to the avail of themselves cheaper computing resources for long-running jobs that could be restarted in the event that they did not finish. An example might be running a secondary data ingestion process on data that was not critical to operations. However, the demand pattern for GPU based instances is different, possibly because of online data mining competitions such as Kaggle. Because GPU instances are not very common, demand spikes much more for GPU instances. This has led to some strange behavior in spot pricing, where the price that people bid for a spot instance can be 10x that of the on-demand price. People do this because they believe that this makes it unlikely that they will be outbid. There are cases where a p2.16xlarge has had a spot price of $144 per hour while the on-demand price is $14.40. The people who set these bids do not want their machines to be terminated and believe that they will still pay less on average for spot instances than on-demand instances. This is not something I would encourage if you use spot instances as you can get a very nasty surprise if demand goes up! However, you should be aware of this pricing quirk – do not think that setting the bid price to just above the on-demand price guarantees that your machine will not be terminated.

AWS provides you help in setting up your spot request bid by providing pricing history charts that advise you on the on-demand price and the bid prices. In the following screenshot, we can see how the price has changed over the past 3 months for a particular region (us-east). There are 6 availability zones (us-east-1a to us-east-1f) and the current spot price of this instance type (**p2.16xlarge**) varies from $4.32-$14.40, while the on-demand price is $14.40:

Figure 10.3: Pricing history for spot bids for p2.16xlarge instance type

Looking at the preceding graph for this resource, I would consider the following:

- I would use the availability zone **us-east-1a** if possible, as it has the lowest price volatility.
- I would set the price to $7.21 per hour, which is just over 50% of the on-demand price. I would probably only pay $4.32 per hour as it has been 1 month since the bid price in us-east-1a has gone over $4.32 per hour. Setting it at the higher price would make it less likely that my spot instance would be terminated.

Regions and availability zones: AWS arranges its services in regions (**us-east1**, **eu-west1**, and so on). Currently, there are 18 different regions and in each region, there are multiple availability zones, which you can consider as physical data centers. For some use cases (for example, websites, disaster recovery, and so on) and regulatory requirements, regions and availability zones are important. For deep learning, they are not so important, as you can usually run your deep learning models at any location. The bid price for spot instances is different for regions/availability zones, and some resources are more expensive in some regions. You also need to be aware that there is a cost in transferring data between regions, so keep your data and instances in the same region.

Creating a deep learning GPU instance in AWS

This section will use AWS to train a deep learning model from Chapter 9, *Anomaly Detection and Recommendation Systems*. This will include setting up the machine, accessing the machine, downloading the data, and running the model. We are going to use a pre-built AWS AMI from RStudio that has TensorFlow and Keras already installed. For details on this AMI, go to this link: https://aws.amazon.com/marketplace/pp/B0785SXYB2. You will need to sign up for an AWS account if you do not already have one at https://portal.aws.amazon.com/billing/signup. Once you have signed up, follow these steps to create a virtual machine that has a GPU on AWS:

Note that when you set up an instance in AWS, you will be billed for as long as it is running! Always ensure that you shut down your instances, otherwise you will continue to be charged. Check the AWS console to ensure you have no running instances when you are finished using the virtual instance.

1. Log in to the AWS console and select EC2. You should see a screen similar to the following. This is the web interface for creating new virtual machines:

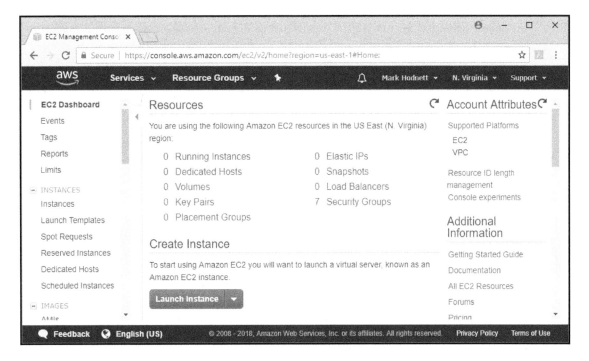

Figure 10.4: AWS EC2 dashboard

2. Click on the launch instance button and the following page will load.
3. Click **AWS Marketplace** on the left and in the search box type `rstudio` (see the following screenshot).
4. Select **RStudio Server with Tensorflow-GPU for AWS**. Be aware that there is another option with the word **Pro** – this is a paid subscription with additional costs, so do not select this AMI:

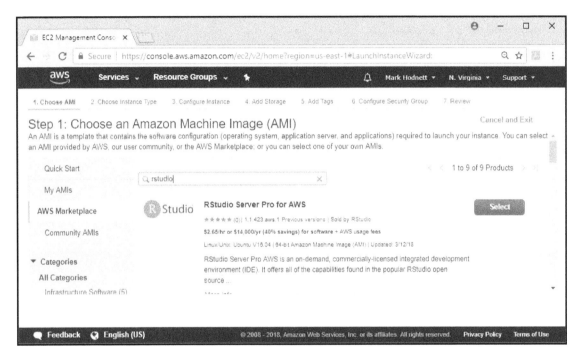

Figure 10.5: AWS launch instance wizard, Step 1

5. Once you click **Select**, the following screen may appear with some additional information on accessing the instance. Read the instructions carefully, as they may have changed from what's shown in the screenshot that follows:

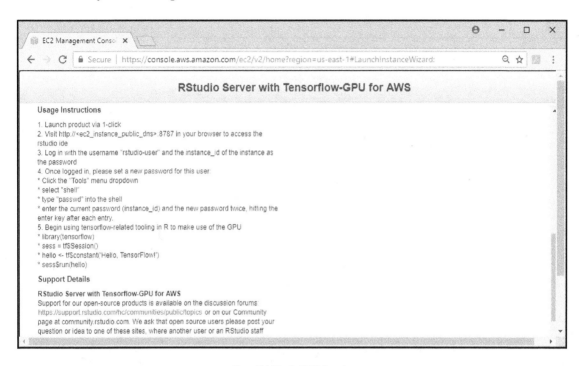

Figure 10.6: RStudio AMI information

6. When you click **Continue**, the following screen will appear for the machine type. It is vital to select a machine that has a GPU, so from the **Filter by:** option, select GPU compute and then select **p2.xlarge** from the list. Your options should look similar to the following screenshot:

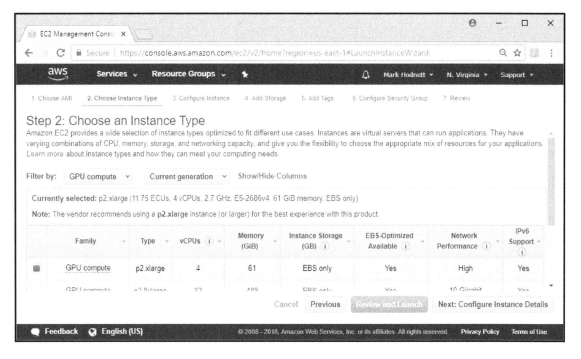

Figure 10.7: AWS launch instance wizard, Step 2

7. When you click **Next**, you will get to the following screen with various configuration options. The default options are OK, so just press **Next** again:

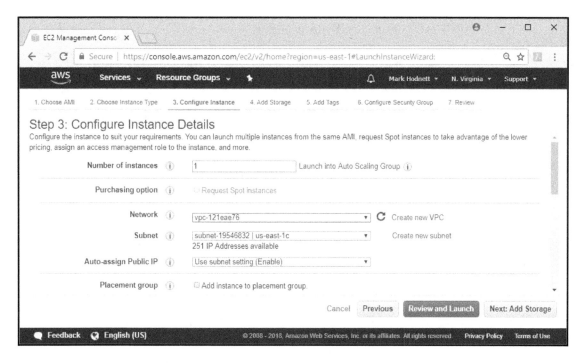

Figure 10.8: AWS launch instance wizard, Step 3

8. This screen allows you to change the storage options. You may need to add additional storage depending on the size of the data. Storage is relatively cheap, so I recommend going with 3x-5x the size of the input data.

9. Click **Next** to go to the following screenshot:

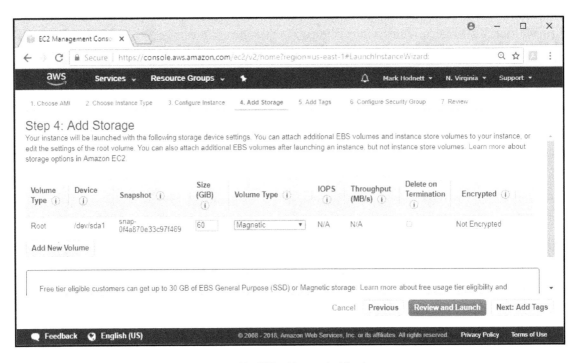

Figure 10.9: AWS launch instance wizard, Step 4

10. The following screen is not important – tags are used to keep track of resources in AWS, but we do not need them. Click Next to go to the following screenshot:

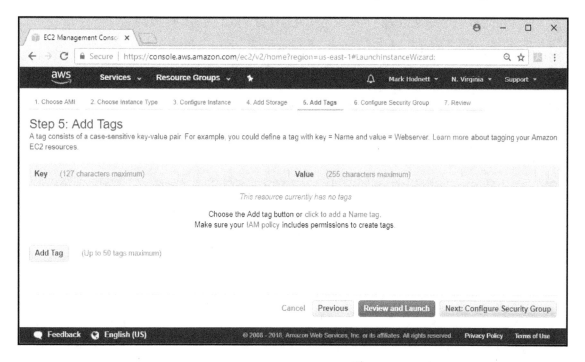

Figure 10.10: AWS launch instance wizard, step 5

11. The following screenshot shows security options. AWS restricts access to instances, so you must open any needed ports. The defaults provided here allow access to port 22 (SSH) to access the shell and also for port 8787, which is the web port that RStudio uses. Click **Review and Launch** to continue:

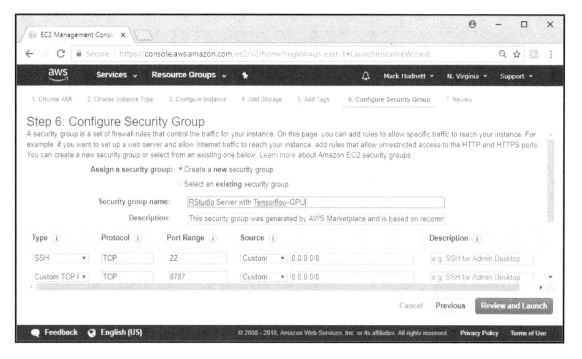

Figure 10.11: AWS launch instance wizard, Step 6

The following screenshot will appear. Note the warning messages regarding security – in a production environment, you would probably want to address these.

12. Click the **Launch** button to continue:

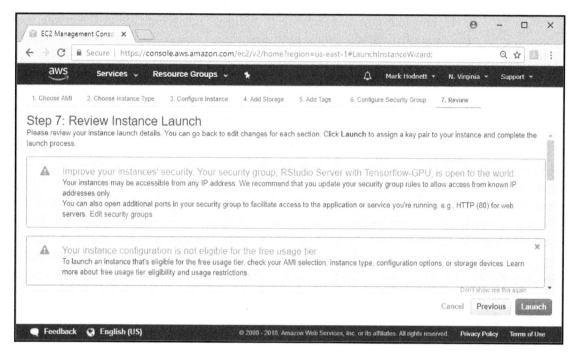

Figure 10.12: AWS launch instance wizard, Step 7

13. You will be asked for a key pair. If you have not already created a key pair, then select the option to do so. Give it a descriptive name and press the **Download Key Pair** button. Then, click on **Launch Instances**:

A key pair is used to access the instance using SSH. You should guard this very carefully, as if someone manages to get your private key, then they will be able to log in to any of your instances. You should delete your key pair occasionally and create a new one.

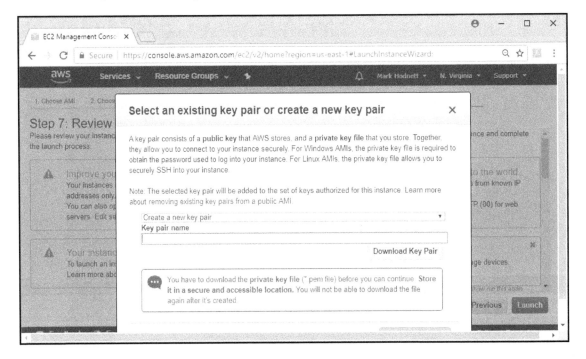

Figure 10.13: AWS launch instance wizard, select key pair

14. Once you have completed this, you can go back to the EC2 dashboard and you will see that you have **1 Running Instances**. Click on that link to move on to the details of the instance:

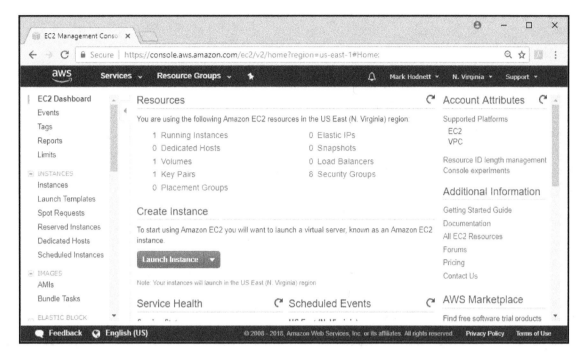

Figure 10.14: AWS EC2 dashboard

15. Here, you will see the details of the instance. In this case, the IP address is
`34.227.109.123`. Also note down the instance ID that is highlighted, as this is
the password that is used to connect to the RStudio instance:

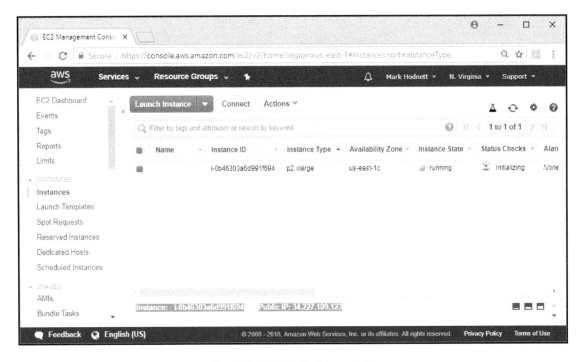

Figure 10.15: AWS EC2 dashboard, instance details

16. Open another web page and browse to the IP address of your machine and add
`:8787` to access the link. In my example, the link is
`http://34.227.109.123:8787/`. Instructions for logging in are in *Figure 10.6*,
that is, use rstudio-user as the username and the instance ID as the password.
You should also consider changing the password as per the instructions.

17. When you log in, you will see a familiar interface – it is similar to the RStudio desktop program. One difference you have is the **Upload** button on the bottom-right pane, which allows you to upload files. In the following example, I have uploaded the data and the script from `Chapter 9`, *Anomaly Detection and Recommendation Systems*, for the Keras recommender example and ran it successfully:

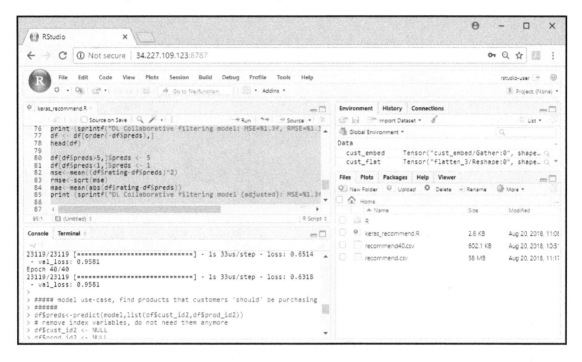

Figure 10.16: Accessing deep learning instance in the cloud using RStudio Server

The web interface in RStudio is similar to using RStudio on your local computer. In *Figure 10.16*, you can see data files that I have uploaded (`recomend.csv`, `recomend40.csv`) and the R script in the **Files** in the bottom-left window. We can also see the code that was executed in the Console window in the bottom-left.

This finishes our example on how to set up a deep learning machine in AWS. Again, remember that you will be billed for as long as the computer is running. Ensure that your instances are terminated, otherwise you will continue to be charged. To do so, go back to the EC2 dashboard, find the instance, and click on the **Actions** button. A pop-up menu will appear, where you can select **Instance State** and then select **Terminate**:

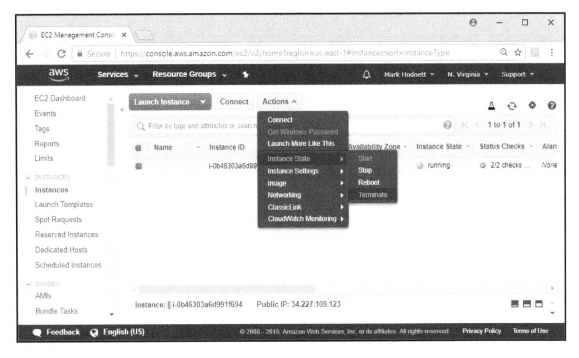

Figure 10.17: Terminating the AWS instance

Creating a deep learning AMI in AWS

In the previous example, we used an **Amazon Machine Image** (**AMI**) that was built by RStudio. In AWS, you can also create your own AMI's. When you create an AMI, you can install the software you want, load data onto it, and set it up as you wish. This section will show you how to use an AMI to use MXNet on AWS.

1. The first step in creating an AMI is to select the base image that you are going to use. We could start with a base image that just has the operating system installed, but instead we are going to use the **RStudio Server with Tensorflow-GPU for AWS** that we used previously and add the MXNet package to it.

2. The instructions to install MXNet were adapted from `https://mxnet.incubator.apache.org/install/index.html`. The first step is to create the instance from the **RStudio Server with Tensorflow-GPU for AWS** AMI as per the previous section.

3. Once you have done this, you need to SSH into the machine. How you do this depends on the operating system on your own computer. For Linux and macOS, you can execute a local command on the shell, and in Windows you can use Putty.

4. Once you have logged in to the machine, run the following command:

```
vi ~/.profile
```

5. Add the following line to the end of this file and save the file:

```
export CUDA_HOME=/usr/local/cuda
```

6. Once you are back at the shell, run the following lines one by one:

```
sudo apt-get update
sudo dpkg --configure -a
sudo apt-get install -y build-essential git
export CUDA_HOME=/usr/local/cuda
git clone --recursive https://github.com/apache/incubator-mxnet
cd incubator-mxnet
make -j $(nproc) USE_OPENCV=1 USE_CUDA=1
USE_CUDA_PATH=/usr/local/cuda USE_CUDNN=1
```

7. The last command could take up to 2 hours to complete. Once it is done, run the last few lines:

```
sudo ldconfig /usr/local/cuda/lib64
sudo make rpkg
sudo R CMD INSTALL mxnet_current_r.tar.gz
```

The second line may take up to 30 minutes. The final line may return a warning about a missing file, which can be ignored.

8. To test if everything installed correctly, go to the RStudio page for the instance and type in the following code:

```
library(mxnet)
a <- mx.nd.ones(c(2,3), ctx = mx.gpu())
b <- a * 2 + 1
b
```

9. You should get the following output:

```
     [,1] [,2] [,3]
[1,]    3    3    3
[2,]    3    3    3
```

10. Now go back to the EC2 dashboard, click on **Running Instances**, and select the machine in the list. Click on the **Action** button, select **Image** from the drop-down menu, and select **Create Image**. This is shown in the following screenshot:

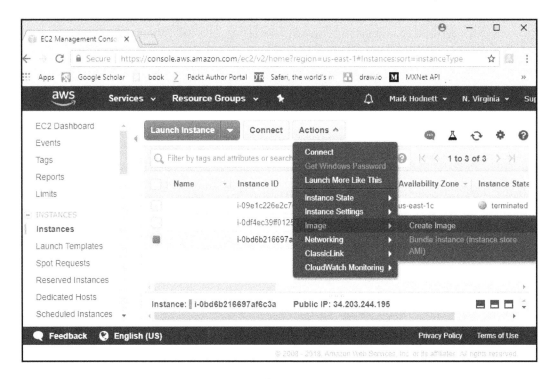

Figure 10.18: Creating an AMI

11. The image may take 15-20 minutes to complete. When it is done, click on AMIs on the left menu selection to show the list of AMIs associated with your account. You should see the AMI you just created. This AMI can then be used to create a new on-demand instance or a new spot instance. The following screenshot shows the menu option to create a spot instance for the AMI:

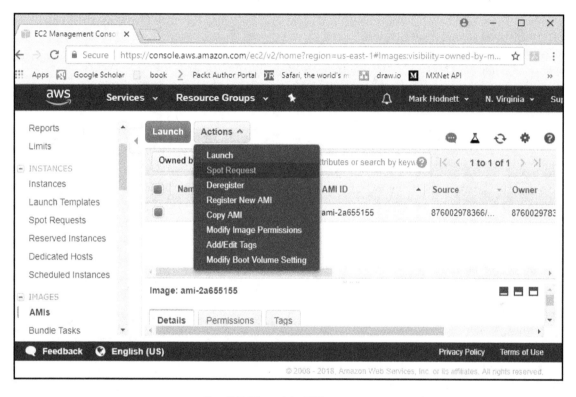

Figure 10.19: Using an existing AMI for a spot request

This AMI is now available so that you can create new deep learning instances. You should be aware that there is an ongoing cost in storing the AMI, even if you do not use it.

Using Azure for deep learning

Azure is the brand name for Microsoft's cloud services. You can use Azure for deep learning and, similar to AWS, it provides deep learning virtual machines that is pre-configured with deep learning libraries installed. In this example, we are going to create a Windows instance that can be used for Keras or MXNet. This assumes that your local computer is also a Windows computer, as you will be using **Remote Desktop Protocol (RDP)** to access the cloud instance.

1. The first step is to create an account in Azure and then log in to Azure at `https://portal.azure.com`. You will see a screenshot similar to the following. Click **Create a resource** and search for **Deep Learning Virtual Machine**:

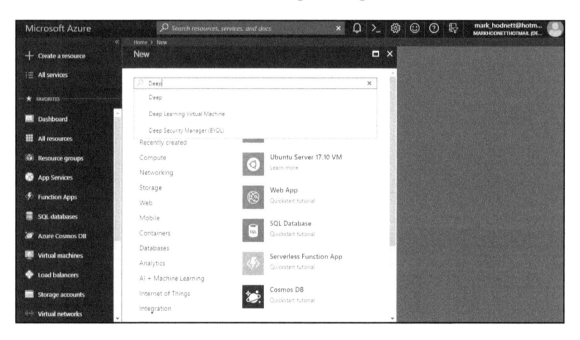

Figure 10.20: Azure portal website

2. When you select **Deep Learning Virtual Machine**, the following screen will appear. Click **Create**:

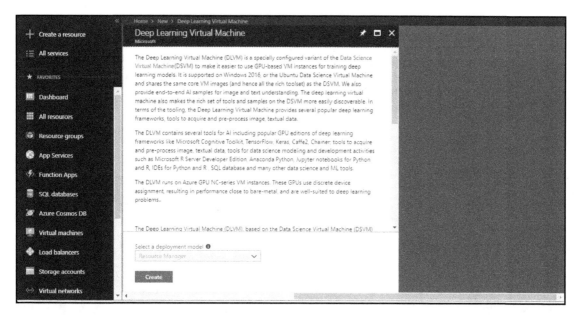

Figure 10.21: Provisioning a deep learning instance on Azure, step 0

3. You will now start a 4-step wizard to create the new instance.

    The first step (Basics), asks for some basic details. It is OK to enter the same values as I have done, but fill in the username and password carefully as you will need them later:

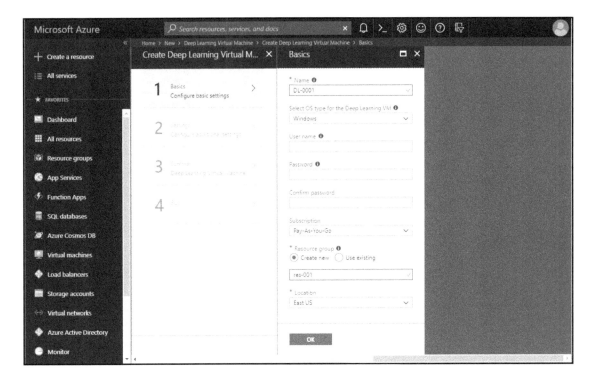

Figure 10.22: Provisioning a deep learning instance on Azure, step 1

For Step 2 (Settings), ensure that the virtual machine size is 1 x Standard NC6 (1 GPU), and click **OK** to continue:

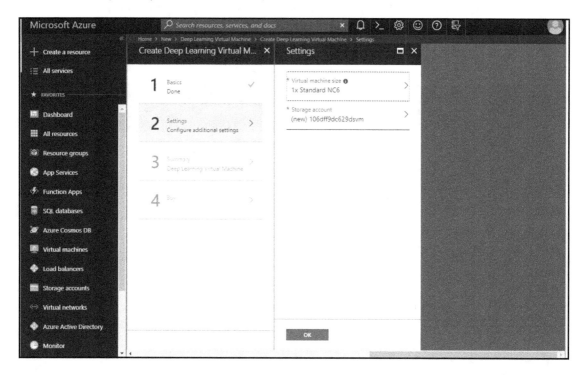

Figure 10.23: Provisioning a deep learning instance on Azure, step 2

For Step 3 (Summary), there is a brief validation check. You may be told that your account does not have sufficient Compute/VM (cores/vCPUs) resources available, which is because Microsoft may have restricted your account when it was first created. Create a support ticket to increase your resources and try again. If you have passed this step, click **OK** to continue. You are now on the final step, so just click **Create**:

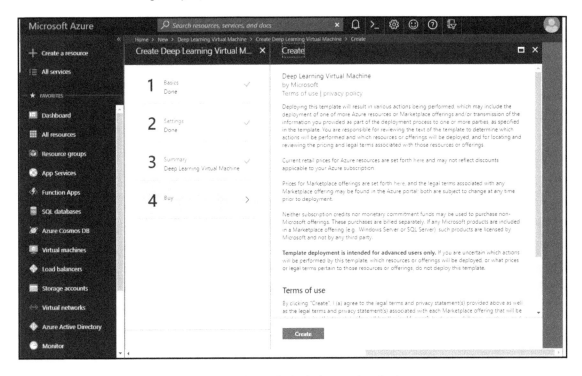

Figure 10.24: Provisioning a deep learning instance on Azure, Step 4

You may have to wait 30-40 minutes until the resources are created. When this is complete, select **All resources** on the left and you will see that all of the objects have been created. The following screenshot shows an example of this. Click on the one where the type is **Virtual Machine**:

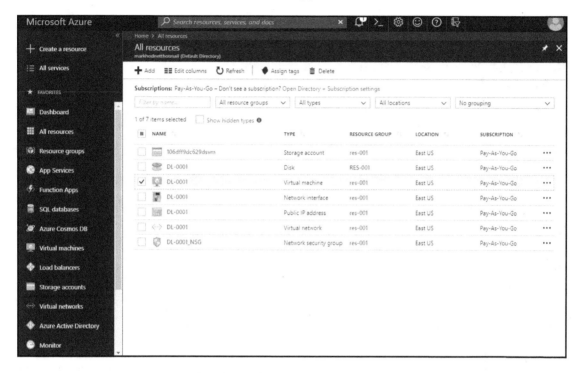

Figure 10.25: List of currently provisioned resources on Azure

4. You will then see the following screenshot. Click on the **Connect** button on the top of the screen.

5. A pane will open up on the right and give you an option to **Download RDP File**. Click on that, and when the file is downloaded, double-click on it:

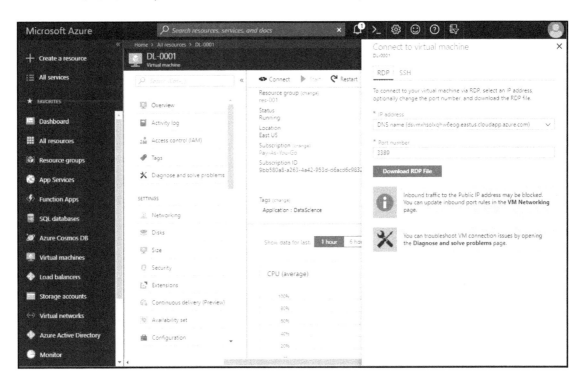

Figure 10.26: Downloading the RDP file to connect to the cloud instance in Azure

6. This should bring up a login window to connect to the cloud instance. Enter the username and password that you created in step 1 to connect to the instance. When you connect, you will see a desktop similar to the following screenshot:

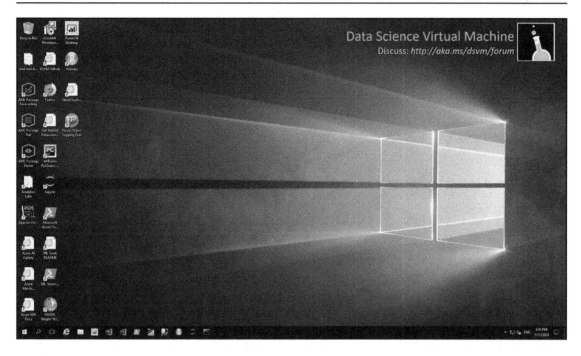

Figure 10.27: The remote desktop of the deep learning instance (Azure)

Great! RStudio is already installed. Keras is already installed, so any Keras deep learning code you have will run. Let's try and run some MXNet code. Open RStudio and run the following commands to install MXNet:

```
cran <- getOption("repos")
cran["dmlc"] <-
"https://apache-mxnet.s3-accelerate.dualstack.amazonaws.com/R/CRAN/GPU/cu90
"
options(repos = cran)
install.packages("mxnet")

# validate install
library(mxnet)
a <- mx.nd.ones(c(2,3), ctx = mx.gpu())
b <- a * 2 + 1
b
```

This will not work on the version of R installed. If you want to use MXNet, you must download the latest version of R (3.5.1 at the time of writing) and install it. Unfortunately, this will disable Keras, so only do this if you want to use MXNet instead of Keras. Once you download R from https://cran.r-project.org/, then re-run the code above to install MXNet.

 Note: The software installed on these AMI's change very frequently. Before installing any deep learning library, check the version of CUDA that is installed. You need to ensure that they deep learning library is compatible with the version of CUDA installed on the machine.

Using Google Cloud for deep learning

Google Cloud also has GPU instances. At the time of writing this book, the price of an instance with an NVIDIA Tesla K80 GPU card (which is also the GPU card in an AWS p2.xlarge instance) is $0.45 per hour on-demand. This is significantly cheaper than the AWS on-demand price. Further details of Google Cloud's GPU instances are at `https://cloud.google.com/gpu/`. However, for Google Cloud, we are not going to use instances. Instead, we are going to use the Google Cloud Machine Learning Engine API to submit machine learning jobs to the cloud. One big advantage of this approach over provisioning virtual machines is that you only pay for the hardware resources that you use and do not have to worry about setting up and terminating instances. More details and pricing can be found at `https://cloud.google.com/ml-engine/pricing`.

Go through the following steps to sign up for Google Cloud and enable the API:

1. Sign up for an account with Google Cloud.
2. You need to login to the portal at `https://console.cloud.google.com` and enable the **Cloud Machine Learning Engine** API.
3. Select **APIs & Services** from the main menu and click on the **Enable APIs and services** button.
4. The APIs are contained in groups. Select **View All** for the **Machine Learning** group, then select **Cloud Machine Learning Engine** and ensure that the API is enabled.

Once the API is enabled, execute the following code from RStudio:

```
devtools::install_github("rstudio/cloudml")
library(cloudml)
gcloud_init()
```

This should install the Google Cloud SDK, and you will asked to connect your Google account to the SDK. Then, you will be taken through a menu of options in the Terminal window. The first option is as follows:

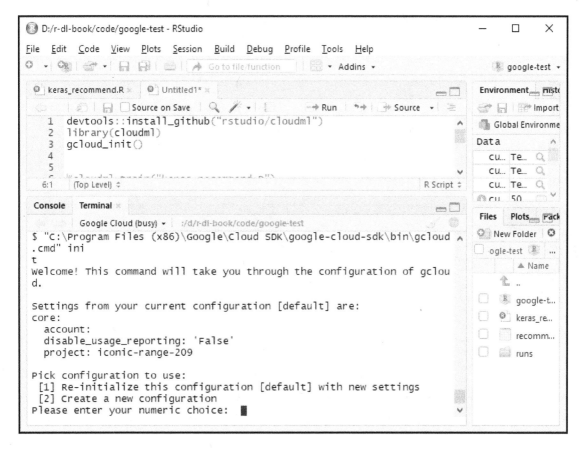

Figure 10.28: Accessing Google Cloud SDK from RStudio

For now, do not create any new projects or configurations, just select the ones that already exist. Once you have linked your Google account to the Google SDK on your machine and enabled the services, you are ready to go. The Cloud Machine Learning Engine allows you to submit a job to Google Cloud without having to create any instances. All the files in the working folder (R scripts and data) will be zipped up and sent to Google Cloud as a package.

For this example, I took a the recommendation file from the project in `Chapter 8`, *Deep Learning models using TensorFlow in R*. I copied this file and the `keras_recommend.R` script into a new directory and created a new RStudio project in that directory. I then opened the project in RStudio. You can see these two files and the RStudio project file in the previous screenshot. Then, I executed the following line in RStudio to submit the deep learning job:

```
cloudml_train("keras_recommend.R", master_type = "standard_gpu")
```

This will collect the files within the current working directory and send them to the Cloud Machine Learning Engine. As the job is executed, some progress information will be sent back to RStudio. You can also monitor the activity on the console page on `https://console.cloud.google.com` by selecting **ML Engine** | **Jobs**. Here is a screenshot of this web page showing two finished jobs and one that was canceled:

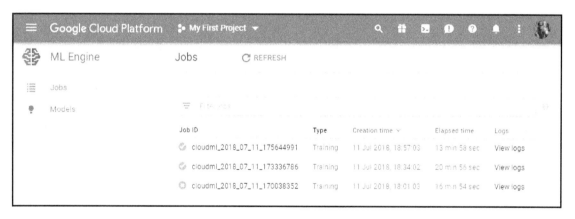

Figure 10.29: The ML Engine/Jobs page on the Google Cloud Platform web page

When the job is finished, the logs will be downloaded to your local machine. A nice summary web page is automatically created showing statistics for the job, as shown in the following screenshot:

Figure 10.30: Web summary page from the machine learning job

We can see the graph showing the progress of the model during training, the model summary, some hyperparameters (**epochs**, **batch_size**, and so on), as well as the cost (**ml_units**). The web page also contains the output from the R script. Select **Output** from the menu to see it. In the following screenshot, we can see the R code and the output from that code:

Figure 10.31: Web summary page from the machine learning job showing the R code and output

This is only a brief introduction to using the Google Cloud Machine Learning Engine. There is an excellent tutorial at `https://tensorflow.rstudio.com/tools/cloudml/articles/tuning.html` that explains how you can use this service for hyperparameter training. Using this service rather than cloud instances for hyperparameter training is simpler and probably cheaper than trying to manage it yourself using virtual instances. You do not have to monitor it and coordinate the different runs of the model training. More information on using this service is available at `https://tensorflow.rstudio.com/tools/cloudml/articles/getting_started.html`.

Using Paperspace for deep learning

Paperspace is another interesting way to perform deep learning in the cloud. It might be the easiest way to train deep learning models in the cloud. To set up a cloud instance with Paperspace, you can log in to their console, provision a new machine, and connect to it from your web browser:

1. Start by signing up for a Paperspace account, log in to the console, and go into the Virtual Machine section by selecting Core or Compute. Paperspace has an RStudio TensorFlow template with NVIDIA GPU libraries (CUDA 8.0 and cuDNN 6.0) already installed, along with the GPU version of TensorFlow and Keras for R. You will see this machine type when you select **Public Templates**, as shown in the following screenshot:

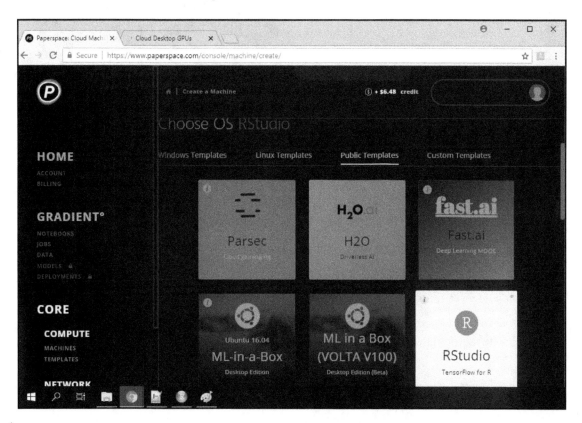

Figure 10.32: Paperspace portal

2. You will be given a choice of three GPU instances and the choice of pay by the hour or monthly. Select the cheapest option (currently P4000 at $0.40 per hour) and the hourly pricing. Scroll down to the bottom of the page and press the **Create** button. After a few minutes, your machine will be provisioned and you will be able to access it through your browser. An example of an RStudio Paperspace instance is shown as follows:

Figure 10.33: Accessing the virtual machine's desktop from a web page and running RStudio for a Paperspace instance

By default, Keras is already installed, so you can go ahead and train deep learning models using Keras. However, we are also going to install MXNet on our instance:

1. The first step is to open RStudio and install a few packages. Execute the following commands from RStudio:

```
install.packages("devtools")
install.packages(c("imager","DiagrammeR","influenceR","rgexf"))
```

2. The next step is to access the Terminal (or shell) for the instance you just created. You can go back to the console page and do it from there. Alternatively, click on the circle target in the top right corner of the desktop (see the previous screenshot). This also gives you other options such as synchronizing copy-and-paste between your local computer and the VM.

3. Once you have logged in to the Terminal for the instance, running the following commands will install MXNet:

```
sudo apt-get update
sudo dpkg --configure -a
sudo apt-get install -y build-essential git
export CUDA_HOME=/usr/local/cuda
git clone --recursive https://github.com/apache/incubator-mxnet
cd incubator-mxnet
make -j $(nproc) USE_OPENCV=1 USE_BLAS=blas USE_CUDA=1
USE_CUDA_PATH=/usr/local/cuda USE_CUDNN=1

sudo ldconfig /usr/local/cuda/lib64
sudo make rpkg
```

4. You also need to add the following line to the end of the .profile file:

```
export CUDA_HOME=/usr/local/cuda
```

When you are done, restart the instance. You now have a machine that can train Keras and MXNet deep learning models in the cloud. For more details on using RStudio in Paperspace, see https://tensorflow.rstudio.com/tools/cloud_desktop_gpu.html.

Summary

We have covered a lot of options for training deep learning models in this chapter! We discussed options for running it locally and showed the importance of having a GPU card. We used the three main cloud providers to train deep learning models in R on the cloud. Cloud computing is a fantastic resource – we gave an example of a super-computer costing $149,000. A few years ago, such a resource would have been out of reach for practically everyone, but now thanks to cloud computing, you can rent a machine like this on an hourly basis.

For AWS, Azure, and Paperspace, we installed MXNet on the cloud resources, giving us the option of which deep learning library to use. I encourage you to use the examples in the other chapters in this book and try all the different cloud providers here. It is amazing to think that you could do so and your total cost could be less than $10!

In the next and final chapter, we build an image classification solution from image files. We will demonstrate how to apply transfer learning, which allows you to adapt an existing model to a new dataset. We will show how to deploy a model to production using a REST API and briefly discuss Generative Adversarial Networks, reinforcement learning and provide some further resources if you wish to continue on your deep learning quest.

11
The Next Level in Deep Learning

We have almost come to the end of our journey in deep learning with R. This chapter is a bit of a mixed bag of topics. We will begin this chapter by revisiting an image classification task and building a complete image classification solution image files rather than tabular data. We will then move on to explaining transfer learning, where you can use an existing model on a new dataset. Next we discuss an important consideration in any machine learning project - how will your model be used in deployment, that is, production? We will show how to create a REST API that allows any programming language to call a deep learning model in R to predict on new data. We will then move on to briefly discussing two other deep learning topics: Generative Adversarial Networks and reinforcement learning. Finally, we will close this chapter and the book by providing a few other resources that you may be interested in.

In this chapter, we will cover the following topics:

- Building a complete image classification solution
- The ImageNet dataset
- Transfer learning
- Deploying TensorFlow models
- Generative adversarial networks
- Reinforcement learning
- Additional deep learning resources

Image classification models

We covered image classification in Chapter 5, *Image Classification Using Convolutional Neural Networks*. In that chapter, we described convolutional and pooling layers that are essential for deep learning tasks involving images. We also built a number of models on a simple dataset, the MNIST dataset. Here, we are going to look at some advanced topics in image classification. First, we will build a complete image classification model using image files as input. We will look at callbacks, which are a great aid in building complex deep learning models. A call-back function will be used to persist (save) a model to file, which will be loaded back later. We then use this model in our next example, which is transfer learning. This is where you use some of the layers in a pre-trained model on new data.

Building a complete image classification solution

We have built a few image classification models, but they used the MNIST dataset that was loaded from Keras or from CSV files. The data was always in tabular format. Obviously that is not how images are stored in most situations. This section looks at how to build an image classification model using a collection of image files. The first task is to acquire a set of image files. We are going to load the CIFAR10 data that is included in Keras and save the data as image files. We will then use those files to build a deep learning model. After this exercise, you will know how to create a deep learning image classification task with your own image files.

The deep learning model in this chapter is not a complex model. The focus is to show how the data pipeline for an image classification task is structured. We look at how to arrange the image files, how to use data augmentation and how callbacks can be used during training.

Creating the image data

The first step is to create the image files. The code for this section is in the Chapter11/gen_cifar10_data.R folder. We will load the CIFAR10 data and save the image files in the data directory. The first step is to create the directory structure. There are 10 classes in the CIFAR10 dataset: we will save 8 classes for building a model and we will use 2 classes in a later section (*Transfer learning*). The following code creates the following directories under data:

- cifar_10_images
- cifar_10_images/data1

- cifar_10_images/data2
- cifar_10_images/data1/train
- cifar_10_images/data1/valid
- cifar_10_images/data2/train
- cifar_10_images/data2/valid

This is the structure that Keras expects image data to be stored in. If you use this structure, then the images can be used to train a model in Keras. In the first part of the code, we create these directories:

```
library(keras)
library(imager)
# this script loads the cifar_10 data from Keras
# and saves the data as individual images

# create directories,
# we will save 8 classes in the data1 folder for model building
# and use 2 classes for transfer learning
data_dir <- "../data/cifar_10_images/"
if (!dir.exists(data_dir))
  dir.create(data_dir)
if (!dir.exists(paste(data_dir,"data1/",sep="")))
  dir.create(paste(data_dir,"data1/",sep=""))
if (!dir.exists(paste(data_dir,"data2/",sep="")))
  dir.create(paste(data_dir,"data2/",sep=""))
train_dir1 <- paste(data_dir,"data1/train/",sep="")
valid_dir1 <- paste(data_dir,"data1/valid/",sep="")
train_dir2 <- paste(data_dir,"data2/train/",sep="")
valid_dir2 <- paste(data_dir,"data2/valid/",sep="")

if (!dir.exists(train_dir1))
  dir.create(train_dir1)
if (!dir.exists(valid_dir1))
  dir.create(valid_dir1)
if (!dir.exists(train_dir2))
  dir.create(train_dir2)
if (!dir.exists(valid_dir2))
  dir.create(valid_dir2)
```

Under each of the train and valid directories, a separate directory is used for each category. We save the images for 8 classes under the data1 folder, and save the images for 2 classes under the data2 folder:

```
# load CIFAR10 dataset
c(c(x_train,y_train),c(x_test,y_test)) %<-% dataset_cifar10()
# get the unique categories,
```

```
# note that unique does not mean ordered!
# save 8 classes in data1 folder
categories <- unique(y_train)
for (i in categories[1:8])
{
  label_dir <- paste(train_dir1,i,sep="")
  if (!dir.exists(label_dir))
    dir.create(label_dir)
  label_dir <- paste(valid_dir1,i,sep="")
  if (!dir.exists(label_dir))
    dir.create(label_dir)
}
# save 2 classes in data2 folder
for (i in categories[9:10])
{
  label_dir <- paste(train_dir2,i,sep="")
  if (!dir.exists(label_dir))
    dir.create(label_dir)
  label_dir <- paste(valid_dir2,i,sep="")
  if (!dir.exists(label_dir))
    dir.create(label_dir)
}
```

Once we have created the directories, the next step is to save the images in the correct directories, which we will do in the following code:

```
# loop through train images and save in the correct folder
for (i in 1:dim(x_train)[1])
{
  img <- x_train[i,,,]
  label <- y_train[i,1]
  if (label %in% categories[1:8])
    image_array_save(img,paste(train_dir1,label,"/",i,".png",sep=""))
  else
    image_array_save(img,paste(train_dir2,label,"/",i,".png",sep=""))
  if ((i %% 500)==0)
    print(i)
}

# loop through test images and save in the correct folder
for (i in 1:dim(x_test)[1])
{
  img <- x_test[i,,,]
  label <- y_test[i,1]
  if (label %in% categories[1:8])
    image_array_save(img,paste(valid_dir1,label,"/",i,".png",sep=""))
  else
    image_array_save(img,paste(valid_dir2,label,"/",i,".png",sep=""))
```

```
   if ((i %% 500)==0)
      print(i)
}
```

Finally, as we have done previously, we will do a validation check to ensure that our images are correct. Let's load in 9 images from one category. We want to check that the images display correctly and that they are from the same class:

```
# plot some images to verify process
image_dir <- list.dirs(valid_dir1, full.names=FALSE, recursive=FALSE)[1]
image_dir <- paste(valid_dir1,image_dir,sep="")
img_paths <- paste(image_dir,list.files(image_dir),sep="/")

par(mfrow = c(3, 3))
par(mar=c(2,2,2,2))
for (i in 1:9)
{
   im <- load.image(img_paths[i])
   plot(im)
}
```

This produces the following plot:

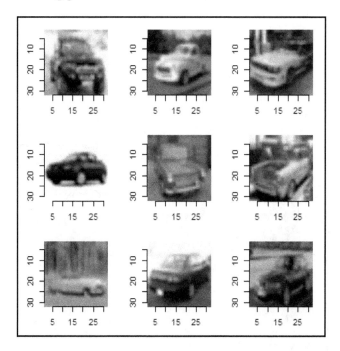

Figure 11.1: Sample CIFAR10 images

This looks good! The images display correctly and we can see that these images all appear to be of the same class, which is cars. The images are out of focus, but that is because they are only thumbnail images of size 32 x 32.

Building the deep learning model

Once you have run the script from the preceding section, you should have 40,000 images for training in the `cifar_10_images/data1/train` directory and 8,000 images for validation in the `cifar_10_images/data1/valid` directory. We will train a model with this data. The code for this section is in the `Chapter11/build_cifar10_model.R` folder. The first section creates the model definition, which should be familiar to you:

```
library(keras)

# train a model from a set of images
# note: you need to run gen_cifar10_data.R first to create the images!
model <- keras_model_sequential()
model %>%
  layer_conv_2d(name="conv1", input_shape=c(32, 32, 3),
    filter=32, kernel_size=c(3,3), padding="same"
  ) %>%
  layer_activation("relu") %>%
  layer_conv_2d(name="conv2",filter=32, kernel_size=c(3,3),
              padding="same") %>%
  layer_activation("relu") %>%
  layer_max_pooling_2d(pool_size=c(2,2)) %>%
  layer_dropout(0.25,name="drop1") %>%
  layer_conv_2d(name="conv3",filter=64, kernel_size=c(3,3),
              padding="same") %>%
  layer_activation("relu") %>%
  layer_conv_2d(name="conv4",filter=64, kernel_size=c(3,3),
              padding="same") %>%
  layer_activation("relu") %>%
  layer_max_pooling_2d(pool_size=c(2,2)) %>%
  layer_dropout(0.25,name="drop2") %>%
  layer_flatten() %>%
  layer_dense(256) %>%
  layer_activation("relu") %>%
  layer_dropout(0.5) %>%
  layer_dense(256) %>%
  layer_activation("relu") %>%
  layer_dropout(0.5) %>%
  layer_dense(8) %>%
  layer_activation("softmax")

model %>% compile(
```

```
  loss="categorical_crossentropy",
  optimizer="adam",
  metrics="accuracy"
)
```

The model definition was adapted from the VGG16 architecture, which we will see later. I used a smaller number of blocks and fewer nodes. Note that the final dense layer must have 8 nodes, because there are only 8, not 10 classes in the data1 folder.

The next part sets up a data generator; the purpose of this is to load batches of image files into the model as it is being trained. We can also apply data augmentation to the train dataset in the data generator. We will select to create artificial data by randomly flipping the images horizontally, shifting images horizontally/vertically, and rotating the images by up to 15 degrees. We saw in Chapter 6, *Tuning and Optimizing Models*, that data augmentation can significantly improve existing models:

```
# set up data generators to stream images to the train function
data_dir <- "../data/cifar_10_images/"
train_dir <- paste(data_dir,"data1/train/",sep="")
valid_dir <- paste(data_dir,"data1/valid/",sep="")

# in CIFAR10
# there are 50000 images in training set
# and 10000 images in test set
# but we are only using 8/10 classes,
# so its 40000 train and 8000 validation
num_train <- 40000
num_valid <- 8000
flow_batch_size <- 50
# data augmentation
train_gen <- image_data_generator(
  rotation_range=15,
  width_shift_range=0.2,
  height_shift_range=0.2,
  horizontal_flip=TRUE,
  rescale=1.0/255)
# get images from directory
train_flow <- flow_images_from_directory(
  train_dir,
  train_gen,
  target_size=c(32,32),
  batch_size=flow_batch_size,
  class_mode="categorical"
)

# no augmentation on validation data
valid_gen <- image_data_generator(rescale=1.0/255)
```

```
valid_flow <- flow_images_from_directory(
  valid_dir,
  valid_gen,
  target_size=c(32,32),
  batch_size=flow_batch_size,
  class_mode="categorical"
)
```

Once the data generators have been set up, we will also use two callback functions. Callback functions allow you to run custom code after a specific number of batches / epochs have executed. You can write your own callbacks or use some predefined callback functions. Previously, we used callbacks for logging metrics, but here the callbacks will implement model checkpointing and early stopping, which are are often used when building complex deep learning models.

Model checkpointing is used to save the model weights to disk. You can then load the model from disk into memory and use it for predicting new data, or you can continue training the model from the point it was saved to disk. You can save the weights after every epoch, this might be useful if you are using cloud resources and are worried about the machine terminating suddenly. Here, we use it to keep the best model we have seen so far in training. After every epoch, it checks the validation loss, and if it is lower than the validation loss in the existing file, it saves the model.

Early stopping allows you to stop training a model when the performance no longer improves. Some people refer to it as a form of regularization because early stopping can prevent a model from overfitting. While it can avoid overfitting, it works very differently to the regularization techniques, such as L1, L2, weight decay, and dropout, that we saw in Chapter 3, *Deep Learning Fundamentals*. When using early stopping, you usually would allow the model to continue for a few epochs even if performance is no longer improving, the number of epochs allowed before stopping training is known as *patience* in Keras. Here we set it to 10, that is, if we have 10 epochs where the model has failed to improve, we stop training. Here is the code to create the callbacks that we will use in our model:

```
# call-backs
callbacks <- list(
  callback_early_stopping(monitor="val_acc",patience=10,mode="auto"),
  callback_model_checkpoint(filepath="cifar_model.h5",mode="auto",
                    monitor="val_loss",save_best_only=TRUE)
)
```

Here is the code to train the model:

```
# train the model using the data generators and call-backs defined above
history <- model %>% fit_generator(
  train_flow,
```

```
    steps_per_epoch=as.integer(num_train/flow_batch_size),
    epochs=100,
    callbacks=callbacks,
    validation_data=valid_flow,
    validation_steps=as.integer(num_valid/flow_batch_size)
)
```

One thing to note here is that we have to manage the steps per epoch for the train and validation generators. When you set up a generator, you don't know how much data is actually there, so we need to set the number of steps for each epoch. This is simply the number of records divided by the batch size.

This model should take less than an hour to train on a GPU and significantly longer if training on a CPU. As the model is training, the best model is saved in cifar_model.h5. The best result on my machine was after epoch 64, when the validation accuracy was about 0.80. The model continued to train for another 10 epochs after this but failed to improve. Here is a plot of the training metrics:

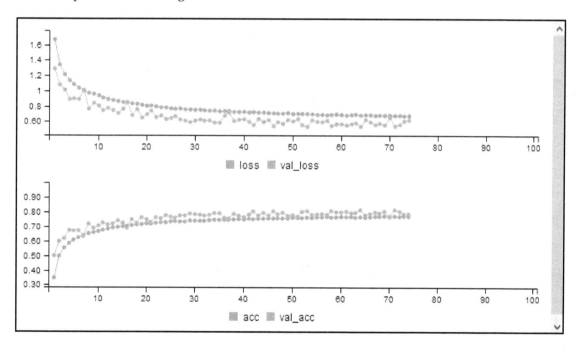

Figure 11.2: Output metrics during model training

Using the saved deep learning model

Now that we have built our deep learning model, we can restart R and reload the model from disk. The code for this section is in the `Chapter11/use_cifar10_model.R` folder. We will load the model that was created in the previous section by using the following code:

```
library(keras)

# load model trained in build_cifar10_model.R
model <- load_model_hdf5("cifar_model.h5")
```

We will use this model to generate a prediction for an image file from the validation set. We will pick the first directory in the validation folder and then pick the 7th file from that folder. We load the image and apply the same preprocessing to it as we did when preprocessing the images during training, which is to normalize the data by dividing the pixel values by 255.0. Here is the code that loads the image and generates the prediction:

```
> valid_dir <-"../data/cifar_10_images/data1/valid/"
> first_dir <- list.dirs(valid_dir, full.names=FALSE, recursive=FALSE)[1]
> valid_dir <- paste(valid_dir,first_dir,sep="")
> img_path <- paste(valid_dir,list.files(valid_dir)[7],sep="/")

# load image and convert to shape we can use for prediction
> img <- image_load(img_path, target_size = c(32,32))
> x <- image_to_array(img)
> x <- array_reshape(x, c(1, dim(x)))
> x <- x / 255.0
> preds <- model %>% predict(x)
> preds <- round(preds,3)
> preds
      [,1] [,2] [,3] [,4] [,5] [,6] [,7]  [,8]
[1,] 0.997    0    0    0    0    0    0 0.003
```

The model predicts that the input is from the first class with 99.7% certainty. Since we chose the first directory in the validation set, the prediction is correct.

The final thing we will do with our model is to evaluate it on a directory of image files. We will also show how to generate predictions for an entire directory of image files. This code loads the images from the directories using data generators, similar to how we trained the model. Here is the code that evaluates and predicts categories by using the model for the validation images we saved to disk:

```
> valid_dir <-"../data/cifar_10_images/data1/valid/"
> flow_batch_size <- 50
> num_valid <- 8000
>
> valid_gen <- image_data_generator(rescale=1.0/255)
> valid_flow <- flow_images_from_directory(
    valid_dir,
    valid_gen,
    target_size=c(32,32),
    batch_size=flow_batch_size,
    class_mode="categorical"
 )
>
> evaluate_generator(model,valid_flow,
    steps=as.integer(num_valid/flow_batch_size))
$`loss`
[1] 0.5331386

$acc
[1] 0.808625
```

The validation accuracy is 80.86%, which is similar to what we observed during model training, this confirms that the model was saved correctly to disk. Here is the code that generates predictions for all 8,000 validation images:

```
> preds <- predict_generator(model,valid_flow,
    steps=as.integer(num_valid/flow_batch_size))
> dim(preds)
[1] 8000 8

> # view the predictions,
> preds <- round(preds,3)
> head(preds)
      [,1]  [,2]  [,3]  [,4]  [,5]  [,6]  [,7]  [,8]
[1,] 0.000 0.000 0.000 0.000 0.000 0.000 0.999 0.001
[2,] 0.000 0.007 0.001 0.002 0.990 0.000 0.000 0.000
[3,] 0.000 0.855 0.069 0.032 0.021 0.017 0.002 0.002
[4,] 0.134 0.001 0.000 0.000 0.000 0.000 0.001 0.864
[5,] 0.011 0.064 0.057 0.226 0.051 0.515 0.004 0.073
[6,] 0.108 0.277 0.135 0.066 0.094 0.091 0.052 0.179
```

We can see that our prediction output has 8,000 rows and 8 columns, so for each validation image, there is a probability for each category. We can see that the sum for each row is 1.0 and that there is usually one class that has a significant probability. For example, the model is predicting that the first image is in class 7 with a probability of 99.9%.

We have now built a complete image classification solution using image files. This template can be reused for other tasks once the image data is stored in the same directory structure. If the new task had a different number of categories, then all you would need to change is the number of nodes in the last dense layer and possibly the softmax activation. However, if you did have a new image classification task that involved real-life images, then you probably would get better results by using an existing model and using transfer learning. Before I explain how to do that, I will provide some background on the ImageNet dataset, which is often used to train complex models which are then used in transfer learning.

The ImageNet dataset

From 2010, an annual image classification competition has been run called the **ImageNet Large Scale Visual Recognition Challenge** (**ILSVRC**). The image set consists of over 14 million images that have been labelled with over 1,000 categories. Without this dataset, there would not be the huge interest in deep learning that there is today. It has provided the stimulus for research in deep learning through the competition. The models and weights learnt on the Imagenet dataset have then been used in thousands of other deep learning models through transfer learning. The actual history of ImageNet is an interesting story. The following link (`https://qz.com/1034972/the-data-that-changed-the-direction-of-ai-research-and-possibly-the-world/`) explains how the project originally got little attention, but that changed with a number of linked events:

- The ILSVRC became the benchmark for image classification for researchers.
- NVIDIA had released libraries that allowed access to **graphical processing units** (**GPUs**). GPUs are designed to do massive parallel matrix operations, which is exactly what is needed to create deep neural networks.
- Geoffrey Hinton, Ilya Sutskever, and Alex Krizhevsky from the University of Toronto created a deep convolutional neural network architecture called **AlexNet** that won the competition in 2012. Although this was not the first use of convolutional neural networks, their submission beat the next approach by a huge margin.
- Researchers noticed that when they trained models using the ImageNet dataset, they could use them on other classification tasks. They almost always got much better performance from using the ImageNet model and then using transfer learning than just training a model from scratch on the original dataset.

The advances in image classification can be tracked with some notable entries in the ILSVRC competition:

Team	Year	Error rate
2011 ILSVRC winner (not deep learning)	2011	25.8%
AlexNet (7 layers)	2012	15.3%
VGG Net (16 layers)	2014	7.32%
GoogLeNet / Inception (19 layers)	2014	6.67%
ResNet (152 layers)	2015	3.57%

VGGNet, Inception, and Resnet are all available in Keras. A complete list of available networks can be found at `https://keras.rstudio.com/reference/index.html#section-applications`.

The models for these networks can be loaded in Keras and used to classify a new image into one of the 1,000 categories in ImageNet. We will look at this next. If you have a new classification task with a different set of images, then you can also use these networks and then use transfer learning, which we will look at later in this chapter. The number of categories can be different; you do not need to have 1,000 categories for your task.

Perhaps the simplest model to begin with is VGGNet, as it is not that different to what we saw in `Chapter 5`, *Image Classification Using Convolutional Neural Networks*.

Loading an existing model

In this section, we will load an existing model (VGGNet) in Keras and use it to classify a new image. The code for this section can be found in the `Chapter11/vgg_model.R`. We will begin by loading the model and looking at its architecture:

```
> library(keras)
> model <- application_vgg16(weights = 'imagenet', include_top = TRUE)

> summary(model)

Layer (type)                    Output Shape               Param #
=================================================================
input_1 (InputLayer)            (None, 224, 224, 3)          0

block1_conv1 (Conv2D)           (None, 224, 224, 64)         1792

block1_conv2 (Conv2D)           (None, 224, 224, 64)         36928
```

block1_pool (MaxPooling2D)	(None, 112, 112, 64)	0
block2_conv1 (Conv2D)	(None, 112, 112, 128)	73856
block2_conv2 (Conv2D)	(None, 112, 112, 128)	147584
block2_pool (MaxPooling2D)	(None, 56, 56, 128)	0
block3_conv1 (Conv2D)	(None, 56, 56, 256)	295168
block3_conv2 (Conv2D)	(None, 56, 56, 256)	590080
block3_conv3 (Conv2D)	(None, 56, 56, 256)	590080
block3_pool (MaxPooling2D)	(None, 28, 28, 256)	0
block4_conv1 (Conv2D)	(None, 28, 28, 512)	1180160
block4_conv2 (Conv2D)	(None, 28, 28, 512)	2359808
block4_conv3 (Conv2D)	(None, 28, 28, 512)	2359808
block4_pool (MaxPooling2D)	(None, 14, 14, 512)	0
block5_conv1 (Conv2D)	(None, 14, 14, 512)	2359808
block5_conv2 (Conv2D)	(None, 14, 14, 512)	2359808
block5_conv3 (Conv2D)	(None, 14, 14, 512)	2359808
block5_pool (MaxPooling2D)	(None, 7, 7, 512)	0
flatten (Flatten)	(None, 25088)	0
fc1 (Dense)	(None, 4096)	102764544
fc2 (Dense)	(None, 4096)	16781312
predictions (Dense)	(None, 1000)	4097000

```
=================================================================
Total params: 138,357,544
Trainable params: 138,357,544
Non-trainable params: 0
```

This model looks complicated, but when you look at it in detail, there is nothing that we haven't seen before. There are two blocks with two convolutional layers, which are then followed by a max pooling layer. These are followed by three blocks with three convolutional layers, which are then followed by a max pooling layer. Finally, we have a flatten layer and three dense layers. The last dense layer has 1,000 nodes, which is the number of categories in the ImageNet dataset.

Let's use this model to make a prediction for a new image. This image is a bicycle, albeit an unusual one – it is a time trial bicycle:

Figure 11.3: Test image for classification

The following code block processes the image into a suitable format to use in the VGG model. It loads the image and resizes it to the dimensions of the images used to train the model (224, 224). We then have to preprocess the image data before calling the predict function. Finally, there is a helper function in Keras called imagenet_decode_predictions that we can use to get the prediction categories and the probabilities:

```
> img_path <- "image1.jpg"
> img <- image_load(img_path, target_size = c(224,224))
```

```
> x <- image_to_array(img)
> x <- array_reshape(x, c(1, dim(x)))
> x <- imagenet_preprocess_input(x)

> preds <- model %>% predict(x)
> imagenet_decode_predictions(preds, top = 5)
[[1]]
  class_name       class_description        score
1  n02835271  bicycle-built-for-two 0.31723219
2  n03792782  mountain_bike             0.16578741
3  n03891332  parking_meter             0.12548350
4  n04485082  tripod                    0.06399463
5  n09193705  alp                       0.04852912
```

The top prediction is `bicycle-built-for-two` at just over 30%, and the second best prediction is `mountain_bike` at 16.5%. ImageNet has a category for a tricycle and unicycle (and even a `Model_T` car!), but does not seem to have a category for a bicycle, so this prediction is a not a bad result. However, `mountain_bike` is probably a more accurate category for this image as it definitely is not a bicycle for two people!

Transfer learning

One of the few disadvantages deep learning has over traditional machine learning is that it requires lots of data. Transfer learning is one way to overcome this, by using the weights of a previously trained model (usually trained on ImageNet data) and then applying them to a new problem set.

The ImageNet dataset consists of 15 million images in 1,000 classes. Since we can reuse parts of a model that has been trained on this amount of data, it may be possible to train the new model with just a few hundred images per category. This would depend on the images being somewhat related to the data used in the original model. For example, trying to use transfer learning from ImageNet models (which is trained on photographs) on data from other domains (for example, satellite or medical scans), would be more difficult and would require much more data. Some of the concerns we raised in Chapter 6, *Tuning and Optimizing Models*, about different data sources also applies. If the data is from a different type of data distribution, for example, mobile images, off-center photos, different lighting conditions, and so on, this will also matter. This is where creating more synthetic data through data augmentation can make a big difference.

We will now apply transfer learning using the model we built in the *Building the deep learning model* section. Recall that we only used 8/10 of the classes in building and evaluating this model. We will now build a new model using transfer learning that will differentiate between the 2 remaining classes. The code for this section can be found in the `Chapter11/cifar_txr.R` folder:

1. We will use the model we built in the previous section and load it using the following code:

```
library(keras)

# load model trained in build_cifar10_model.R
model <- load_model_hdf5("cifar_model.h5")
```

2. Next, we will call `trainable_weights` on the model object to get the number of trainable layers. This will count all the non-activation layers in our model.

```
> length(model$trainable_weights)
[1] 14
```

3. Next, we freeze the early layers in our model. Freezing the layers in a model means that the weights will not be updated during back-propagation. We freeze the convolutional blocks, but do not freeze the dense layers at the end of the model. We use the names we set in the model definition to set the first and last layers to freeze.

4. We then call `trainable_weights` on the model once more to confirm that the number changed from the preceding value, `14`, to `6`. Here is the code for freezing the layers:

```
freeze_weights(model,from="conv1", to="drop2")
length(model$trainable_weights)
[1] 6
```

5. Next, we will remove the last dense layer and last activation layer from our model by calling the `pop_layer` function twice in the following code. We need to do this because our new task has 2 classes and not 8:

```
# remove the softmax layer
pop_layer(model)
pop_layer(model)
```

6. Now, we can add a new layer with 2 nodes (because we have 2 classes in the new task) by using the following code:

```
# add a new layer that has the correct number of nodes for the new
task
model %>%
   layer_dense(name="new_dense",units=2, activation='softmax')
summary(model)
```

7. The following code block compiles the model again and sets up the generators to load the data. This is similar to what we saw when we built the model. One difference is that we do not use data augmentation here:

```
# compile the model again
model %>% compile(
   loss = "binary_crossentropy",
   optimizer="adam",
   metrics=c('accuracy')
)

# set up data generators to stream images to the train function
data_dir <- "../data/cifar_10_images/"
train_dir <- paste(data_dir,"data2/train/",sep="")
valid_dir <- paste(data_dir,"data2/valid/",sep="")

# in CIFAR10, # there are 50000 images in training set
# and 10000 images in test set
# but we are only using 2/10 classes,
# so its 10000 train and 2000 validation
num_train <- 10000
num_valid <- 2000
flow_batch_size <- 50
# no data augmentation
train_gen <- image_data_generator(rescale=1.0/255)
# get images from directory
train_flow <- flow_images_from_directory(
   train_dir,
   train_gen,
   target_size=c(32,32),
   batch_size=flow_batch_size,
   class_mode="categorical"
)

# no augmentation on validation data
valid_gen <- image_data_generator(rescale=1.0/255)
valid_flow <- flow_images_from_directory(
   valid_dir,
   valid_gen,
```

```
  target_size=c(32,32),
  batch_size=flow_batch_size,
  class_mode="categorical"
)
```

8. Finally, we can train the model by using the following code:

```
> history <- model %>% fit_generator(
+ train_flow,
+ steps_per_epoch=as.integer(num_train/flow_batch_size),
+ epochs=10,
+ validation_data=valid_flow,
+ validation_steps=as.integer(num_valid/flow_batch_size)
+ )
Found 10000 images belonging to 2 classes.
Found 2000 images belonging to 2 classes.
Epoch 1/10
200/200 [==============================] - 5s 27ms/step - loss:
0.3115 - acc: 0.8811 - val_loss: 0.1529 - val_acc: 0.9425
Epoch 2/10
200/200 [==============================] - 4s 20ms/step - loss:
0.1971 - acc: 0.9293 - val_loss: 0.1316 - val_acc: 0.9550
Epoch 3/10
200/200 [==============================] - 4s 20ms/step - loss:
0.1637 - acc: 0.9382 - val_loss: 0.1248 - val_acc: 0.9540
Epoch 4/10
200/200 [==============================] - 4s 20ms/step - loss:
0.1367 - acc: 0.9497 - val_loss: 0.1200 - val_acc: 0.9575
Epoch 5/10
200/200 [==============================] - 4s 20ms/step - loss:
0.1227 - acc: 0.9543 - val_loss: 0.1148 - val_acc: 0.9605
Epoch 6/10
200/200 [==============================] - 4s 20ms/step - loss:
0.1161 - acc: 0.9559 - val_loss: 0.1110 - val_acc: 0.9625
Epoch 7/10
200/200 [==============================] - 4s 20ms/step - loss:
0.1022 - acc: 0.9622 - val_loss: 0.1118 - val_acc: 0.9620
Epoch 8/10
200/200 [==============================] - 4s 20ms/step - loss:
0.0996 - acc: 0.9655 - val_loss: 0.1068 - val_acc: 0.9645
Epoch 9/10
200/200 [==============================] - 4s 20ms/step - loss:
0.0861 - acc: 0.9687 - val_loss: 0.1095 - val_acc: 0.9655
Epoch 10/10
200/200 [==============================] - 4s 20ms/step - loss:
0.0849 - acc: 0.9696 - val_loss: 0.1189 - val_acc: 0.9620
```

The best accuracy was on epoch 9 when we got 96.55% accuracy. This is significantly better than what we got on the multi-classification model (approximately 81%), but binary classification tasks are much easier than multi-classification tasks. We can also see that the model was very quick to train, because it only had to update the weights in the last few layers.

Deploying TensorFlow models

Historically, one of the perceived disadvantages of using R for data science projects was the difficulty in deploying machine learning models built in R. This often meant that companies used R mainly as a prototyping tool to build models which were then rewritten in another language, such as Java and .NET. It is also one of the main reasons cited for companies switching to Python for data science as Python has more *glue code*, which allows it to interface with other programming languages.

Thankfully, this is changing. One interesting new product from RStudio, called RStudio Connect, allows companies to create a platform for sharing R-Shiny applications, reports in R Markdown, dashboards, and models. This allows companies to serve machine learning models using a REST interface.

The TensorFlow (and Keras) models we have created in this book can be deployed without any runtime dependency on either R or Python. One way of doing this is TensorFlow Serving, which is an open source software library for serving TensorFlow models. Another option is to use the Google CloudML interface that we saw in Chapter 10, *Running Deep Learning Models in the Cloud*. This allows you to create a publicly available REST API that can be called from your applications. TensorFlow models can also be deployed to iPhones and Android mobile phones.

There are two basic options for scoring models in production:

- **Batch mode**: In batch mode, a set of data is scored offline and the prediction results are stored and used elsewhere
- **Real-time mode**: In real-time mode, the data is scored immediately, usually a record at a time, and the results are immediately used.

For a lot of applications, batch mode is more than adequate. You should carefully consider if you really need a real-time prediction system as it is requires more resources and needs constant monitoring. It is much more efficient to score records in a batch rather than individually. Another advantage of batch mode is that you know the demand on the application beforehand and can plan resources accordingly. With real-time systems, a spike in demand or a denial of service attack can cause problems with your prediction model.

We have already seen batch mode for a saved model in the *Using the saved deep learning model* section in this chapter. So, let's look at how we can build a REST interface to get a prediction on new data from a deep learning model in real-time. This will use the tfdeploy package. The code for this section can be found in the Chapter11/deploy_model.R. We are going to build a simple model based on the MNIST dataset and then create a web interface where we can submit a new image for classification. Here is the first part of the code that builds the model and prints out the predictions for the first 5 rows in the test set:

```
library(keras)
#devtools::install_github("rstudio/tfdeploy")
library(tfdeploy)

# load data
c(c(x_train, y_train), c(x_test, y_test)) %<-% dataset_mnist()

# reshape and rescale
x_train <- array_reshape(x_train, dim=c(nrow(x_train), 784)) / 255
x_test <- array_reshape(x_test, dim=c(nrow(x_test), 784)) / 255

# one-hot encode response
y_train <- to_categorical(y_train, 10)
y_test <- to_categorical(y_test, 10)

# define and compile model
model <- keras_model_sequential()
model %>%
  layer_dense(units=256, activation='relu',
input_shape=c(784),name="image") %>%
  layer_dense(units=128, activation='relu') %>%
  layer_dense(units=10, activation='softmax',name="prediction") %>%
  compile(
    loss='categorical_crossentropy',
    optimizer=optimizer_rmsprop(),
    metrics=c('accuracy')
  )

# train model
history <- model %>% fit(
```

```
    x_train, y_train,
    epochs=10, batch_size=128,
    validation_split=0.2
)
preds <- round(predict(model, x_test[1:5,]),0)
head(preds)
     [,1] [,2] [,3] [,4] [,5] [,6] [,7] [,8] [,9] [,10]
[1,]    0    0    0    0    0    0    0    1    0     0
[2,]    0    0    1    0    0    0    0    0    0     0
[3,]    0    1    0    0    0    0    0    0    0     0
[4,]    1    0    0    0    0    0    0    0    0     0
[5,]    0    0    0    0    1    0    0    0    0     0
```

There is nothing new about this code. Next, we will create a JSON file for one image file in the test set. JSON stands for JavaScript Object Notation, and is the accepted standard for serializing and sending data over a network connection. If HTML is the language for computers-to-human web communication, JSON is the language for computers-to-computers web communication. It is heavily used in microservice architecture, which is a framework for building a complex web ecosystem from lots of small web services. The data in the JSON file must have the same preprocessing applied as what was done during training – since we normalized the training data, we must also normalize the test data. The following code creates a JSON file with the values for the first instance in the testset and saves the file to `json_image.json`:

```
# create a json file for an image from the test set
json <- "{\"instances\": [{\"image_input\": ["
json <- paste(json,paste(x_test[1,],collapse=","),sep="")
json <- paste(json,"]}]}",sep="")
write.table(json,"json_image.json",row.names=FALSE,col.names=FALSE,quote=FA
LSE)
```

Now that we have a JSON file, let's create a REST web interface for our model:

```
export_savedmodel(model, "savedmodel")
serve_savedmodel('savedmodel', browse=TRUE)
```

Once you do this, a new web page should pop up that is similar to the following:

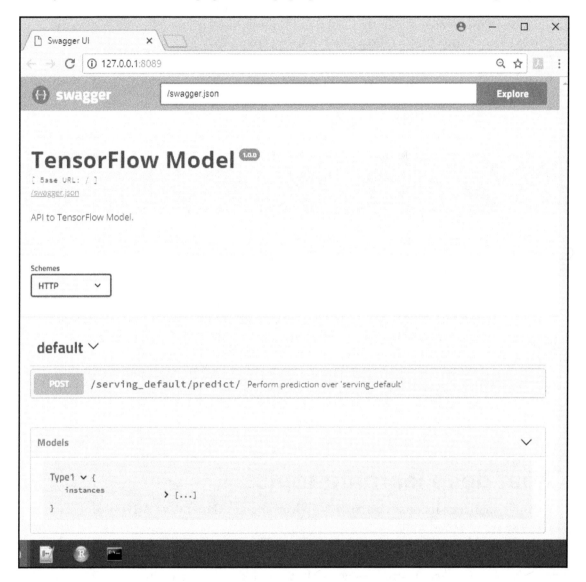

Figure 11.4: Swagger UI for the TensorFlow model REST web service

This is a Swagger UI page showing the RESTful web services for the TensorFlow model. This allows us to test our API. While we could try to use this interface, it is easier to use the JSON file we just created. Open up Command Prompt on your machine, browse to the Chapter11 code directory, and run the following command:

```
curl -X POST -H "Content-Type: application/json" -d @json_image.json
http://localhost:8089/serving_default/predict
```

You should get the following response:

The REST web interface returns another JSON string with these results. We can see that the 8th entry in the list is 1.0 and that all the other numbers are extremely small. This matches the prediction for the first row that we saw in the code at the start of this section.

I imagine that half of the people reading this are very excited about this and the other half couldn't care less! The half that really like this can see how R can be used to serve model predictions that interface with web applications. This opens up huge possibilities for using R, where beforehand it was believed that you either had to use Python or you had to redevelop models in other languages. The half that couldn't care less probably never had to deal with these issues with R, but in time they will see how important this is as well!

Other deep learning topics

Two topics that get a lot of attention in deep learning are **Generative Adversarial Networks (GANs)** and reinforcement learning. We only briefly introduce both topics, there is no code for this section for a couple of reasons. Firstly both topics are very advanced and trying to create a use-case that is non-trivial would require a few chapters for each topic. Secondly, reinforcement learning is not well supported in R, so creating an example would be difficult. Despite this, I include both of these topics in the book because I believe they are important emerging areas in deep learning that you should definitely be aware of.

Generative adversarial networks

Generative Adversarial Networks have been called *the coolest thing since sliced bread* by Yann LeCunn, one of the most prominent people in deep learning. If he believes that, then we should all take notice!

Most of our models in this book have been discriminative models, that is, we try to differentiate one class from another. However in `Chapter 9`, *Anomaly Detection and Recommendation Systems* we created a generative model in the anomaly detection use-case. This model could create new data, albeit a different representation of the input data. Creating complex generative models is a very hot research topic in deep learning. Many believe that generative models can solve many problems in deep learning, including one of the biggest, which is the lack of correctly labelled data. However before GANs, it was difficult to judge how good a generative model actually was. A group of researchers led by Ian Goodfellow proposed Generative Adversarial Networks (GANs) (Goodfellow, Ian, et al. *Generative adversarial nets.* Advances in neural information processing systems. 2014) that could be used to create realistic artificial data.

In GANs, two models are trained together, the first is a generative model G that creates new data. The second model is a discriminative model D that tries to predict if an example is from the real dataset, or has been created by the generative model G. The basic GAN idea is for the generative model to try to fool the discriminative model, while the discriminative model must try to tell the differences from fake data and real data. The generator keeps creating new data and refining its process until the discriminative model can no longer tell the difference between the generated data and the real training data.

In the paper, the process is compared to a team of counterfeiters creating fake currency (the generative model) and the police who are trying to detect the counterfeit currency (the discriminative model). Both models improve incrementally until it is impossible to differentiate between the counterfeit currency and the real currency.

GANs are notoriously hard to train. One paper that documented a working approach to training GANs on image data called their approach deep convolutional generative adversarial networks (Radford, Alec, Luke Metz, and Soumith Chintala. *Unsupervised representation learning with deep convolutional generative adversarial networks.* arXiv preprint arXiv:1511.06434 (2015)). In this paper, they recommended a number of guidelines to train stable deep convolutional generative adversarial networks (DCGANs):

- Replace any pooling layers with strided convolutions (discriminator) and fractional-strided convolutions (generator).
- Use batchnorm for both models.
- Remove fully connected hidden layers for deep architectures.

- For the generator, use tanh activation in the output layer and ReLU elsewhere.
- For the discriminator, use LeakyReLU activation for all layers.

Training DCGANs is an iterative process, the following steps are repeated:

- First the generator creates some new examples.
- The discriminator is trained using real data and generated data.
- After the discriminator has been trained, both models are trained together. The discriminator's weights are frozen, but its gradients are used in the generator model so that the generator can update it's weights.

During this loop, it is vital that one model does not dominate the other model, they should both improve together. If the discriminator is too smart and is very confident that the instances from the generator are fakes, then there is no signal passed back to the generator and it can no longer improve. Similarly, if the generator finds a clever trick to fool the discriminator, it may generate images that are too similar, or of only one input category and the GAN again fails to improve. This shows the difficulty in training any GAN's, you have to find a set of parameters that works for the data and keeps two models synchronized. A good reference from one of the authors of the DCGAN paper on advice to make GANs work is `https://github.com/soumith/ganhacks`.

GANs have many potential use-cases including being able to train with less data. They also could be used to predict missing data, e.g. add definition to blurred images / videos. They in reinforcement learning, which we discuss in the next section.

Reinforcement learning

Reinforcement learning has a deceptively simple definition: an agent interacts with its environment and changes its behaviors based on the the consequences of its actions. This is actually how humans and animals behave in the real world and is why many people believe that reinforcement learning is the key to achieving artificial general intelligence (AGI).

Artificial general intelligence (AGI) will be achieved if and when computers can perform complex tasks as well as people. This also requires that computers be able to adapt their current knowledge to new problems, just as humans do. Experts disagree on whether AGI is even possible. If we take the very first image from Chapter 1, *Getting Started with Deep Learning,* we can see that the definition of artificial intelligence (... *performing functions that require intelligence when performed by people*) closely resembles the definition of reinforcement learning:

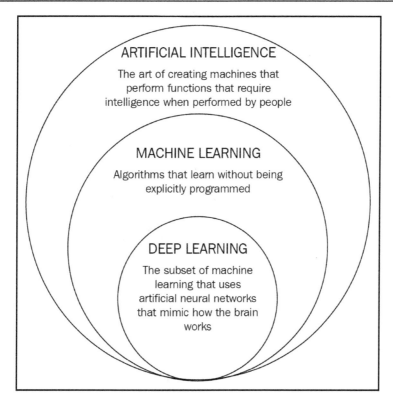

Figure 11.5: The relationship between artificial intelligence, machine learning, and deep learning

David Silver, one of the most prominent people in reinforcement learning and one of the main people involved in AlphaGo, coined the following formula:

Artificial intelligence = Reinforcement learning + Deep learning

One well-known example of reinforcement learning is an algorithm that can play a number of Atari 2600 video games better than most people by just using image pixels as input to the algorithm. The reinforcement learning algorithm learns by playing the game thousands, maybe millions of times, and learns what actions it needs to take to achieve rewards, which could be to collect points or to keep its avatar alive as long as possible. Perhaps the best known example in reinforcement learning is AlphaGo, which defeated one of the best players in the world in Go. AlphaGo is a hybrid artificial system that was composed of neural networks, reinforcement learning, and heuristic search algorithms. It is much harder to program a computer to win in a game of Go than other games, such as chess, because brute-force approaches are not feasible. An additional problem in Go is the difficulty in evaluating the current position.

A formal definition of reinforcement learning is where an agent observes a state s_t at timestep t. When in state s_t, the agent interacts with its environment by taking action, which means that the agent transitions to the new state s_{t+1}. The movement into a new state is linked with a reward, and the goal of the agent is to learn a policy that maximizes the expected rewards. The rewards could be cumulative and/or discounted; for example, near-time rewards are worth more than far-off returns. The value function is the prediction of the future reward. If the new state s_{t+1} is dependent only on the previous state s_t and the action a_t, then it becomes a Markov process. However, one of the major problems in reinforcement learning is that rewards may be sparse and that there may a long delay between an action and achieving the reward. There is also the problem where an immediate reward might cause the agent to go down a path that could ultimately be destructive. For example, in a computer game, the agent could take an immediate step of trying to maximize a score, but this ultimately means that the character *dies* sooner. In a more real-life scenario, for example, a self-driving car, if the goal is to get to a location quickly, then the agent might decide to drive dangerously, putting passengers and other road users at risk.

The core elements in reinforcement learning include the following:

- Rewards are the gains that an agent can achieve in the near-term.
- A value function is the expected reward an agent can expect to achieve from the current state. The value function looks at the long-term rewards / goals, so this may mean taking actions that do not maximize rewards in the short-term.
- A policy guides the actions that an agent can take, it maps the states to possible actions from that state.
- The model is encapsulation of the environment that the agent interacts with. As such it is an incomplete representation of the physical world, but as long as it can accurately simulate the next step given an action, and calculate the reward, then it is an adequate representation that can be used for reinforcement learning.

Other important mechanisms in reinforcement learning include multi-label classification, memory, unsupervised learning, knowledge transfer (using knowledge learned from one problem to solve related problems), search (to select the next best action by looking at all possible permutations x moves ahead), multi-agent RL, and learning to learn. We will not go into detail on these tasks, some may already be familiar to you. However, this list does highlight the complexity involved in reinforcement learning.

Deep learning can be used as a component in reinforcement learning to work on subtasks, such as object detection, speech recognition, NLP, and so on. Deep learning can also be an integral part of reinforcement learning when it is used in the key components of reinforcement learning, which are the value function, policy, and the environmental model. This is called deep reinforcement learning (deep RL). For example, by using recurrent connections between hidden units, Hausknecht and Stone built a deep recurrent Q-network (DRQN) that could predict the speed of the ball in the computer game **Pong**. Another research area in linking deep learning with RL is for imitation learning. In imitation learning, an agent learns by observing an *expert*. It is especially useful where there are delayed rewards and evaluating the current position is hard. But imitation learning can be costly, so one approach is to use GANs to produce artificial data to be used in reinforcement learning.

Even though AlphaGo managed to beat the world champion in Go, it is nowhere near solving the problem of artificial general intelligence. DeepMind are a dedicated artificial intelligence company who combined experts in reinforcement learning, supervised learning and tree search functions and huge hardware resources to solve a single problem. AlphaGo was trained on a dataset of 30 million game states and simulated millions of games. The version that beat one of the best players in the world in Go used almost 2,000 CPUs and 300 GPUs. Before it could beat the world champion, it was coached by the European champion, although the early version did beat him first. However, AlphaGo solves only one problem, it cannot even generalize to other board games. Therefore, it does not come anywhere near solving artificial general intelligence.

One of the more honest appraisals of AlphaGo is from Andrej Karpathy, who is a distinguished researcher in deep learning and currently is director of artificial intelligence at Tesla. He posted a blog called **AlphaGo, in context** (https://medium.com/@karpathy/alphago-in-context-c47718cb95a5) after AlphaGo defeated the number one ranked player in 2017. Karpathy listed the following limitations of Go compared to other artificial intelligence tasks:

- The game is fully deterministic, that is, rules are fixed and fully known beforehand. In comparison, most real-world problems are not
- The game is fully observable, that is, complete information is known to all parties, there are no hidden variables or states.
- The games has a discrete action space, that is, there is a fixed number of allowable actions
- A perfect simulator exists, that is, you can model millions of examples in a safe space. Real-life artificial intelligence does not have this.
- The game is relatively short.
- There are historical datasets from previous games

If we consider self-driving cars as an artificial intelligence task, it probably does not match any of these properties.

One unusual quirk in AlphaGo games with the world champion is that it sometimes passed on moves that would have captured board space. As humans, when we play games, we sometimes crave immediate feedback and therefore make moves to achieve short-term rewards. AlphaGo was programmed to win the game, regardless of the margin, so was quite content to pass on making such moves during the games. It is interesting that some expert Go players believe that they can improve by studying the strategies of AlphaGo. We have come full circle – humans trying to imitate the actions of computers, which in turn are modeled on the actions of humans.

Additional deep learning resources

This section consists of some recommendations if you wish to continue your development in deep learning. My first recommendation is that you ensure that you have run all the code examples in this book. You are getting less than 50% of the benefit if you just read this book without running the code. Go through the examples, change the code to try and beat the results I got, re-write the MXNet code to Keras code, and so on.

I strongly recommend *Deep Learning Specialization* on Coursera by Andrew Ng (`https://www.coursera.org/specializations/deep-learning`). Unfortunately, it is in Python, but it still is a great resource. Also in Python are two excellent courses on fast.ai (`http://www.fast.ai/`) from Jeremy Howard. These two options take opposite approaches: the *Deep Learning* specialization on Coursera takes a bottom-up approach that goes from theory to practice, and the fast.ai courses show you practical examples from the start and only afterwards shows you the theory.

Another excellent resource is Kaggle (`https://www.kaggle.com/competitions`). Kaggle hosts competitions where data scientists compete to get the best score in machine learning competitions. Many of these tasks are computer vision tasks. I am not a huge fan of the competitions, because I think that they ignore a lot of the work in preparing and acquiring datasets and also ignore how models are deployed. However, two notable features in Kaggle are its Kernels and forums/blogs. Kernels are Python or R scripts from other people. These scripts often have very interesting approaches to machine learning tasks. It is well worth following a competition and just looking at how other competitors approach these problems. The second notable feature is the forums/blogs on Kaggle. Again, some interesting approaches are discussed on the competition forums, and after every competition, there's usually a blog post from one of the winning competitions discussing their approach in winning the competition.

Going back to R, another fantastic resource is the RStudio website. These guys do fantastic work in keeping R relevant to data science and machine learning. RStudio put a lot of output back into the R ecosystem; for example, the excellent work by Hadley Wickham, their Chief Scientist. The founder of RStudio (J.J. Allaire) is the author of the R API's to TensorFlow and Keras. We have used some of their excellent tools in this book, including RStudio IDE, RShiny, RMarkdown, the tidy universe of packages, and so on. Here are some links with examples that you should check out:

- `https://keras.rstudio.com/`
- `https://keras.rstudio.com/articles/examples/index.html`
- `https://tensorflow.rstudio.com/`
- `https://tensorflow.rstudio.com/tfestimators/`
- `https://tensorflow.rstudio.com/tensorflow/`
- `https://tensorflow.rstudio.com/tools/`
- `https://tensorflow.rstudio.com/learn/resources.html`

My final suggestion is looking at research papers. Here are a number of good papers to begin with:

- Krizhevsky, Alex, Ilya Sutskever, and Geoffrey E. Hinton. *ImageNet Classification with Deep Convolutional Neural Networks*. Advances in neural information processing systems. 2012.
- Szegedy, Christian, et al. *Going Deeper with Convolutions*. Cvpr, 2015.
- LeCun, Yann, et al. *Learning Algorithms for Classification: A Comparison on Handwritten Digit Recognition*. Neural networks: the statistical mechanics perspective 261 (1995): 276.
- Zeiler, Matthew D., and Rob Fergus. *Visualizing and Understanding Convolutional Networks*. European conference on computer vision. Springer, Cham, 2014.
- Srivastava, Nitish, et al. *Dropout: A Simple Way to Prevent Neural Networks from Overfitting*. The Journal of Machine Learning Research 15.1 (2014): 1929-1958.
- Simonyan, Karen, and Andrew Zisserman. *Very deep convolutional networks for large-scale image recognition*. arXiv preprint arXiv:1409.1556 (2014).
- Szegedy, Christian, et al. *Going deeper with convolutions*. Proceedings of the IEEE conference on computer vision and pattern recognition. 2015.
- He, Kaiming, et al. *Deep residual learning for image recognition*. Proceedings of the IEEE conference on computer vision and pattern recognition. 2016.

- Goodfellow, Ian, et al. *Generative adversarial nets*. Advances in neural information processing systems. 2014.
- LeCun, Yann, Yoshua Bengio, and Geoffrey Hinton. Deep learning. nature 521.7553 (2015): 436.
- Goldberg, Yoav. *A primer on neural network models for natural language processing*. Journal of Artificial Intelligence Research 57 (2016): 345-420.

Summary

In this chapter, the reader has seen some advanced deep learning techniques. First, we looked at some image classification models and looked at some historical models. Next, we loaded an existing model with pre-trained weights into R and used it to classify a new image. We looked at transfer learning, which allows us to reuse an existing model as a base on which to build a deep learning model for new data. We built an image classifier model that could train on image files. This model also showed us how to use data augmentation and callbacks, which are used in many deep learning models. Finally, we demonstrated how we can build a model in R and create a REST endpoint for a prediction API that can be used from other applications or across the web.

We have come to the end of the book, and I really hope it was useful to you. R is a great language for data science and I believe it is easier to use and allows you to develop machine learning prototypes faster than the main alternative, Python. Now that it has support for some excellent deep learning frameworks in MXNet, Keras and TensorFlow, I believe that R will continue to be an excellent choice for data scientists and machine learning practioners.

Other Books You May Enjoy

If you enjoyed this book, you may be interested in these other books by Packt:

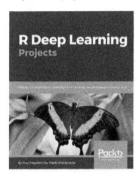

R Deep Learning Projects
Yuxi (Hayden) Liu, Pablo Maldonado

ISBN: 9781788478403

- Instrument Deep Learning models with packages such as deepnet, MXNetR, Tensorflow, H2O, Keras, and text2vec
- Apply neural networks to perform handwritten digit recognition using MXNet
- Get the knack of CNN models, Neural Network API, Keras, and TensorFlow for traffic sign classification
- Implement credit card fraud detection with Autoencoders
- Master reconstructing images using variational autoencoders
- Wade through sentiment analysis from movie reviews
- Run from past to future and vice versa with bidirectional Long Short-Term Memory (LSTM) networks
- Understand the applications of Autoencoder Neural Networks in clustering and dimensionality reduction

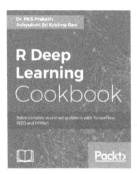

R Deep Learning Cookbook
Dr. PKS Prakash, Achyutuni Sri Krishna Rao

ISBN: 9781787121089

- Build deep learning models in different application areas using TensorFlow, H2O, and MXnet.
- Analyzing a Deep boltzmann machine
- Setting up and Analyzing Deep belief networks
- Building supervised model using various machine learning algorithms
- Set up variants of basic convolution function
- Represent data using Autoencoders.
- Explore generative models available in Deep Learning.
- Discover sequence modeling using Recurrent nets
- Learn fundamentals of Reinforcement Leaning
- Learn the steps involved in applying Deep Learning in text mining
- Explore application of deep learning in signal processing
- Utilize Transfer learning for utilizing pre-trained model
- Train a deep learning model on a GPU

Leave a review - let other readers know what you think

Please share your thoughts on this book with others by leaving a review on the site that you bought it from. If you purchased the book from Amazon, please leave us an honest review on this book's Amazon page. This is vital so that other potential readers can see and use your unbiased opinion to make purchasing decisions, we can understand what our customers think about our products, and our authors can see your feedback on the title that they have worked with Packt to create. It will only take a few minutes of your time, but is valuable to other potential customers, our authors, and Packt. Thank you!

Index

ctx parameter 79
customer lifetime value (CLV) 170

D

data augmentation
  about 176
  test time augmentation 181
  training data, increasing 177, 178, 180
  using, in deep learning libraries 183
data distributions 171, 172
data leakage 176
data partitioning 174
data preparation 170
deep belief networks (DBNs) 20
deep feedforward neural networks 99, 100
deep learning AMI
  creating, in AWS 307, 309
deep learning frameworks, R
  Keras 27
  MXNet 26, 27
deep learning GPU instance
  creating, in AWS 292, 294, 296, 298, 300, 302,
    303, 305, 306
deep learning layers 106, 107
deep learning libraries
  data augmentation, using 183
deep learning model
  base model 154, 155
  building 107, 108, 109
deep learning networks
  visualizing, TensorBoard used 231, 233, 234,
    235, 236, 237
deep learning NLP architectures
  comparing 226
deep learning text classification 206, 207
deep learning
  about 8, 9, 78
  AWS, using for 288
  Azure, using for 310, 311, 312, 313, 314, 315,
    316, 318
  Google Cloud, using for 318, 319, 320, 322
  local computer, setting up for 284, 285, 287
  myths 21, 22
  Paperspace, using for 323, 324, 325
  reinforcement learning 352, 353

versus traditional text classification 210, 211,
  212
deep neural network (DNN) 19
dense layer 106
dimensionality-reduction 37
document classification 198
dropout
  used, for improving out-of-sample model
    performance 92, 94, 95, 96

E

Emacs 23
epoch.end.callback parameter 81
eval.data parameter 80
eval.metric parameter 80
evaluation metrics
  about 166
  types 166, 167

F

fashion MNIST dataset
  using, in classification 159, 160, 161, 163
fast.ai
  reference 356
forward-propagation 16

G

Gated Recurrent Units (GR's) 220
generative adversarial networks (GANs) 350
Google Cloud
  using, for deep learning 318, 319, 320, 322
GPUs 28
graphical processing units (GPUs) 338

H

h2o
  reference 26
hyperparameters, tuning
  about 183
  grid search 184
  random search 185

increasing, data augmentation used 177, 178, 180
training run 250
transfer learning 342, 344, 345

undercomplete auto-encoder 255
unsupervised learning 9, 254

weight decay 87, 88
word vectors 208, 209

www.ingramcontent.com/pod-product-compliance
Lightning Source LLC
LaVergne TN
LVHW081514050326
832903LV00025B/1480